Teaching Games for Understanding

Theory, Research, and Practice

Linda L. Griffin, PhD

University of Massachusetts, Amherst

Joy I. Butler, EdD

University of British Columbia

Editors

Human Kinetics

Library of Congress Cataloging-in-Publication Data

Teaching Games for Understanding : theory, research, and practice / Linda L. Griffin, Joy I. Butler, editors.

p. cm.

Includes bibliographical references and index.

ISBN 0-7360-4594-5 (soft cover)

1. Sports--Study and teaching. 2. Physical education and training--Study and teaching. 3. Student-centered learning. I. Griffin, Linda L., 1954- II. Butler, Joy.

GV361.T34 2005

796'.071--dc22

2004014897

ISBN-10: 0-7360-4594-5

ISBN-13: 978-0-7360-4594-0

The Web addresses cited in this text were current as of September 2004, unless otherwise noted.

Acquisitions Editor: Bonnie Pettifor; **Developmental Editor:** Melissa Feld; **Assistant Editors:** Bethany J. Bentley and Kathleen D. Bernard; **Copyeditor:** Patsy Fortney; **Proofreader:** Anne Rogers; **Indexer:** Betty Frizzéll; **Permission Manager:** Dalene Reeder; **Graphic Designer:** Fred Starbird; **Graphic Artist:** Dawn Sills; **Photo Manager:** Kareema McLendon; **Cover Designer:** Keith Blomberg; **Photographer (cover):** © Human Kinetics; **Photographer (interior):** © Human Kinetics; **Art Managers:** Kelly Hendren and Kareema McLendon; **Illustrator:** Tara Welsch; **Printer:** Versa Press

Printed in the United States of America   10   9   8   7   6

Human Kinetics
Web site: www.HumanKinetics.com

United States: Human Kinetics
P.O. Box 5076
Champaign, IL 61825-5076
800-747-4457
e-mail: humank@hkusa.com

Canada: Human Kinetics
475 Devonshire Road, Unit 100
Windsor, ON N8Y 2L5
800-465-7301 (in Canada only)
e-mail: info@hkcanada.com

Europe: Human Kinetics
107 Bradford Road
Stanningley
Leeds LS28 6AT, United Kingdom
+44 (0)113 255 5665
e-mail: hk@hkeurope.com

Australia: Human Kinetics
57A Price Avenue
Lower Mitcham, South Australia 5062
08 8372 0999
e-mail: info@hkaustralia.com

New Zealand: Human Kinetics
Division of Sports Distributors NZ Ltd.
P.O. Box 300 226 Albany
North Shore City, Auckland
0064 9 448 1207
e-mail: info@humankinetics.co.nz

Contents

Preface

For more than two decades various professionals have advocated the Teaching Games for Understanding (TGfU) model as a sound idea built on assumptions (particular beliefs) about games education. In fact, more than two decades have passed since the release of Bunker and Thorpe's (1982) *Teaching Games for Understanding,* which introduced TGfU as a means of conceptualizing games teaching and learning. With that in mind, we welcome you to *Teaching Games for Understanding: Theory, Research, and Practice.* This book is a celebration of TGfU as an innovation in games learning, and it examines ways in which we can work toward making TGfU a more legitimate model for games learning.

This book brings together several international scholars with a passion for sharing their knowledge, research, and insights about TGfU with teachers (preservice and inservice), teacher educators, and coaches. The chapters include topics spanning the fields of research, theory, and practice from various perspectives (including elementary and secondary education and assessment). Each chapter opens with a scenario or quote that sets the stage for the rest of the chapter. All chapters end with questions to stimulate reflective discussion.

Chapter 1 explains the true spirit behind this learner-centered model. Griffin and Patton acquaint you with TGfU's past by providing an overview of the major underpinnings of the model. They bring you up to the present by discussing ideas related to the recent reconceptualization of TGfU. Finally, they present a possible research challenge that focuses on exploring the learner's development of games knowledge as one way to improve games teaching and learning.

In chapter 2 Richard and Wallian examine TGfU from a constructivist teaching–learning perspective and explore pedagogical principles that emphasize students' engagement in the construction of knowledge and skills. Richard and Wallian then shape the scaffolding of a socioconstructivist approach applied to games teaching by focusing on the notions of observation and debate that can be used to improve the TGfU model.

In chapter 3 Butler and McCahan examine how the inherent assumptions and values of TGfU can help teachers develop a healthy, vital, and inclusive games curriculum. Butler and McCahan compare TGfU with the technique model in terms of purpose, objectives, outcomes, and games framework; examine the classification system; show how to create a spiral curriculum that will obviate the need for physical educators to cover all games; provide planning considerations using a sample TGfU games program; describe the learning steps involved in TGfU; and offer guidelines for implementation.

In chapter 4 Mitchell presents a research-based rationale for using the TGfU model at the elementary level, along with strategies for implementing TGfU. Mitchell urges that the implementation of TGfU at the elementary level is best accomplished by taking a thematic approach to content development.

Chapter 5 addresses the implementation of the TGfU model at the secondary level. Turner provides a rationale for using TGfU and highlights research that supports the model. He also provides insight into some of the misconceptions about TGfU that have made teachers reluctant about using the approach. The chapter presents a tactical framework that provides secondary teachers with adequate knowledge to start using this approach and a unit plan based on the tactical components of invasion.

In chapter 6 Howarth addresses the attractions and barriers preservice teachers face when they are introduced to the TGfU model. Howarth shows us how the assimilation of this model into our own teaching can be stimulating, demanding, and informing for both preservice teachers and the teacher educators who teach and work with them.

In chapter 7 Tan shares how teachers made sense of and experienced change as they attempted to negotiate a new curriculum initiative mandated by Singapore's central government agency. Tan describes the context of change, the research study, and individual and school characteristics related to the teachers' implementation of the new curriculum. Unique stories of four teachers, which include their beliefs, rationales, decisions, and actions during the change process, are featured.

In chapter 8 Oslin shares her perspective as a teacher and teacher educator on the challenge of finding resources for designing games, practice drills, and assessments that are aligned with the TGfU approach. Oslin describes aspects of games that ought to be considered in the selection and design of student assessments.

In chapter 9 Collier describes and analyzes the processes and questions surrounding the integration of the Tactical Games model (TGM; Griffin, Mitchell, & Oslin, 1997; Mitchell, Oslin, & Griffin, 2003) and the Sport Education model (SEM; Siedentop, 1994). This chapter describes methods for determining the compatibility of SEM and TGM, the key similarities and differences between them, the benefits and challenges associated with the integration of SEM and TGM, and considerations for integrating these models.

In chapter 10 Dyson explains the integration of cooperative learning (CL) with TGfU and provides an overview of CL as an instructional model. Dyson reviews the research on CL in physical education, makes theoretical connections between CL and TG, emphasizes the pedagogical integration of the models, and provides practical examples of the integration of TG and CL (Griffin, Mitchell, & Oslin, 1997; Mitchell, Oslin, & Griffin, 2003).

In chapter 11 Light provides insight about Game Sense from a coaching perspective. Among the strengths are the ability to "work off the ball," the transfer of training to the game, and the development of independent players. Among the challenges are the repositioning of the role of coach, the chaotic nature of game sense training, and the time required for long-term player development.

In chapter 12 Metzler provides some thoughtful critique of research regarding TGfU as an instructional model. Metzler argues that while some of this research can use questions and methods taken from earlier research on teaching in physical education, those questions and methods must be refined when applied to research on various instructional models.

In chapter 13 Kretchmar analyzes the theory and practice of TGfU as "pedagogy for delight." Kretchmar examines the significance of the subjective domain and the notion of delight, reviews examples of activity-based delight, surveys the potential of TGfU methodologies to promote delight, reviews criticisms of TGfU as a resource for delight, and draws conclusions about TGfU and delight.

In chapter 14 Kirk explores the future of TGfU. Kirk considers the way we do research and how we design research studies. He discusses the need to continue to develop the TGfU model, and he explores some new concepts for thinking about, and ways to measure, learning in games. He then considers the challenges of incorporating TGfU into teacher and coach education programs.

We believe that there is cause for a TGfU celebration. This celebration stems from our own beliefs about TGfU and our enthusiasm for spreading the TGfU word. We hope that insights and enthusiasm presented in these chapters inspire readers to start on their own TGfU journey.

References

Bunker, D., & Thorpe, R. (1982). A model for the teaching of games in the secondary school. *Bulletin of Physical Education, 18* (1), 5-8.

Griffin, L., Mitchell, S., & Oslin, J. (1997). *Teaching sport concepts and skills: A tactical games approach.* Champaign, IL: Human Kinetics.

Mitchell, S., Oslin, J., & Griffin, L.L. (2003). *Sport foundations for elementary physical education: A tactical games approach.* Champaign, IL: Human Kinetics.

Acknowledgments

First, I would like to acknowledge the entire international TGfU community for sharing their passion and enthusiasm for this growing TGfU movement. I hope that we will continue to learn as a community. Second, I would like to acknowledge Jennifer S. Cook for her thoughtful and careful editing skills during the early chapter drafts.

—Linda

I give thanks to the friends, colleagues, and students with whom I have worked at Plymouth State University for the last ten years. In particular, I have enjoyed and benefited from both the support and the philosophical debates provided by the members of the TFU Major's Club, HPER department chair, Barbara McCahan, and Claire Robson.

—Joy

chapter

1

Two Decades of Teaching Games for Understanding: Looking at the Past, Present, and Future

Linda L. Griffin and Kevin Patton

"Tell me, I forget. . . . Show me, I understand. . . . Involve me, I remember."

Every time one of your students asks to play a game, the student is asking to be more involved in the action. Playing the game gives meaning to their performance and actively involves them in the learning process. By involving learners in games and in the decision-making process required to play games, teachers can encourage both game appreciation and physical skill development. As students gain experience, they become better decision makers and more competent games players, and thus are motivated to play more games and reap the rewards of participation.

Teaching Games for Understanding (TGfU) is a learner- and game-centered approach to sport-related games learning with strong ties to a constructivist approach to learning. Two decades have passed since TGfU was introduced in the *Bulletin of Physical Education* (by Bunker and Thorpe in 1982 and by Thorpe, Bunker, and Almond in 1984) as a means to conceptualize games teaching and learning. TGfU highly values the role of the teacher as the facilitator and the role of the learner as active and involved in the learning process.

The purpose of this first chapter is to explain the true spirit behind this learner-centered model. First, we will orient you to TGfU's past by providing an overview of the major underpinnings of the model. Second, we will discuss the latest ideas related to the recent reconceptualization

TGfU is a learner- and game-centered approach to sport-related games learning with strong ties to a constructivist approach to learning.

of TGfU. Finally, we will present potential research that focuses on exploring the learner's development of games knowledge as one way to improve games teaching and learning.

Overview of the Past

This overview of the TGfU model includes an introduction of the original model, a discussion of the guiding principles, and an exploration of the various events and ideas that shaped the development of the model. The TGfU model shifts games learning from an approach based on the development of techniques or content with highly structured lessons to a more student-based approach that links tactics and skills in game contexts (Bunker & Thorpe, 1982; Thorpe & Bunker, 1989).

Original TGfU Model

The original TGfU model presented by Bunker and Thorpe (1982) is a step-by-step procedural model for teachers to enable students or players to become skillful games players (i.e., develop skillful performance) (see figure 1.1). The key aspect of the model lies in the design of well-structured (i.e., conditioned) games that require students to make decisions to elevate their understanding of games (i.e., increase tactical awareness).

Step 1—the game. The game is introduced; it should be modified to represent the advanced form of the game and meet the developmental level of the learner.

Step 2—game appreciation. Students should understand the rules (e.g., conditions such as boundaries, scoring, and so on) of the game to be played.

Step 3—tactical awareness. Students must consider the tactics of a game (i.e., creating space or defending space) to help them work through the principles of play, thus increasing their tactical awareness.

Step 4—making appropriate decisions. Students must focus on the decision-making process in games. Students are asked what to do (i.e., tactical awareness) and how to do it (i.e., appropriate response selection and skill execution) to help them make appropriate game decisions.

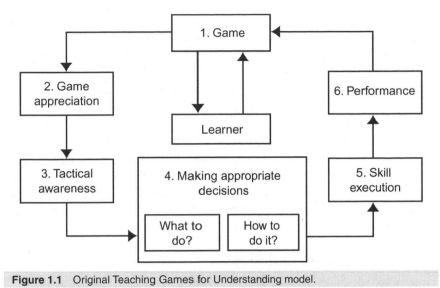

Figure 1.1 Original Teaching Games for Understanding model.

Reprinted, by permission, from D. Bunker and R. Thorpe, 1982, *Bulletin of physical education*, (Worcester,UK: British Association of Advisers & Lecturers in Physical Education).

> *Step 5—skill execution*. In this step, the focus is on *how to* execute specific skills and movements. Knowing how to execute is different from performance in that the focus is limited to a specific skill or movement. Skill execution is always viewed in the context of the game.

> *Step 6—performance*. Finally, performance is based on specific criteria according to the goals of the game, lesson, or unit. Ultimately, these specific performance criteria lead toward competent and proficient games players.

Pedagogical Principles

Thorpe and Bunker (1989) also introduced four pedagogical principles (sampling, representation, exaggeration, and tactical complexity) associated with TGfU.

▪ Game *sampling* can provide students with an opportunity to explore the similarities and differences among games (Thorpe, Bunker, & Almond, 1984). Exposure to various game forms helps students learn to transfer their learning from one game to another.

▪ *Representation* involves developing condensed games that contain the same tactical structure of the advanced form of the game (e.g., reduced number of players, modified equipment). The games classification system described by Thorpe, Bunker, and Almond (1984) can facilitate the representation process by providing a selection of various games with similar tactical problems rather than the traditional selection of teaching one specific sport as a unit topic.

- *Exaggeration* involves changing the secondary rules of the game to overstate a specific tactical problem (e.g., long and narrow courts, narrow or wide goals).
- *Tactical complexity* involves matching the game to the developmental level of the student. Some tactical problems are too complex for novice players to understand, but as students develop an understanding of tactical problems and appropriate solutions, the complexity of the game can be increased. Thus, all games and game forms are designed to be developmentally appropriate.

Influential Events and Ideas

These have been particular events and ideas that have strongly influenced the development of the TGfU model which is crucial to understanding TGfU as a games teaching innovation. Thorpe and Bunker were influenced by Worthington and Wigmore, who challenged them to consider the benefits of small-sided games (Thorpe & Bunker, 1986). Wade (1967), Morris (1976), and Mauldon and Redfern (1981) also influenced Thorpe and Bunker (1986) in the conceptualization of TGfU. Wade (1967) introduced the notion of principles of play in soccer. Morris (1976) proposed that games could have a range of educational purposes. Mauldon and Redfern (1981) suggested an approach that outlines a way to develop skills within the structure of a game.

As teachers during the late 1960s and early 1970s, Thorpe and Bunker grew dissatisfied with traditional teaching approaches, which they viewed to be unproductive. Early influences helped Thorpe and Bunker to develop their own ideas about games teaching and to recognize that a technical focus in the teaching of games often neglected other essential areas of games. They sought ways to increase motivation and make games more relevant to students across all ability levels. In 1979 Almond formed a partnership with Thorpe and Bunker, and a clearer theoretical perspective on TGfU began to take shape (Almond, 2001).

Thorpe, Bunker, and Almond brought different skills to their vision of games teaching. Thorpe and Bunker are practitioners knowledgeable about a wide range of games and passionately committed to practice. Almond (2001) stated, "Thorpe and Bunker watched Australian Rules football on television and in 15 minutes, they could tell you exactly how the game was played, the major principles, and various tactical considerations. And they could do the same analysis in any game" (p. 4). Thorpe and Bunker had a strong practical and theoretical perspective from their immersion in skill acquisition and social psychology, which they taught to the undergraduates at Loughborough University in England.

Whereas Thorpe and Bunker provided a practical perspective, Almond was concerned with professional and curriculum development. In an interview, Thorpe (personal communication, October, 12, 2000) reflected on Almond's contribution when he stated, "I don't think we would have published anything if Len hadn't come in and said, 'you've got a major curriculum development.'" Almond's interests stemmed from philosophy and cognitive psychology, and he was committed to getting teachers to reflect on their practice. His notion of professional development was to have teachers explore alternative views and debate ideas. Almond believed that if teachers listened to each other, they would begin to enrich and enlighten their perspectives, thus learning more about games and pedagogy (Almond, 2001).

An event that showcased Thorpe, Bunker, and Almond's contributions and influenced TGfU's development occurred in 1982 when a group of teachers from Coventry, England, were invited to take part in a "Project on Games Teaching" initiated by the staff at Loughborough University (Jeffray & Almond, 1986). The purpose of the Project on Games Teaching was to help formulate a model of professional development in which teachers monitored their own practice. The goals for this project were to

- examine the ways teachers think about games teaching,
- produce case studies of games teaching,
- examine the use of case studies as a means of developing a games curriculum, and
- identify the issues related to teacher inquiry.

All teachers in the project attended a one-day workshop in which they examined different perspectives on games teaching and explored TGfU. Teachers were also provided with ground rules for conducting teacher inquiry (i.e., action research) and were presented with guidelines for case study writing. Almond (2001) believed that teacher educators and researchers needed to recognize the value of action research, and that teachers needed a way of critiquing practice in a safe environment. He believed that this safe environment could promote professional practice and motivate teachers to really study and reflect on their own practice.

Thorpe, Bunker, and Almond were strongly influenced by educational gymnastics because it uses a problem-solving approach. Thorpe stated, "I think the biggest influence on my games teaching is educational gymnastics. The logic of it . . . The game sets the problem; you've got to see what the problem is, and then you've got to see an answer" (personal communication, October, 12, 2000). The ideas generated from educational gymnastics led to a discussion about the nature of games and their problem-solving capabilities. Thorpe, Bunker, and Almond viewed games as problem-solving activities in which players learn how to make intelligent decisions. They were not interested in techniques or skills, only in the tactical demands of the game.

The modification principles from Ellis (1986) were very influential in Thorpe, Bunker, and Almond's development of the notion of primary and secondary rules and their exploration of the idea of modifying the technical demands of the game. Thorpe, Bunker, and Almond believed that games needed to be broken down to their simplest form and represented in a game form that students (children) could play with modified equipment to reduce the technical demands of the activity. Representation and exaggeration were the basic principles for building modified games that children wanted to and could play. For example, in badminton, key principles explored are aspects of the long and short game. Whether the player is at the net or at the back of the court, the question is, Where do I put the shuttle? To introduce these principles, Thorpe and Bunker (1986) set up an exaggerated court (i.e., very long and narrow). The goal was to progress students' understanding and technical competence to higher levels.

Bunker and Thorpe (1982) also believed that in games playing, knowing what to do and when to do it are as valuable as knowing how to do it. Kirk (1983) connected these ideas and introduced the notion of intelligent performance, which takes into account various principles of play (e.g., appropriate timing) relevant to a given situation in a game. This notion provided a broader understanding of performance.

Present Reconceptualization of TGfU

The TGfU model and associated pedagogical principles have remained unchanged for approximately 15 years and only recently received some close examination, critique, and reconceptualization (Gréhaigne & Godbout, 1995; Griffin, Mitchell, & Oslin, 1997; Holt, Strean, & Bengoechea, 2002; Kirk & MacPhail, 2002; Light & Fawns, 2003; Mitchell, Oslin, & Griffin, 2003).

From a broader games teaching and learning perspective, Gréhaigne and Godbout (1995) substantiated that games involve teams operating as competency networks engaged in high-strategy sports (e.g., invasion or net/wall games) against opponents in a contest, and that learning occurs for both individuals and teams. Four components of games (cooperation with teammates, opposition to opponents, attacking opponents' space, and defending a team's own space) can be taken as highly sophisticated goal structures using forms of declarative and procedural knowledge

(Gréhaigne, Godbout, & Bouthier, 1999). Gréhaigne and colleagues (1999) reiterated the importance of strategic and tactical knowledge as key components of expert game play. They asserted that these can be taught by carefully structuring learning environments to facilitate the use of players' knowledge structures when representing and solving problems related to game play, thus expanding their knowledge structures.

The Team Sport Assessment Procedure (TSAP) was developed to assess students' performance in actual contexts within different assessment scenarios (i.e., diagnostic, formative, and summative), thus helping to expand students' knowledge (Gréhaigne & Godbout, 1998; Richard, Godbout, & Griffin, 2002). Gréhaigne, Godbout, and Bouthier (2001) also explored more specifically the role of decision making during game play, concluding that decisions are grounded in dynamic, fluid configurations of game play related to player positions and ball location.

Specifically related to TGfU, Griffin and colleagues (1997) proposed a simplified three-stage model that focuses on the essential lesson components of the model, namely modified game play, development of tactical awareness and decision making through questioning, and development of skill. They also advocated for the need to assess students' game performance through the use of an authentic assessment instrument known as the Game Performance Assessment Instrument (GPAI). The GPAI was developed to be a comprehensive assessment tool for teachers to use and adapt in assessing a variety of games. Teachers can use the GPAI for different types of games across the classification system (e.g., invasion and net/wall) (Griffin et al., 1997; Mitchell, Oslin, & Griffin, 2003).

Mitchell and colleagues (2003) also proposed the use of a thematic approach to teaching in elementary grades that shifts teaching discrete games (e.g., soccer, volleyball, and softball) to teaching units of invasion, net/wall, striking/fielding, and target games, which are focused on specified tactical problems. This thematic approach is intended to develop more knowledgeable and adaptable games players who can switch among different games within the same classification (e.g., invasion or net/wall) and who can retain a degree of understanding and generalization from one game to another (e.g., soccer to ultimate Frisbee).

Situated learning has emerged as a framework with which to theorize and analyze a TGfU model (Dyson, Griffin, & Hastie, 2004; Kirk & MacPhail, 2002). Situated learning theory is conceptualized as one component of a broader constructivist theory of learning in physical education (Kirk & MacDonald, 1998). The mastery of knowledge and skills requires that novices move toward fuller (i.e., advanced) participation in the sociocultural practices of the community (Lave & Wenger, 1991). Individuals are considered part of a holistic learning enterprise, not isolated actors or participants. The assumptions and organizational structures of TGfU allow for participation to occur in a student-centered "learning curriculum" as opposed to a teacher-centered "teaching curriculum" (Lave & Wenger, 1991, p. 97).

Using the situated learning perspective, Kirk and MacPhail (2002) (also see chapter 14) modified and extended aspects of the original TGfU model. In this view of the model they argued for explicit attention to the learner's perspective, game concept, thinking strategy, cue recognition, technique selection, and skill development as the intersection of tactics and technique. Kirk and MacPhail (2002) also believe that situated performance provides the learner with opportunities to gain game playing experiences (e.g., legitimate peripheral participation in games).

Holt, Strean, and Bengoechea (2002) outlined an expanded model that incorporates the curriculum model (six-step model) and the four fundamental pedagogical principles (sampling, representation, exaggeration, and tactical complexity) proposed by Thorpe and Bunker (1989). This expanded model represents a more holistic view of the learner. Holt and colleagues (2002) also urged researchers to explore the learner-centered feature of the model across the learning domains, but specifically to focus on the affective domain (i.e., affect and enjoyment in sport).

Griffin and Sheehy (2004) proposed a conceptual framework to help the teacher foreground problem solving using the pedagogical principles in the tactical games model across the learning domains. The primary features of this framework include

- the games classification system,
- the tactical problems and levels of tactical complexity,
- a game or game form focus,
- game or game form modification,
- questioning as teaching, and
- problem-solving skills as outcomes.

Light and Fawns (2003) suggested that using TGfU in games teaching offers a holistic learning experience for students that focuses on the mind and body. Using a holistic perspective, the TGfU lesson links movement in games with the verbalization of understanding to form an educational conversation linking the mind and body through speech and action. In this form, TGfU pedagogy is based in a way of discourse (i.e., perceptions and decision making) rather than in the teaching of a skill as an object or a state.

All of the events and ideas just discussed have shaped and situated TGfU as a major games teaching movement. Advocates of the TGfU model have set themselves apart by considering an alterative to teach sport-related games to teachers, coaches, students, and players. Ultimately, the goal of games teaching is to enable students and players to enjoy participation and a level of success so that they will have increased motivation to play and gain the benefits of participation (Rink, 1996).

> **A**dvocates of the TGfU model are concerned with issues related to how best to teach sport-related games to teachers, coaches, students, and players.

Future TGfU Research and Development

In this section we will outline the assumptions of TGfU as it relates to learning and argue for continued research and development work specifically focused on exploring the development of games knowledge. If we believe that TGfU has the potential as a best practice model, then we need to engage in research focused on sport-related games learning.

The TGfU model was built on the basic assumption that "students learn best if they understand what to do before they understand how to do it" and puts an emphasis on "the engagement of students through the affective domain" (Butler, Griffin, & Nastasi, 2003, p. 215). The model centers on getting students in gamelike situations, thinking about the tactical problem on which instruction is focused, and answering questions designed to develop tactical awareness (i.e., decision making). Like all teaching methodologies, TGfU makes some assumptions about how students learn (Rink, 2001).

Absent from current discourse about TGfU are efforts to support assumptions about how students learn games while engaged in the TGfU approach. Although TGfU is built on a constructivist theory of knowledge and learning, there is limited empirical support to back up an intuitive sense that this approach works for students. In a recent examination of TGfU, Butler and colleagues (2003) made a call for such support by raising several relevant pedagogical questions about TGfU and the learning process:

> Do students understand better if they discover a concept and skill within the context of a game situation? What is the balance between cognition and physical engagement? How much information can students absorb at one time? In what order should this information be offered? How much is the effectiveness of learning dependent on factors such as imagination and discovery, and which lie within the affective domain? (p. 214)

To further our understanding of the TGfU approach, we must employ multiple theoretical perspectives in the design and interpretation of TGfU research. An area of investigation with particularly strong implications focuses on how individuals learn and how the prior knowledge that learners bring to instruction influences the teaching and learning process.

Exploring Learners' Game Knowledge Development

As research on the TGfU approach to games teaching evolves, and as the debate concerning technical versus tactical approaches to games instruction subsides, sport pedagogists must begin to move forward and explore new and important avenues of study. As Rink (2001) argued, "When you spend all of your effort proving that a particular kind of teaching is better than another kind of teaching, you limit what you can learn about the very complex teaching/learning process" (p. 123). Grounding work in the learning theories that underlie different teaching methods will enable researchers, teachers, and curriculum experts to create a knowledge base. This broader view extends beyond identifying direct links between what a teacher does and what a student learns to begin to test the assumptions of different methodologies. In the case of TGfU, application of a theory of learning may enable researchers to examine questions largely identified as assumptions of the model. For example, does the constructivist nature of this model lend itself to more motivated learners? How do learners construct knowledge of games?

Grounding work in the learning theories that underlie different teaching methods and approaches to teaching will enable researchers, teachers, and curriculum experts to create a knowledge base that extends beyond identifying direct links between what a teacher does and what a student learns to begin to test the assumptions of different methodologies.

Physical education researchers have argued that instructional strategies should be based on learning theory because without a clear understanding of how students and teachers learn, one cannot expect to achieve intended learning outcomes (Kirk & MacPhail, 2002; Rink, 2001). Researchers with a learning orientation emphasize understanding what students know, what they can do, what prior knowledge they bring to physical education, and how their knowledge changes as a function of physical education instruction (see Griffin & Placek, 2001).

Information processing theory from cognitive psychology provides a theoretical framework for investigating domain-specific knowledge and contributes to ideas of what learners know and how they learn cognitive aspects of movement activities. Information processing suggests that humans represent the world through knowledge structures stored in long-term, intermediate, and short-term

Students in a physical education setting in the same class in school will differ greatly in their knowledge structures of sport-related games.

memory (Shuell, 1986). These knowledge structures are formed by gathering and combining forms of new information and then relating the newly acquired information to prior knowledge already stored in long-term memory (Sternberg, 1984). These knowledge structures consist of nodes that represent particular concepts, facts, or theories and relate hierarchically to other nodes in an array of relationships (Anderson, 1976; Dodds, Griffin, & Placek, 2001).

Research on information processing reports that complex knowledge structures internally represent the outside world and can be changed under various conditions over time (Dodds, Griffin, & Placek, 2001). Further, knowledge can be broadly characterized as declarative, procedural, conditional, and strategic (Alexander & Judy, 1988; Anderson, 1976). Sport pedagogy research reveals that people may simultaneously be highly knowledgeable about some aspects of sport and physical education and far less knowledgeable about others. For example, students in a physical education setting in the same class in school will differ greatly in their knowledge structures of sport-related games. A student could be highly knowledgeable about the tactics involved in invasion games and yet have many gaps in her knowledge structures relating to the tactics of net/wall games.

From a perspective related more directly to instruction, Gréhaigne and colleagues' (1995, 1998, 1999, 2001) theoretical papers have explored players' acquisition and use of knowledge, expanding on views of how to teach strategic and tactical knowledge in the context of game play. They advocated that many elements are involved in the "construction" of a player. These concepts are amenable to an information processing interpretation in that players use appropriate cues from the environment (e.g., game play) to activate portions of their knowledge structure to select and execute appropriate responses.

Our colleagues in motor learning have used the information processing perspective to study expert and novice sport performance, which has implications for TGfU. The following is a summary of their research findings:

- Expert performers plan, whereas novice performers "wait and see."
- Expert performers continuously monitor relevant current and past response, and build and modify their game status. Novice performers react to game events rather than plan for response selection (McPherson, 1999a, 1999b).
- Expert performers use a specific approach to problem solving that is highly contextual, whereas novice performers use a global approach to problem solving (McPherson & Thomas, 1989).
- Expert performers process information at a deeper, more tactical level, whereas novice performers process events in the environment or surface features of a game situation (McPherson & Thomas, 1989).
- Expert performers make faster and more accurate decisions, whereas novice performers have slower access to the information needed to make accurate decisions.
- Expert performers have specialized search and retrieval abilities (if-then-do statements) from past game situations, whereas novice performers do not have these abilities or the game experiences to draw from in their long-term memories (McPherson & Thomas, 1989; Rink, French, & Tjeerdsma, 1996).
- Expert performers (1) have high success at performing skills correctly during games, (2) perform effortless and more automatic movements (i.e., they make it look easy), (3) show greater consistency and adaptability in performing movement patterns, and (4) are better at monitoring their own performance as well as error detection and correction compared with novices (Rink et al., 1996).
- In early work Thomas, French, and McPherson suggested that knowledge and decision-making processes may develop faster than motor skills (French & Thomas, 1987; McPherson & French, 1991; McPherson & Thomas, 1989). They later stated that this assertion was wrong, reporting that knowledge and decision making develop much more slowly than motor skill (French & McPherson, 2004).
- Different instructional approaches produce different knowledge representations that influence the performer's view and interpretation of game events (French, Spurgeon, & Nevett, 1995; French & Thomas, 1987; French, Werner, Taylor, Hussey, & Jones, 1996; McPherson, 1994; McPherson & French, 1991; Rink et al., 1996).

We believe that understanding the development of learners' domain-specific knowledge provides teachers and researchers with an additional means to facilitate learning and to find out what children know about physical education at the outset of instruction and as instruction unfolds over time (Griffin & Placek, 2001). This strategy acknowledges that learners are active participants in the teaching–learning process (Weinstein & Mayer, 1986) and come to every new learning experience with some knowledge about the topic. In a physical education context, players' knowledge is important in building overall game skills

In a physical education context, players' knowledge is important in building overall game skills and in knowing what to do and when to do it, how to perform particular motor skill components of the game, and how to apply these tactically and strategically to their own advantage during game play.

and in knowing what to do and when to do it, how to perform particular motor skill components of the game, and how to apply these tactically and strategically to their own advantage during game play.

Implications for Learning and Teaching

From the research base using the information processing perspective, French and McPherson (2004) provided what they referred to as "best guess approaches" to sport-related games learning, which are directly related to a TGfU model. First, teachers and coaches should design game play situations that foreground decision making. Second, teachers and coaches should use questions to gain insight and information from students about what they are processing or not processing. Much more research and development work is needed to understand how to facilitate the development of game knowledge. A challenging but important question is, What types of learning situations (i.e., games or practice) elicit what types of improvement in game performance (i.e., decision making and execution) (French & McPherson, 2004)?

Application of a better theory for games learning has implications for physical education teachers, teacher educators, and students. First, application of theory may add to the knowledge of how teachers and students learn games and will aid in curriculum development and creating better ways of teaching games.

Second, teachers who know more about the prior knowledge their students bring to class have better opportunities to provide a quality learning environment that extends and deepens knowledge during instruction. When teachers understand students' knowledge structures, they can build on what students already know, making bridges to new learning. Physical educators, whose curricula largely rely on games in various forms (Rovegno, Nevett, & Babiarz, 2001), could thus design learning tasks that challenge students to increase and better connect their knowledge of rules, strategies and tactics, motor skill selection and execution, and decision making in games contexts.

Physical education teachers should consider students' prior knowledge to identify gaps in students' knowledge structures so that they can tailor instruction and practice opportunities to address these gaps. For example, teachers who know that students lack a particular aspect of tactical knowledge might design and cater instruction to fill this knowledge void.

A better theory of games learning has implications for teacher educators as well. If students' prior knowledge is in part a result of their earlier experiences in physical education, and if their knowledge structures seem to lack details of strategies and tactics, then we are left wondering how preservice teachers are taught to teach these aspects of games. Teacher educators should perhaps examine their own content knowledge and pedagogical content knowledge to be sure they are current in all components of games understanding. Then they must decide how to teach both content knowledge and pedagogical content knowledge to preservice teachers so that they deliver the best possible instruction.

Finally, a better theory of games learning has implications for physical education students. As physical education teachers learn how to access and make meaning of students' prior knowledge structures, they will have a more complete picture of where gaps exist within the knowledge of groups of students. As a result, they may become more adept at providing challenging learning environments that will facilitate students' learning and skill development. As students gain expertise in games, they are more likely to enjoy activity inside and outside of school contexts, thus strengthening the possibility of lifelong participation in games and other physical activities.

We also believe that as teachers there are times when telling and showing are appropriate; however, students are most empowered when they are involved.

Conclusion

Approximately 20 years ago a group of educators from Loughborough University in the United Kingdom created the innovative approach to games teaching and learning known as Teaching Games for Understanding (TGfU). The overview of the original model, discussion of pedagogical principles, and explorations of influential events and ideas offered in this chapter provide you with a way to reflect on your own game experiences, which can serve as a starting point for you to reexamine your games teaching. The present reconceptualizations and ideas for research suggest that TGfU has been highly successful in stimulating a solid professional debate around games teaching and learning.

We believe that TGfU as a problem-solving approach to learning has great potential for physical education and sport. The potential lies in the involvement of the learner in game and game form experiences with meaningful teacher/coach facilitation. We also believe that as teachers there are times when telling and showing are appropriate; however, students are most empowered when they are involved.

Discussion Questions

1. Provide an example of the representation principle. How might you use this principle in your teaching?
2. Provide an example of the exaggeration principle. What are three game factors that might be modified to accommodate this principle when designing a games curriculum?
3. Identify the necessary steps to ensure that games are presented at an appropriate level of tactical complexity. How might you alter or modify a game that is too easy? How about too difficult?
4. How might you as a teacher or coach use the expert and novice research to inform your teaching or coaching? Provide an example.

References

Alexander, P., & Judy, J. (1988). The interaction of domain-specific and strategic knowledge in academic performance. *Review of Educational Research, 58*, 375-404.

Almond, L. (2001, August). Teaching for understanding: An historical perspective. Keynote presentation at the Teaching Games for Understanding in Physical Education and Sport International Conference, Waterville Valley, NH, USA.

Anderson, J.R. (1976). *Language, memory, and thought.* Hillsdale, NJ: Erlbaum.

Bunker, D., & Thorpe, R. (1982). A model for the teaching of games in the secondary school. *Bulletin of Physical Education, 18* (1), 5-8.

Butler, J., Griffin, L., & Nastasi, R. (Eds.). (2003). *Teaching games for understanding in physical education and sport.* Reston, VA: National Association for Sport and Physical Education.

Dodds, P., Griffin, L., & Placek, J. (2001). A selected review of the literature on development of learners' domain-specific knowledge. *Journal of Teaching in Physical Education, 20* (4), 301-313.

Dyson, B., Griffin, L.L., & Hastie, P. (2004). Sport education, tactical games and cooperative learning: Theoretical and pedagogical considerations. *Quest, 56*, 226-240.

Ellis, M. (1986). Making and shaping games. In R. Thorpe, D. Bunker, & L. Almond (Eds.), *Rethinking games teaching* (pp. 61-65). Loughborough, England: University of Technology, Department of Physical Education and Sports Science.

French, K.E., & McPherson, S.L. (2004). The development of expertise. In M.R. Weiss (Ed.), *Developmental sport and exercise psychology: A lifespan perspective.* Morgantown, WV: Fitness Information Technology.

French, K., Spurgeon, J., & Nevett, M. (1995). Expert-novice differences in cognitive and skill execution components of youth baseball performance. *Research Quarterly for Exercise and Sport, 66,* 194-201.

French, K., & Thomas, J. (1987). The relation of knowledge development to children's basketball performance. *Journal of Sport Psychology, 9,* 15-32.

French, K.E., Werner, P.H., Taylor, K., Hussey, K., & Jones, J. (1996). The effects of a 6-week unit of tactical, skill, or combined tactical and skill instruction on badminton performance of ninth-grade students. *Journal of Teaching in Physical Education, 15,* 439-463.

Gréhaigne, J., & Godbout, P. (1995). Tactical knowledge in team sports from a constructivist and cognitivist perspective. *Quest, 47,* 490-505.

Gréhaigne, J., & Godbout, P. (1998). Formative assessment in team sport in a tactical approach context. *Journal of Physical Education, Recreation and Dance, 69* (1), 46-51.

Gréhaigne, J., Godbout, P., & Bouthier, D. (1999). The foundations of tactics and strategy in team sports. *Journal of Teaching in Physical Education, 18,* 159-174.

Gréhaigne, J., Godbout, P., & Bouthier, D. (2001). The teaching and learning of decision making in team sports. *Quest, 53,* 59-76.

Griffin, L., Mitchell, S., & Oslin, J. (1997). *Teaching sport concepts and skills: A tactical games approach.* Champaign, IL: Human Kinetics.

Griffin, L., & Placek, J. (2001). The understanding and development of learners' domain-specific knowledge: Introduction. *Journal of Teaching in Physical Education, 20* (4), 299-300.

Griffin, L.L., & Sheehy, D. (2004). Using a tactical games model to teach problem solving in physical education. In J. Wright, D. MacDonald, & L. Burrows (Eds.), *Critical inquiry and problem solving in physical education: Working with students in schools.* London: Routledge.

Holt, N.L., Strean, W.B., & Bengoechea, E.G. (2002). Expanding the Teaching Games for Understanding model: New avenues for future research and practice. *Journal of Teaching in Physical Education, 21* (2), 162-176.

Jeffray, S., & Almond, L. (1986). Introduction to *Coventry Curriculum Development, Games: Coventry teachers explore . . . teaching for understanding.* Coventry, England: Elm Bank Teachers' Centre.

Kirk, D. (1983). Theoretical guidelines for Teaching Games for Understanding. *Bulletin of Physical Education, 19* (1), 41-45.

Kirk, D., & MacDonald, D. (1998). Situated learning in physical education. *Journal of Teaching in Physical Education, 17,* 376-387.

Kirk, D., & MacPhail, A. (2002). Teaching games for understanding and situated learning: Rethinking the Bunker-Thorpe model. *Journal of Teaching in Physical Education, 21,* 117-192.

Lave, J., & Wenger, E. (1991). *Situated learning: Legitimate peripheral participation.* New York: Cambridge University Press.

Light, R., & Fawns, R. (2003). Knowing the game: Integrating speech and action in games teaching through TGfU. *Quest, 55,* 161-176.

Mauldon, E., & Redfern, H.B. (1981). *Games teaching: A new approach for the primary school.* London: MacDonald and Evans.

McPherson, S. (1994). The development of sport expertise: Mapping the tactical domain. *Quest, 46,* 223-240.

McPherson, S. (1999a). Expert-novice differences in performance skills and problem representations of youth and adults during tennis competition. *Research Quarterly for Exercise and Sport, 70,* 233-251.

McPherson, S. (1999b). Tactical differences in problem representations and solutions in collegiate varsity and beginner women tennis players. *Research Quarterly for Exercise and Sport, 70,* 369-384.

McPherson, S., & French, K. (1991). Changes in cognitive strategies and motor skills in tennis. *Journal of Sport & Exercise Psychology, 13,* 26-41.

McPherson, S., & Thomas, J. (1989). Relation of knowledge and performance in boys' tennis: Age and expertise. *Journal of Experimental Child Psychology, 48,* 190-211.

Mitchell, S., Oslin, J., & Griffin, L.L. (2003). *Sport foundations for elementary physical education: A tactical games approach.* Champaign, IL: Human Kinetics.

Morris, G.S.D. (1976). *How to change the games children play.* Minneapolis: Burgess Publishing Company.

Richard, J.-F., Godbout, P., & Griffin, L.L. (2002). An introduction to the Team Sport Assessment Procedure (TSAP). *Physical and Health Education Journal, 68,* 12-18.

Rink, J.E. (1996). Tactical and skill approaches to teaching sport and games [Monograph]. *Journal of Teaching in Physical Education,* 15 (4).

Rink, J.E. (2001). Investigating the assumptions of pedagogy. *Journal of Teaching in Physical Education, 20,* 112-128.

Rink, J., French, K.E., & Tjeerdsma, L. (1996). Foundations for learning and instruction of sport games. *Journal of Teaching in Physical Education, 15,* 399-417.

Rovegno, I., Nevett, M., & Babiarz, M. (2001). Learning and teaching invasion-game tactics in 4th grade: Introduction and theoretical perspective [Monograph]. *Journal of Teaching in Physical Education 20,* 341-351.

Shuell, T. (1986). Cognitive conceptions of learning. *Review of Educational Research, 56,* 411-436.

Sternberg, R.J. (1984). A theory of knowledge acquisition in the development of verbal concepts. *Developmental Review, 4,* 113-138.

Thorpe, R., & Bunker, D. (1986). Is there a need to reflect on our games teaching? In R. Thorpe, D. Bunker, & L. Almond (Eds.), *Rethinking games teaching* (pp. 25-34). Loughborough, England: University of Technology, Department of Physical Education and Sport Science.

Thorpe, R.D., & Bunker, D. (1989). A changing focus in games teaching. In L. Almond (Ed.), *The place of physical education in schools* (pp. 42-71). London: Kogan Page.

Thorpe, R.D., Bunker, D., & Almond, L. (1984). A change in the focus of teaching games. In M. Pieron & G. Graham (Eds.), *Sport pedagogy: Olympic Scientific Congress proceedings* (Vol. 6, pp 163-169). Champaign, IL: Human Kinetics.

Wade, A. (1967). *The FA guide to training and coaching.* London: Heinemann.

Weinstein, C.E., & Mayer, R.E. (1986). The teaching of learning strategies. In M.C. Wittrock (Ed.), *Handbook of research on teaching* (3rd ed., pp. 315-327). New York: Macmillan.

2

Emphasizing Student Engagement in the Construction of Game Performance

Jean-François Richard and Nathalie Wallian

To truly modify and improve their game performance, learners must be given the chance to take what they have learned from their observations and reflections, and to then integrate this new knowledge through a debate of ideas. Intentionally setting up this debate of ideas in the teaching–learning process will help students to verbalize what they have learned and to modify their performance.

Over the past 20 years, conceptions about teaching and learning have changed. As a result of the influences of philosophy, psychology, and semiotics, the perspective of the teaching–learning process has evolved from a teacher-centered approach to a more student-centered approach. Students now have to not only memorize the right solution for a prescribed task but also develop autonomous learning strategies to find available solutions in relation to more complex tasks. Consequently, new teaching–learning approaches have emerged to develop students' autonomy of thought and problem-solving skills. In fact, teachers are confronted with new expectations of their students and of curricula, and consequently, physical education teacher training has opened its boundaries to cross-disciplined scientific and technological approaches. This paradigm shift has forced teachers to adapt their teaching practices to evolving mentalities and bodies of knowledge while still incorporating a reflexive approach.

In physical education, practice and research has shifted from questions about the process/product paradigm (Dunkin & Biddle, 1974), subject-matter knowledge (Schempp, 1993), and the corresponding assessment modalities (Desrosiers, Genet-Volet, & Godbout, 1997; Godbout, 1988) to questions about the way learners build their knowledge in relation to their environment. A distinction has evolved between providing students with experiences and supporting students' development of understanding. For many teachers and teacher educators, the significant focus of research has been to explore *if* and *what* students have learned but rarely *how* they actually learned. Consequently, the relationship between students and how they learn has now been questioned and investigated more thoroughly.

Increasingly, both teachers and teacher educators have become interested in exploring how students learn so that they can better assess and describe students' reasoning from the students' points of view. The basic postulate is that no one can take the student's place because learning is a singular and personal process. To understand how a student develops reflective thinking and adapting strategies, researchers use new paradigms and methods extracted from language and cognitive sciences, such as socioconstructivism and metacognition, which address the social interactions surrounding action.

The purpose of this chapter is to examine the Teaching Games for Understanding (TGfU) model from a constructivist teaching–learning perspective and to explore different concepts and pedagogical principles that emphasize student engagement in the construction of knowledge and skills. We will then shape the scaffolding of a *socioconstructivist approach* applied to games teaching by focusing on the notions of *observation* and the *debate of ideas*. Both of these notions are vital to the construction of knowledge and will be explained in light of improving the current TGfU model.

Constructivism and TGfU

In his discussion of what it means to teach for understanding, Good (1996) explained that "teaching for student understanding" is associated with a constructivist view of the teaching–learning process. According to Lemlech (1998),

> Constructivism and inquiry go hand and hand; they are two parts of the same coin. The teacher assesses what students know, and with this knowledge of the learner, the teacher plans new experiences and knowledge to be gained by the student. Constructivist teaching uses the student's prior knowledge as a building block to integrate new understandings with prior

learning. To accomplish this, the teacher plans active experiences to involve students in explorations, theory building, and experimentation so that students can generate and organize data, and communicate with others. As the learner gains new knowledge, previously held beliefs and ideas may change as new interpretations are made. (p.136)

Constructivism asks for students to be engaged in activities that require higher level thinking and reflective processes. Ultimately, students must demonstrate their understanding by applying the new knowledge in new situations (Lemlech, 1998). Cobb (1986) differentiated between two different constructivist perspectives:

1. To propose to students the discovery of *one solution* (tactical response) that applies in a specific situation. This option is associated with an indirect teaching approach, combining a subject-matter-centered and a student-centered perspective. This perspective could be considered an *empiricist-constructivist approach* to teaching (Cobb, 1986), in which knowledge is an external reality and exists independently of the student's cognitive ability.

2. To propose to students the construction of *suitable personal tactical responses* that apply in a specific situation (there may be more than one plausible response from a student's point of view). This option is also referred to as indirect teaching. It is considered a more *radical constructivist approach* (Cobb, 1986), in which the knowledge constructed by students is the result of the interaction between their cognitive activities and reality (Gréhaigne & Godbout, 1995; Piaget, 1971, 1974a, 1974b).

Given these definitions, we argue that the current TGfU model has more of an empiricist-constructivist connotation. The current TGfU model is characterized by the following:

- The presentation of a tactical problem
- Students' involvement in an adapted game setting that emphasizes the tactical problem at hand
- A series of questions leading to the *specific response* students should be using to address the specific problem

When compared with the traditional "technical" model of games teaching, the TGfU model is more focused on students' development and understanding of game play. Even though most research comparing tactical and technical approaches to teaching games has been inconclusive with regard to the tactical approaches' influence on learning (Rink, 1996), it is noteworthy that most studies were conducted in a very limited time frame (i.e., 6 to12 weeks). Considering the current paradigm shift toward more constructivist approaches to teaching, the classroom culture clearly has to be altered. Hence, the effects of learning as a result of a "new" approach might not occur in a short period of time. This being said, it is important not to forget the basic premise of the constructivist paradigm in education: the development of autonomous learners through their own appropriation of knowledge and skills. TGfU possesses this characteristic when compared to more traditional approaches to games teaching (i.e., technical models). How can TGfU, however, have a more constructivist connotation, and more specifically, a more radical constructivist connotation than it has presently?

Recent work on games teaching by Kirk and MacPhail (2002) presents the TGfU model in relation to a situated learning perspective. This perspective assumes that learning involves the active engagement of learners with their environment. Rather than receiving information from another source and internalizing that information, learners in a situated learning experience actively appropriate information and thus become authors of their own learning (Kirshner & Whitson, 1998). These elements are essential to the process of knowledge construction in any domain. In relation to game performance construction, Gréhaigne and Godbout (1998) specified that this process requires the following:

- Presenting students with problems to solve or putting them in situations favoring the recognition of such problems
- Presenting students with the results of their actions
- Inviting students to appreciate their performance and to decide whether it is satisfactory
- In the case of unsatisfactory results, giving students the opportunity to experiment further and to search for better solutions

Based on this process, two essential components must be included in the teaching and learning of games to enable students to construct their games knowledge and competencies and to become authors of their own learning: (1) observation of game play behaviors and (2) critical thinking through the *debate of ideas*.

Observation As a Critical Moment in the Teaching–Learning Process

Teachers are the facilitators of emergent learning strategies because they organize favorable conditions in relation to problem-solving scenarios (Good, 1996). The difficulty for the teacher is to identify where the problem lies with regard to student understanding and to elucidate the obstacles to constructing efficient responses to particular tactical problems.

Teacher observation of student behavior does not, by itself, provide the teacher with enough data to interpret students' learning strategies and the intentions of their action. To create a learning environment in which students construct their own knowledge and competencies, teachers must integrate students into the systematic observation of game play behavior. As Gréhaigne and Godbout (1998) stated, observation represents a critical moment in the teaching–learning process because it allows both the student and the teacher to retrieve information. From a radical constructivist perspective (i.e., knowledge constructed by students through interactions between their cognitive activities and reality), students must make their own observations (see figure 2.1) if they are to construct their own personal frames of reference in relation to the tactical problems at hand. Gréhaigne and Godbout (1998) added that during or after a performance, students should be asked to collect or recollect information based on their personal observations. The teacher or other student observers can provide additional information. Remember, however, that a constructivist perspective requires interaction between the subject and the environment. Although additional information from other observers can be useful to a student in constructing a frame of reference, outside observers

As Gréhaigne and Godbout (1998) stated, observation represents a critical moment in the teaching–learning process because it allows both the student and the teacher to retrieve information.

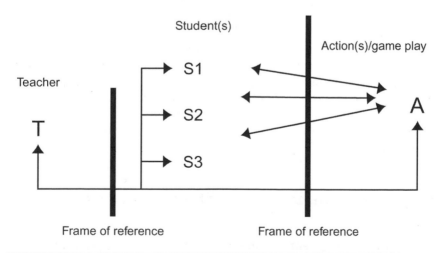

Figure 2.1   A learner-based observational approach.

Gréhaigne & Godbout, 1998.

cannot duplicate the performer's perception of action. Augmented feedback is presented, rather, as additional information that can be processed differently by the learner depending on his perception of the completed action and on the learning stage employed by the teacher (i.e., exploration, construction, consolidation).

If a student is to construct her knowledge and competencies through game play, she needs to develop observational competency not only in describing her behaviors but also in interpreting what makes sense from her point of view. To do this, the student must be directly involved in observing her game play behaviors while in action ("reflection in action," Gréhaigne & Godbout, 1998) with the support of the teacher or peers in the observational process. This support is important in the early stages of the learning process because the student's frame of reference of different game play situations is not innate and final. As a student's learning evolves, so does her observational capabilities. Therefore, as illustrated in figure 2.1, the student is confronted with the construction of a frame of reference with the help of teachers and other students.

Involving students in the observation of game play is certainly beneficial to their learning process. We mentioned in the last paragraph that "reflection in action" is important in the teaching and learning of game concepts. Another important component of observation is related to a student's observations of other students' performances, otherwise known as "reflection on action" (Gréhaigne & Godbout, 1998). From the systematic observation of peers' game play, students can learn about game play and also enhance their peers' learning (Richard, Godbout, Tousignant, & Gréhaigne, 1999). Observation and assessment instruments such as the Team Sport Assessment Procedure (TSAP) (see Gréhaigne, Godbout, & Bouthier, 1997; modified by Richard, Godbout, & Picard, 2000) and the Game Performance Assessment Instrument (GPAI) (see Oslin, Mitchell, & Griffin, 1998) permit teachers to gradually integrate their students into the observation process of selected game behaviors. By using these types of self-/peer assessment procedures, game play data is produced and can be the fuel to create discussion and critical thinking through a debate of ideas (DI) in relation to different game play situations. At the end of a learning scenario, after having a debate of ideas about different game situations, students are able to evaluate their own performances and those of their peers.

Integrating Critical Thinking Through the Debate of Ideas

Critical thinking is a central component of a constructivist approach to learning (Good, 1996). There are many different ways of defining critical thinking. McBride's (1991) position summarizes its application to physical education: " . . . that critical thinking in physical education be defined as reflective thinking that is used to make reasonable and defensible decisions about movement tasks or challenges" (p. 115). How is critical thinking used in the teaching and learning of games? Gréhaigne and Godbout (1998) considered four broad strategies that may be used at various stages of learning:

1. *Letting students explore.* At an early stage of learning pertaining to specified tactical problems, students are put in modified game play situations that present them with a problem. If after some exposure to play, students fail to perceive the problem, the teacher may then let them explore further with or without modification of the play context.

2. *Asking open-ended questions.* Once students have identified a problem, the teacher may ask open-ended questions to encourage debate with the teacher or among the students. Such debates are not directed toward specific, predetermined answers.

3. *Taking part in students' debate and asking specific questions.* After asking open-ended questions, the teacher must be vigilant in moderating the students' debate by discussing the ideas and issues presented by students and asking them more specific questions.

4. *Having students reuse suitable solutions.* Once students have come up with solutions that satisfy selected performance criteria, the teacher may want them to practice these solutions to stabilize their use.

Strategies 2 and 3 are at the core of a constructivist view of the TGfU approach to games education. General discussions, debates within groups, and debriefings can complement one another in enhancing critical thinking and learning (Plummer & Rougeau, 1997). As Schunk (1986) stated, many studies have demonstrated that verbalization can improve children's learning of information, their learning of modeled actions and strategies, and their self-efficacy for performing tasks. Consequently, these findings indicate that verbalization is a key process that can help develop self-regulated learning in children.

Debate of Ideas (DI)

Observation of game play is the basis for student dialogue (i.e., verbalization) about their performance (behaviors), *but it is insufficient for building efficient strategies.* Verbalizing intentions-in-action helps to explain a player's reality from his point of view and is useful for understanding his reasoning. However, teachers must then interpret the positive elements of game play performance to formulate *proper ways to perform a task (action rules)* and to share this information with other students

(Gréhaigne & Godbout, 1998). Consequently, the interpretation of information collected within action is a determinant factor in a constructivist approach to learning.

A student's process of making sense of his responses to particular game situations depends on the interpretation of his intentions-in-action, which are not necessarily expressed in actual game play. In fact, the challenge for the teacher is to understand the reasons a player intended a certain action and the reasons he did not choose a certain alternative. Consequently, the teacher must bring to the forefront, from the player's point of view, the common practical knowledge emerging from game play. DI is a critical component to the construction of game performance because it makes explicit what could remain implicit within the player's mind.

Definition of Debate of Ideas

In the DI setting students exchange and confront their interpretations about the learning activity. Gréhaigne and Godbout (1998) defined this notion as "situations in which students express themselves (overt verbalization), and exchange facts and ideas, based on observation or on personal activity experienced. The debate may concern the results obtained during the action setting, the process involved, and so on" (p. 114). Based on a student's competencies in communicating her thoughts and critical thinking skills, DI allows the student to make explicit her knowledge-in-action. In fact, when a student is confronted with a game situation in which she has to produce efficient strategies and act within her teammates' performance limitations, she is given the opportunity to share her reflections about the action with other students.

The debate of ideas is characterized by situations in which students express themselves (overt verbalization), and exchange facts and ideas, based on observation or on personal activity experienced.

Three Steps for Introducing a Debate of Ideas Setting

To facilitate a postperformance debate of ideas, teachers should explain to the students the tactics they will use in the modified game. The tactics are related to the pursued objectives. During the activity itself, students try to use these tactics adequately at opportune moments. Over a period of time, their game play will evolve and their efficient use of the proposed tactic(s) will be tested. Following a game play sequence, the teacher organizes a time for reflection and a debate of ideas (DI).

The *first step* in creating a DI setting is to invite players to list and describe what happened during game play (observed facts). These descriptions serve as a basis for the sharing of first impressions and for comparing different points of view related to the proposed tactic(s). For example, a team might have lost possession of the ball because of

- a bad pass by the ball carrier,
- a bad decision to pass the ball as a result of the opposing team's defensive configuration,
- a mishandled ball by the ball receiver, or
- a defensive action by the opposing team.

In sharing their ideas and points of view, students build a global picture of what they experienced during game play to help them better understand their own and their teammates' reasoning. During the discussion, each player recognizes other players' roles in the collective action and has an opportunity to consider the points of view of different players. From these descriptions of game events a variety of problematic situations emerge. Different questions can arise from these situations: What is the nature of these problems? What are some of the constraints that hamper a team's success? These types of questions lead to a second phase of critical thinking that consists of attributing possible causes to problematic situations experienced by students during game play.

The *second step* of DI involves students giving their interpretations of the events experienced during game play. This step consists of decoding different processes and attributing meaning to them. Using deductive reasoning, students try to interpret game play problems beyond the surface of observed facts. The students' collective interpretations of game events consist of elaborating different explanations in which actions are justified by specific intentions. The challenge for both teacher and student is to extract significant facts that can explain different alternatives to help students better understand game play behaviors (or nonbehaviors). In fact, the objective in this step is to go beyond observed facts and try to explain the underlying intentions. When doing this, different possibilities may emerge to explain certain actions. Students interpret facts by linking intentions and action; they then estimate the decisional hierarchy by taking into account their own and their teammates' apparent reasoning. The presence of different motor responses to game situations must not distort the reasoning process because it represents the essence of going through such an open, reflexive mental exercise.

The *third step* of DI is to extrapolate efficient strategies from students' interpretations of events. This step serves as a foundation for building plausible responses to future game situations based on the problems encountered in previous play. Students' reasoning is based on cause and effect: "If I respond in a certain way, then this will happen." These connections between causes and effects need to be tested. The only way to test these new strategies is to experiment with them during game play action. This experimentation in action will verify the appropriateness of the strategies and will help to build foundations for future problematic situations of the same nature. DI is a never-ending process of reflective thinking and planning of future action (strategies).

Integrating Observation and the Debate of Ideas Into the Teaching of Games

As Gréhaigne and Godbout (1998) stated, a close relationship might exist between verbalization and observation settings. The use of these two settings can create rich learning situations in which students can build knowledge pertaining to different game situations. Using verbalization through DI in the teaching of team sports may help to meet various needs (Gréhaigne 1996; Gréhaigne & Godbout, 1998), such as the following:

- Building a common frame of reference pertaining to a particular game
- Acknowledging action rules and management rules for the organization of the game
- Developing critical thinking skills that can be used in future game situations

Figure 2.2 illustrates how the observation and verbalization settings can be organized in such an arrangement.

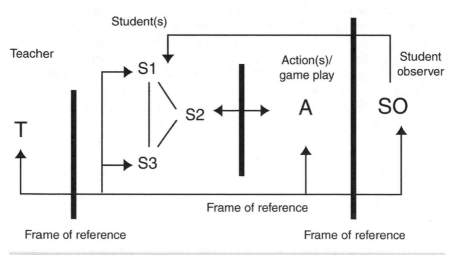

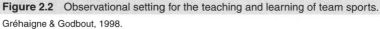
Figure 2.2 Observational setting for the teaching and learning of team sports.
Gréhaigne & Godbout, 1998.

The center of figure 2.2 is represented by the action/game play setting, which involves a certain number of students (e.g., 3v3, 5v5). The teacher and student observers make up the observation setting. They observe the action setting based on their individual (or partly shared) frames of reference. The teacher must be responsible in guiding student observers in their observations of game play. Finally, the various lines connecting the members of a team (S1, S2, S3, etc.) and the team with the teacher and student observers represent the debate of ideas setting (through verbalization), involving reflection on action.

Similar to any approach that teachers may want to integrate into their classroom, developing a DI setting based on systematic observation takes planning to maximize student benefit. To fully integrate a DI approach, teachers will need to use classroom time. Although an important aspect of physical education classes is to provide students with sufficient activity time, time for reflection and discussion is necessary if learning is to be an important aspect of the class (Richard & Picard, 1998).

Conclusion

The notions of observation and the debate of ideas presented in this chapter are fundamental in the development of a constructivist approach to the teaching and learning of games. These are essential components of a situated learning perspective in games education. Integrating observation and the debate of ideas in a classroom setting fosters students' critical thinking. Gréhaigne & Godbout (1998) also added that problem-solving learning requires reflection ("reflection in action" and "reflection on action") on the part of the student. Without reflection, students can only stumble blindly from one trial to another hoping for random success or waiting for an outside observer to tell them what to do next. In either case, no real understanding develops. Although verbalization may facilitate reflection, observation, through informal (noninstrumented) or formal means (instrumented— GPAI, TSAP, or other types of observational tools), will provide the basic data on which to reflect. By offering students a structured learning environment that includes observation and critical thinking, teachers should be able to develop a "reflective reflex" in their students. If so, then teaching for understanding will have occurred, at least from a radical constructivist point of view (Cobb, 1986).

Without reflection, students can only stumble blindly from one trial to another hoping for random success or waiting for an outside observer to tell them what to do next. In either case, no real understanding develops.

In conclusion, we have chosen to emphasize the aspects that we feel are essential in the evolution of TGfU as a constructivist approach and possibly a radical constructivist approach to games learning. We are advocating ways to help make TGfU more of a radical constructivist approach to teaching. If learners are to truly modify and improve their game performance, they must be given the chance to reinvest the notions and realizations they make through observations and critical thinking; that is, the learners must be given the chance to try out the knowledge they have learned (from observations and critical thinking) in game situations. Integrating observation and critical thinking (through DI) as regular features of the teaching–learning process will help students to verbalize what they have learned and to modify their performance. In the spirit of constructing knowledge and know-how, students must have the chance to experiment in action to truly integrate what they have learned through discussion (Richard & Godbout, 2000). Students will have truly learned if, when faced with a problem that is new but compatible with the resources they have at their disposal, they can succeed, thus demonstrating that they have *transformed* and *stabilized* their initial behavior and identified and verbalized the action rules that made their success possible (Gréhaigne & Godbout, 1998). By respecting this process, teachers will create a teaching environment that includes systematic observation and critical thinking and that will potentially help students to more fully understand and integrate their knowledge of different games and sports.

Discussion Questions

1. How do we define constructivism in an educational setting? How is constructivism different from behavioral and cognitive teaching approaches?

2. Differentiate between empiricist-constructivist and radical constructivist teaching perspectives. Typically, where does the TGfU model situate itself within these two perspectives?

3. Some say observation is a key component in a student's construction of game knowledge and understanding. Explain the different roles involved in the observation process (student-player, student-observer, and teacher) and their influence on the student's construction of game concepts.

4. Through observation, information can be retrieved to create a DI setting that is important in the development of critical thinking. Knowing that the time allotted for physical education is often limited in many school settings around the world (i.e., number of periods a week, class time), how can teachers effectively create a DI setting without compromising classroom activity time?

References

Cobb, P. (1986). Making mathematics. Children's learning and constructivist tradition. *Harvard Educational Review, 56,* 301-306.

Desrosiers, P., Genet-Volet, Y., & Godbout, P. (1997). Teachers' assessment practices viewed through the instruments used in physical education classes. *Journal of Teaching in Physical Education, 16,* 211-228.

Dunkin, M.J., & Biddle, B.J. (1974). *The study of teaching.* New York: Holt, Reinhart & Winston.

Godbout, P. (1988). La supervision de l'évaluation en activité physique [The supervision of evaluation in physical activity]. In J. Brunelle, D. Drouin, P. Godbout, & M. Tousignant, (Eds.) *La supervision de l'intervention en activité physique [The supervision of intervention in physical activity]* (pp. 215-317). Montréal, QC: Gaétan Morin.

Good, T. (1996). Teaching effects and teacher evaluation. In J. Sikula, T.J. Buttery, & E. Guyton (Eds.), *Handbook of research on teacher education* (2nd ed.) (pp. 617-665). New York: Simon & Shuster.

Gréhaigne, J.-F. (1996). Les règles d'actions: Un support pour les apprentissages [Action rules: A support for learning]. *Éducation physique et sport, 265,* 71-73.

Gréhaigne, J.-F., & Godbout, P. (1995). Tactical knowledge in team sports from a constructivist and cognitivist perspective. *Quest, 47,* 490-505.

Gréhaigne, J.-F., & Godbout, P. (1998). Observation, critical thinking and transformation: Three key elements for a constructivist perspective of the learning process in team sports. Presented at the 1998 AIESEP world conference. Adelphi University, Long Island, N.Y.

Gréhaigne, J.-F., Godbout, P., & Bouthier, D. (1997). Performance assessment in team sports. *Journal of Teaching in Physical Education, 16,* 500-516.

Kirk, D., & MacPhail, A. (2002). Teaching games for understanding and situated learning: Rethinking the Bunker-Thorpe model. *Journal of Teaching in Physical Education, 21,* 177-192.

Kirshner, D., & Whitson, J.A. (1998). Obstacles to understanding cognition as situated. *Educational Researcher, 27,* 22-28.

Lemlech, J.K. (1998). *Curriculum and instructional methods for the elementary and middle school.* Upper Saddle River, NJ: Prentice Hall.

McBride, R. (1991). Critical thinking: An overview with implications for physical education. *Journal of Teaching in Physical Education, 11,* 112-125.

Oslin, J.L., Mitchell, S.A., & Griffin, L.L. (1998). The Game Performance Assessment Instrument (GPAI): Development and preliminary validation. *Journal of Teaching in Physical Education, 17,* 231-243.

Piaget, J. (1971). *Biology and knowledge: An essay on the relations between organic regulations and cognitive processes.* Chicago: University of Chicago Press.

Piaget, J. (1974a). *La prise de conscience [Sudden awareness].* Paris: PUF.

Piaget, J. (1974b). *Réussir et comprendre [Succeeding and understanding].* Paris: PUF.

Plummer, O.K., & Rougeau, D. (1997). Team building magic for all. *Strategies, 10* (6), 22-24.

Richard, J.-F., & Godbout, P. (2000). Formative assessment as an integral part of the teaching-learning process. *Physical and Health Education Journal, 66* (3), 4-10.

Richard, J.-F., Godbout, P., & Picard, Y. (2000). La validation d'une procédure d'évaluation en sports collectifs [The validation of a team sport assessment procedure]. *Mesure et évaluation en éducation, 23* (1), 43-67.

Richard, J.-F., Godbout, P., Tousignant, M., & Gréhaigne, J.-F. (1999). The try-out of a team-sport assessment procedure in elementary and junior high school PE classes. *Journal of Teaching in Physical Education, 18* (3), 336-356.

Richard, J.-F., & Picard, Y. (1998). Physical education in our schools: Emphasizing the educational outcomes of physical activity. *The Canadian Association for Health, Physical Education, Recreation and Dance Journal, 64* (4), 44-45.

Rink, J.E. (Ed.). (1996). Tactical and skill approaches to teaching sports and games [Monograph]. *Journal of Teaching in Physical Education, 15* (4).

Schempp, P. (1993). Constructing professional knowledge: A case study of an experienced high-school teacher. *Journal of Teaching in Physical Education, 13,* 2-23.

Schunk, D.H. (1986). Verbalization and children's self-regulated learning. *Contemporary Educational Psychology, 11,* 347-369.

3

Teaching Games for Understanding As a Curriculum Model

Joy I. Butler and Barbara J. McCahan

"Welcome back, sixth grade! We're going to start the year with a soccer unit. Like the professionals, we're going to learn how to perform some of the techniques we'll need so that we can play more effectively. I want you to get into pairs, stand about six feet apart, and start by practicing your inside kicks. Right! Let's get set up. One person in each pair go and collect a ball."

As students collect their soccer balls, they can be heard to be mumbling, "We did this last year," and "Can't we just play the game?"

Mr. Pettitt, a fifth-year teacher, overhears one of the students and says, "Now come on, Tony. Listen up! This is going to be fun. Once we have this down, we can start playing."

Clearly, Mr. Pettitt is troubled by the responses of his students but is compelled to teach in this fashion. After all, this is the basic curriculum model he has always used. His instincts tell him to move quickly through the skill progressions so that the class stays motivated. He has often had difficulty integrating students with greater playing experience from extracurricular teams with students whose soccer experience is limited to the scope of their physical education program. Although the less experienced students need time and practice to develop skills, they also need opportunities to transfer those skills into actual play or they will make little, if any, progress in the unit. Mr. Pettitt bemoans the limited time he has available to hone each student's skills and still allow for playing. There just isn't enough time allowed for physical education classes to cover all the games and do any of them justice!

This well-meaning, energetic, and enthusiastic teacher is faced with a dilemma. He wants his students to play games, but he does not want to spend too much of the precious class time having students play because the students clearly need so much work on their skills to play well. As Richard Light and Rod Fawns (2003) stated,

> Despite the potential that games offer as a learning process and the complex higher order thinking that is essential for skillful performance, in team games much teaching is still purely focused on the physical dimensions of games isolated from their social and cognitive dimensions. (p. 161)

What Mr. Pettitt needs is an alternative that can accommodate different learning abilities and focus on the cognitive and social dimensions of a game in addition to the physical dimensions. Using a curriculum model based on a conceptual perspective of games can provide just such an alternative. Thoughtfully implemented, this alternative can free the teacher from the need to address all games specifically. Instead of centering pedagogical work around *how to do it* (techniques practiced), Mr. Pettitt would be able to address the *why* (common concepts) and *what if* (skills and strategies for better play). This paradigm shift would allow Mr. Pettitt to change his teaching focus from correcting what is wrong with the students' actions to encouraging his students to respond with a range of creative actions, generated by their own decisions.

Any curriculum model is based on a conceptual framework and a set of assumptions about educational priorities, presentation mechanisms, instructional methods, and evaluation criteria. Although curriculum models vary in their philosophies, they guide teachers and administrators in delivering and assessing programs. Some curriculum models are highly prescriptive and provide detailed guidelines for teacher behaviors. Others rely on guiding concepts and allow teachers the freedom to determine how to implement these concepts. Curriculum models, regardless of their goals or flexibility, are designed to help structure programs through the use of a plan that will have instructional integrity and predictable learning outcomes.

The purpose of this chapter is to

- examine how the inherent assumptions and values of Teaching Games for Understanding (TGfU) can help teachers develop a healthy, vital, and inclusive games curriculum;

- compare the TGfU model with the technique model in terms of purpose, objectives, outcomes, and games framework;
- examine the TGfU classification system;
- show how to create a spiral curriculum that will obviate the need for physical educators to cover all games;
- provide planning considerations using a sample TGfU games program;
- describe the learning steps involved in the TGfU model; and
- offer guidelines for implementation.

Inherent Assumptions and Values

The philosophy, or system of values, that underlies a curriculum model frames the curriculum design and the teaching process. Effective curriculum models have the potential to align educational priorities (what is taught), educational philosophy (why things are taught), and educational methods (how things are taught) (Butler, 1993). Several other fundamental questions are also addressed when a curriculum model is adopted, including: What is the role of the learner? What is the role of the teacher? What is the social and structural context of the learning environment? How will learning be assessed and evaluated?

The educational philosophy underlying the TGfU model is based on constructivism. This learning theory advocates that comprehension and meaning be built gradually using experiences and contexts that help students become willing and able to learn. Constructivism uses problem solving, tasks, groups, and sharing activities to provide learning that can be structured around basic concepts. Brooks and Brooks (1999) in *The Case for Constructivist Classrooms* say that "Deep understanding, not imitative behavior is the goal. . . . We look not for what students can repeat, but for what they can generate, demonstrate, and exhibit" (p. 16).

An inherent challenge for physical education teachers is to break away from the exclusive use of "direct instruction," which has been the norm for most of the current adult generation. This norm developed under the influence of curriculum reformist Ralph Tyler in the 1940s.

The University of Chicago first published Tyler's *Basic Principles of Curriculum and Instruction* in 1949. Herein Tyler argued that teachers should develop specific objectives for their courses, develop activities and programs to reach the goals, and then prepare tests to determine if the goals had been reached. Tyler's original intent was to help teachers to identify problems in learning and practice creative ways in solving those problems.

Historically, the use of this model has been partly the result of how physical educators interpreted Ralph Tyler's rationale (1949). This led to a step-by-step process for developing a curriculum in physical education that attempted to provide a blueprint for teaching in the form of a technical model. Kirk and Tinning (1992) described the key features of this approach as "the use of objectives in planning programs and instructional episodes; the selection of subject matter and teaching strategies based on intended learning outcomes expressed as behavioral objectives; and assessment of the behavioral outcomes of instruction involving measurement and quantification" (p. 1).

The main emphasis of the technical model has always been performance, and the model has generally yielded good performance results for some. Most physical education teachers came through their early school years with a technique approach and went on to use it to help students master techniques. Generally, students who enjoy games and are inherently good at them have always had positive experiences with the technical approach.

The technical approach, however, allows little room for creativity or for learner empowerment. In 1982, Bunker and Thorpe drew attention to students who are, or who have been, disaffected and disenfranchised in their experiences in games education. Others have also called on physical educators to reexamine the way we teach games and to find ways to enhance our curriculum (Griffin, Mitchell, & Oslin, 1997; Kirk, 1993; Werner & Almond, 1990). To access the many assets of constructivism, a curriculum would build on concepts and strategies that allow both students and teachers to think "out of the box," to step back from the status quo and challenge assumptions about what should be learned and how. In this spirit, Kirk (1993) suggested that future curriculum workers will need "capabilities which allow them to learn from experience, to regenerate, and to imagine beyond experience—in a word, to be reflexive" (p. 262).

To illustrate how the TGfU model can be used as a basis for curriculum development, table 3.1 deliberately polarizes and compares the assumptions and tenets inherent in the technical model and those inherent in the TGfU model. The dichotomy offered in this table is one that could apply equally to other areas of the curriculum, such as reading and writing, in which a similar dialogue is in progress with regard to phonics and whole language.

In essence, the technical model is based on behaviorist learning theory, which advocates the use of direct instruction by teachers, who are the "keepers of knowledge" who will "transmit" information to "receptive" students (Allison & Barrett, 2000). The constructivist TGfU model, conversely, uses conceptual and transactional instruction. Students are viewed as thinkers with emerging theories about the world. Teachers investigate the students' points of view to understand students' present

Table 3.1 Comparison of the Technical Model and the TGfU Model

	Technical model (behaviorist)	TGfU model (constructivist)
Why it is taught (philosophical and historical perspectives)		
Culture	Factory/product model	Village green/progressive education
Belief system	Dualism	Integration of mind, body, and spirit
Context	Isolation; links with coaching and professional sport	Integration of school and community
Training	Efficiency/military influence	Movement education
Experience	Specialism/sport	Integration and inclusiveness
What is taught (curriculum)		
Purpose	Acquisition of knowledge	Construction of meaning
Objective	Defining what we know	Discovering what we don't know and applying what we know
Outcome	Performance	Thinking and decision making
Game frameworks	Seasonal activities	Classification
How it is taught (pedagogy)		
Instruction	Teacher centered	Student centered, developmental, progressive
Strategy	Part–whole	Whole–part–whole
Content	Techniques based	Concept based
Context	Teacher–student interaction	Multidimensional interaction
Teacher role	Transmission of information	Facilitation of problem solving
Learner role	Passive learning	Active learning
Evaluation	Mastery	Demonstration of understanding and contributions to process

From J. Butler, 1998, Factory vs. village green. Two approaches in teaching games education. *Education for life*. Association Internationale des Ecoles Superieures d'Education Physique. World Convention Proceedings. New York. By permission of R. Feingold.

In the same way that a worthy opponent helps define and refine the skills of each player, it is our hope that this comparison will help separate out the distinguishing characteristics of these models and illustrate their impact on the games experience for students.

conceptions for use in subsequent lessons (Brooks & Brooks, 1999). For the purpose of this discussion, the two extremes of these models are polarized in table 3.1, with the understanding that in reality, most school curricula lie somewhere between these extremes. In the same way that a worthy opponent helps define and refine the skills of each player, it is our hope that this comparison will help separate out the distinguishing characteristics of these models and illustrate their impact on the games experience for students.

Curriculum (What Is Taught): Comparing the Technical Model With the TGfU Model

Table 3.1 presents three areas of consideration in building a course of study:

1. Why it is taught (curriculum theories based on philosophical and historical perspectives)
2. What is taught (the curriculum model based on the why and conceptual framework—see table 3.2)
3. How it is taught (pedagogical perspectives including action and reflection)

Keep in mind that curriculum theories are based on assumptions about society, humanity, and education. Curriculum models represent the operational mode of these theories. This chapter will highlight only the curriculum section (what is taught) of table 3.1 and will consider the purpose, objectives, outcomes, and frameworks of each model and their impact on students. The curriculum theories embedded in the *why* section of table 3.1 are left for another, albeit necessary, discussion.

Purpose: Acquisition of Knowledge Versus Construction of Meaning

The purpose of the curriculum is derived from a set of values and beliefs and is a paramount consideration for its designer (Butler, 1998). The underlying question is, Why do we teach games? (Bunker & Thorpe, 1986).

If the purpose is to train students to replicate certain behaviors or skills, then the technical approach, based in behaviorist theory (i.e., stimuli and reinforcements), works well and fulfills the purpose of teaching games, which is seen as acquiring knowledge. Content is broken down into small steps that are then modeled for students who practice them in efficient drills. This allows the teacher maximum time to provide both positive and corrective feedback to each student. The focus is on psychomotor learning, with cognitive learning as a second priority (Metzler, 2005).

> *If the purpose is to train students to replicate certain behaviors or skills, then the technical approach, based in behaviorist theory (i.e., stimuli and reinforcements), works well and fulfills the purpose of teaching games, which is seen as acquiring knowledge.*

If developing deeper understanding, synthesis, decision making, and the ability to use information in a variety of situations is the main purpose of the curriculum, the TGfU model is a better fit than the technical model because it encourages students to construct meaning from the situations in which they are placed. In other words, to encourage students to apply game skills effectively in the context of playing will require attention to a deeper understanding of the game, as provided by TGfU. As Griffin and colleagues (1997) suggested, students using this approach are less likely to ask, Why are we doing this? or When can we play a game? As seen through the constructivist lens, learners make sense of their world by synthesizing new experiences, in a process Piaget and Inhelder (1971) referred to as assimilation and accommodation. Therefore, the purpose of teaching games is to enable students to construct meaning in games education.

> *If developing deeper understanding, synthesis, decision making, and the ability to use information in a variety of situations is the main purpose of the curriculum, the TGfU approach is a better fit than the technical model because it encourages students to construct meaning from the situations in which they are placed.*

Objective: Defining What We Know Versus Discovering What We Don't Know and Applying What We Know

In the technical model, the teacher's objective is to teach the student the information effectively and efficiently. This can be summed up as *transmission*. One can recognize the influence of early 20th-century military and efficiency models in a transmission approach to teaching. Embedded in it are assumptions that all students start with the same knowledge, learn at the same rate, and will learn using this style. In contexts in which players are highly motivated, such as voluntary play situations, the teacher or coach can move efficiently through the skills, thus defining what players know.

The teacher's objective in the TGfU model is to offer all students, regardless of ability or skill level, the opportunity to actively experience, enjoy, and understand games. Student behavior is much less predictable when the TGfU approach is used (e.g., when students are engaged in making tactical decisions in a modified game). Although students may be learning in ways the teacher is unable to foresee, the teacher can channel students' experiences through a process that Kirk (1993) described as "curriculum work as craft." Students are encouraged to listen, explore, discuss, and create ideas. Students' assumptions are challenged, and their decisions are negotiated.

Although many teachers report "understanding" as their primary objective, many don't scaffold or make connections to allow students to truly make sense of what they know and what they're discovering and learning. Many teachers use skill drills out of game context or allow students to "just play" without purposely ensuring the building of connections between skill acquisition and game strategies (Butler, 1997). "Curriculum work does not produce prescriptions for what teachers and students are to do, but provides provisional strategies" (Jewett, Bain, & Ennis, 1995, p. 123).

Outcome: Performance Versus Thinking and Decision Making

The expected outcome of the technical model is that students will become skillful performers. They are also expected to be orderly, compliant, and respectful so that they can learn what to do and how to do it. For example, students may be assessed in a soccer lesson on their ability to execute a kick using the inside of the foot to make accurate and short passes. Various rubrics delineating criteria of this skill will be rated according to the student's performance. If we can imagine this taking place in a fourth-grade class, we can also imagine the application of this in a game. Often

The expected outcome of the technical model is that students will become skillful performers. They are also expected to be orderly, compliant, and respectful so that they can learn what to do and how to do it.

students assume that their role in the game is to kick the ball because that is the focus of the lead-up skills practice. They end up replicating bees around the honey pot!

TGfU's shift in focus—from *how* to *why* or *what if* (Kirk & Tinning, 1992)—encourages students to reflect and to ask questions. As Brooks and Brooks (1999) suggested, when students have to reconsider their prior ideas in

Through a process of teacher questioning, students would learn to think about each game situation using the following questions: What is happening here? How do I help my team move the ball upfield? Where should I move?

the presence of new information to create cognitive structures, deep understanding will occur. Their skills in negotiating, compromising, and listening are developed through small-group work. Students are required to make creative decisions, to question, and to challenge themselves and each other—much like children do at play. The previous example of the soccer lesson would look different in a TGfU class. The assessment focus for student learning would be the thinking process and decision making of the students. Through a process of teacher questioning, students would learn to think about each game situation using the following questions: What is happening here? How do I help my team move the ball upfield? Where should I move?

Game Frameworks: Seasonal Activities Versus Classification

The technical model organizes its curriculum in imitation of the seasonal cycles of professional sport. As reported by one teacher in Butler's study (1993),

> The curriculum varies but it stays the same. I mean I think everyone in the fall plays a little football, plays a little soccer. When you start coming inside you do a little gymnastics, you do a little basketball. In the spring there is field and track, you are doing softball, so I think that is pretty traditional. (p. 145)

Werner and Almond (1990) suggested that "offering an extensive variety of sports in one- or two-week units means that students never have time to become proficient" (p. 23). The TGfU model uses a classification system for its framework and bases the inclusion of games on a systematic selection process. Games with similar intents are grouped together (see table 3.2).

Table 3.2 Essential Components of Games Education (Conceptual Framework)

	Target	Striking	Net/wall	Territorial
Main intention of game	To send away an object and make contact with a specific, stationary target in fewer attempts than the opponent.	To place the ball away from fielders in order to run the bases and score more runs than the opponents.	To send the ball back to the opponent so that the opponent is unable to return it or is forced to make an error. Serving is the only time the object is held.	To invade the opponents' defending area to score a goal while simultaneously protecting own goal.
Concepts and skills	Sending away Skills: drive, release, deliver	I. Placement of the ball in the field Skills: striking, body positioning, hand positions on bat II. Decision making Skills: observation, listening, receiving, throwing III. Covering bases Skills: sprinting, ready position, moving sideways IV. Base running Skills: sliding, sprinting	I. Spatial awareness Skills: throwing, catching on bounce and volley, serving and receiving serve II. Positioning on court Skills: running, stopping, changing directions III. Position of body Skills: balance, footwork, hitting the ball in relation to the body IV. Trajectory Skills: throwing, catching V. Depth Skills: hitting with specific force, lob shot, drop shot, spin shots, volley, drives, dig VI. Angles Skills: control of racket, angle of racket, volley, forehand and backhand	**Offensive Concepts** I. Keeping possession Skills: sending, receiving, traveling II. Penetration/invasion Skills: accurate passing and receiving, dodging, change of speeds **Defensive Concepts** I. Zoning, defending players in area Skills: shuffle, change of speed, running in different directions II. Defending a specific player Skills: footwork III. Transposition concepts Skills: peripheral vision, footwork, running, quick change of directions

Players' roles	Same skill required for all players; no interaction	Variation in roles for defensive team (e.g., pitcher, catcher)	All players require same skills as they rotate positions (e.g., all serve and receive)	Designated goalkeeper; defensive and offensive role or player; midcourt (both roles)
Playing area	Playing area shared; players take turns; variations from golf courses to ice sheets	Area is shared; offensive team has designated track to run; running track varies	Area is divided by a net; opposing players are separated	Area shared by all players; rectangular; often outdoors
Offensive strategies	Hitting a target: archery gold; bowling jack; curling button; golf hole; pool pockets; skittles pins	Fielding positions; forcing play; holding runner from stealing; staying on offense; keeping turn for as long as possible OK	Placing ball farthest away from player(s); placing ball close to boundary lines; moving to volley position at net; intercepting; anticipating; employing spikers	Keeping possession; moving ball or puck to specified area; rapid changing from offensive to defensive; transposition—organization of players moving from offense to defense and vice versa
Defensive strategies	No defensive strategies in individual games. In team games, obstacles prevent own target from being hit.	Stealing; leading; tagging up; quick and accurate receiving and sending skills	Returning object and keeping it in bounds; anticipating where opponents will return object	Intercepting ball or puck before it goes over the line or into the goal; pressuring opponents into making mistakes; closing down distribution options
Examples of games	Archery, bowls, bowling, croquet, curling, golf, pool, billiards	Baseball, cricket, Danish longball, kickball, rounders, softball	Net: badminton, pickleball, tennis, table tennis, volleyball Wall: handball, racquetball, squash	Basketball, field/ice hockey, football, lacrosse, soccer, team handball, water polo, ultimate Frisbee

TGfU Classification of Games

Bunker and Thorpe (1982) categorized games of similar intents into the following headings: invasion, net/wall, striking/fielding, and target sports. Since the publication of the 1982 classification, authors have made various modifications to these headings. To move away from militaristic connotations, Bunker and Thorpe chose to use the term *territorial* instead of *invasion*. Doolittle and Fay adopted the term *team passing sports* in their 2002 publication, *Authentic Assessment of Physical Activity for High School Students*.

Game components used to distinguish the categories include intent, concepts and skills, players' roles, playing area, and offensive and defensive strategies (see table 3.2). With these components in place, the curriculum can be arranged to allow the development and sequencing of concepts and the transfer of ideas and relationships both among games and among the concepts they involve. The common conceptual threads can be presented and mastered in varied contexts. As Thorpe (1989) pointed out, highlighting these relationships increases tactical complexity and greater decision making for students. He suggested that this is what separates the physical education teacher from other providers of games experiences (e.g., coaches and sport leaders).

When read from left to right, table 3.3 (Thorpe, Bunker, and Almond's games classification) reflects a developmental sequence, with target and

Table 3.3   Thorpe, Bunker, and Almond Games Classification

Target	Striking/fielding	Net/wall	Territorial
Archery	Baseball	Net:	Basketball
Billiards	Cricket	Badminton	Football
Bowling	Danish longball	Pickleball	Handball (team)
Croquet	Kickball	Table tennis	Hockey: field, floor, ice
Curling	Rounders	Tennis	Lacrosse
Pool	Softball	Volleyball	Netball
Snooker		Wall:	Rugby
		Handball (court)	Soccer
		Paddleball	Speedball
		Racquetball	Ultimate Frisbee
		Squash	Water polo

Figure 3.1 Magnet soccer.

striking games followed by net/wall games, which are followed by territorial games. The concept and skills embedded in target and striking games form the foundation for the more conceptually sophisticated and complex net and territorial games. Students need to think and respond more quickly in the continuous nature of net/wall games because striking games allow a team to gather itself between plays. Net games are less complex than territorial games because the opposition is contained in one area. Territorial games move further along this continuum; now the opposition can intersect with all spaces on the field.

Children who have not reached Piaget's third stage of cognitive development (concrete-operational—ages 7 to 8) are unable to think about more than one thing at a time (decenter). When introduced to soccer, they are thus likely to focus on one thing (see figure 3.1). If the teacher has taught kicking, then that is what the students will do, all at the same time! The same types of progressions can be applied to each of the behavioral learning domains: psychomotor—closed skills to open; affective—indirect competition in target games versus direct competition in other categories.

Sample TGfU Games Program

With the conceptual framework in place and values established, the selection and structuring of the program content can now occur. Without such a framework (other frameworks have been offered by scholars, such as

Table 3.4   Games Education Program (Time allocation: one period per week)

	3rd grade	4th grade	5th grade	6th grade	
Fall (Sept.–Oct.)	Manipulative skills development: 1v1 games	Intro. to territorial games	Soccer, hockey	Inventing games	
Fall (Oct.–Dec.)	Bowling, skittles	Pickleball (no rackets)	Danish longball, quik cricket	Basketball, hockey, soccer	
Spring (Jan.–Feb.)	Intro. to net games (no rackets)	Basketball, soccer	Floor hockey, soccer, basketball	Pickleball	
Spring (Feb.–April)	1v1	Volleyball–3v3	Pickleball (with rackets)	Danish longball, softball	
Spring (April–June)	Bowling (with angles–intro to wall games)	Intro. to striking games	Kickball	Pickleball, tennis	

☐ = Territorial games   ▨ = Net/wall games

Mauldon & Redfern, 1981; and Ellis, 1983), it is easy to fall into biased selections, choosing games with which we feel familiar or with which we have had more experience. The games education program (see table 3.4) is an attempt to offer a TGfU program for grades 3 through 12 with an allocation of one class period per week. Many programs often allocate a disproportionate 60% to 90% of the physical education program to games education (Fleming 1994; Thorpe, Bunker, & Almond, 1984; Turner & Martinek, 1995; Werner & Almond, 1990; Werner & Thorpe, 1996) and

7th grade	8th grade	9th	10th grade	11th grade	12th grade
Field hockey, lacrosse	Softball, Danish longball, cricket	Foundation course—sport education	Golf, archery	Soccer, hockey, basketball	Tennis, wallyball
Badminton, volleyball	Flag football, hockey		Pickleball, tennis, racquetball	Bowling, archery, golf	Flag football, hockey, soccer
Basketball, soccer, hockey	Badminton, pickleball		Team handball, soccer, basketball	Badminton, volleyball	Racquetball, wallyball
Ultimate Frisbee, hockey, lacrosse	Volleyball, tennis		Volleyball, pickleball, tennis	Basketball, team handball, soccer	Lacrosse, soccer, hockey
Cricket, Danish longball	Archery, golf		Softball, baseball, Danish longball	Cricket, softball	Softball, cricket

███ = Striking games   ███ = Target games

give undue weight to territorial games (Butler, 1993; Jackson, Jones, & Williamson, 1983). A program organized around the following factors will look less cluttered because representations of each category are taught instead of as many games as the program allows. The sample program offered in table 3.4 is a generic example that can be modified to accommodate the specific needs and contexts of any school.

The following factors have been considered when planning the sample program in table 3.4:

1. *Time.* Time is required to develop a game in some depth. Some games need more time than others (e.g., bowling takes less time to understand than basketball).

2. *Focus.* Teachers should focus on a few games at each grade level and let them represent the category (Collier & Oslin, 2001). Less is more.

3. *Sampling.* Children need to experience a number of games to understand their similarities and differences. One game in the classification is selected as the focus for a particular year group, and others from the same classification can be sampled to draw out the similarities. For example, basketball has been chosen as the focus game for the fourth grade (see table 3.4), with soccer as the sampling game. As stated earlier, relationships among the games can be made clear in terms of concepts, strategies, and skills.

4. *Readiness of learners.* Games chosen should be based on the developmental levels of students. For example, as suggested earlier, first- or second-grade students are generally not cognitively ready to learn territorial games.

5. *Intertask transfer (of skills, concepts, and strategies).* The curriculum should maximize the transfer of learning that occurs from one game to another within the classification (and, to a lesser extent, to games from other classifications). For example, the ability to pass to an open teammate and move toward the goal for the return pass (give and go) can be applied to most territorial games.

6. *Intratask transfer (of skills, concepts, and strategies).* The curriculum needs to be arranged so that skills and concepts learned in each game transfer to the next level of difficulty within that game. Skills taught should be given adequate time and should be quickly employed in an appropriate game situation. Central to the TGfU model is the creation of practices that have transfer potential. This will be determined by the "similarities between one practice situation and another or between a practice and the real game" (Launder, 2001, p. 21).

7. *Spiral curriculum* (Bruner, 1977). The ideas, concepts, and strategies within the four categories should be revisited each year. Weight should be given to unifying ideas rather than to any specific game. Each year, the curriculum "spirals" to more advanced levels of instruction and new materials.

8. *Standards.* National, regional, and state/county standards will be an important consideration here (e.g., NASPE, 1995; National Curriculum Council, 1992; Ministry of Education, Singapore, 2003). A conceptual framework such as the TGfU model can provide easy

connections between the games program and designation standards.

The TGfU Model and Its Steps

Bunker and Thorpe (1982) first published the TGfU model for games teaching in the *Bulletin of Physical Education*. Butler (2002) adapted it by adding material related to Rink's (2002) four stages of developing game play. A quick glance at figure 3.2 shows that the TGfU model starts the learning focus with the equivalent of stage 3 of the traditional approach—step 1 of the TGfU model. Step 1 is the playing of (modified) games emphasizing learning on tactical awareness and decision making. The beginning of the traditional approach starts the learning process with stage 1 emphasizing skill acquisition before being given access to the game.

The following are Rink's four stages of game play:

Stage 1 Developing control of the object

Stage 2 Complex control and combination of skills

Stage 3 Beginning offensive and defensive strategies

Stage 4 Complex game play in the context of the TGfU model

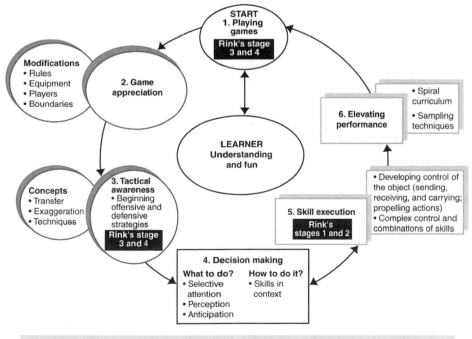

Figure 3.2 Model for games teaching.

Adapted, by permission, from D. Bunker and R. Thorpe, 1982, "A model for the teaching of games in the secondary school," *Bulletin of Physical Education* 10:9-16.

In essence, the TGfU model reverses the traditional order of teaching games and thereby "enables students to learn about the game and practice the technique within the context of a game rather than separate from it" (Thorpe, 2001, p. 23). The game and its tactics are central to the lesson, rather than tagged on to the end or left for extracurricular practice time.

The steps of the TGfU model are as follows:

1. *Game.* All students are able to play the game. Margaret Ellis (1986) outlined the benefits and means of "enabling" every child to participate, regardless of skill level, by modifying such things as rules, equipment, playing areas, and group size.

2. *Game appreciation.* Students learn to understand and respect the necessity of rules because they create, implement, and refine them.

3. *Tactical awareness.* Students come to know and understand the game through solving problems as they are presented in game situations.

4. *Decision making.* Students learn to make good decisions by practicing the elements of decision making. These elements include paying attention to relevant actions (selective attention), anticipating responses by opponents, and choosing appropriate skills (those that will implement the decision most effectively).

5. *Skill execution.* Students are motivated to learn skills because they are learned in context and practiced after the game is played. The skills then enhance game play performance and help students implement the chosen strategy.

6. *Performance.* The level of student performance increases as the cycle continues.

Implementing the TGfU Model

Following are some points that teachers may find helpful as they consider the implementation of a TGfU model within a potentially revitalized games education curriculum. These guidelines are the result of teacher feedback from workshops and from personal experience.

1. Clarify your own educational philosophy. This will help guide your educational decisions.

2. Compare the ideas that make up your educational philosophy with those of others (see Metzler's *Instructional Models for Physical Education,* 2005).

3. Decide what learning outcomes are being sought and determine what kind of learning environment is most likely to foster them.

4. Start with one cooperative class.

5. Start with an activity with strong content and one with which you are comfortable.

6. Combine efforts with other physical educators (not necessarily in the same institution) so that you can share ideas, materials, content knowledge, problems and solutions, experiences, and frustrations.

7. Seek administrative support for implementation, in terms of in-service work, conference attendance, visits to other programs, and moral support. As Brooker, Kirk, Braiuka, and Bransgrove (2000) suggested, the approach must be implemented in "conditions that are receptive and supportive."

8. Involve school district curriculum planners; bring them into the philosophical discussion of values in education and the merits of the TGfU model.

Conclusion

To bring physical education into the present millennium, teachers such as Mr. Pettitt will need to engage in a paradigm shift that makes heavy demands on their energy and motivation. Curricular change is inherently a stressful process. However, the benefits over time can be great. TGfU, with its emphasis on the values of learner-centered teaching and outcome-based planning, is an instructional model that will enable teachers, students, parents, and administrators to promote the holistic and transformational education of children "through the physical." When considering the benefits that the model brings, it is nonetheless important to remember that it is more like a lifestyle change than a "magic bullet medication."

Although TGfU addresses many of the problems inherent in our current physical education programs, it is a process rather than a prescription. The point is not to simply replace a current curriculum with a TGfU curriculum—to jump on the bandwagon, as it were, and let it carry us blindly along for the next few decades. If we believe that it is good for our students to debate and negotiate, to invent and refine—to put understanding at the core of the educational experience—then it should be good for curriculum designers as well. Although it is tempting at times to wish that we could codify the "perfect curriculum," the truth is that we are caught up in the organic process of change that constantly transforms all of our social institutions.

If we believe that it is good for our students to debate and negotiate, to invent and refine—to put understanding at the core of the educational experience—then it should be good for curriculum designers as well. Although it is tempting at times to wish that we could codify the "perfect curriculum," the truth is that we are caught up in the organic process of change that constantly transforms all of our social institutions.

The process of change helps educators to step into learners' shoes and to discern what they believe to be of value. It also helps them teach in accordance with those values. One of the most striking findings of Butler's 1993 study was that, although many teachers believed that learning should be "child-centered," in reality they taught using a directive approach. As Laws (1990) put it, they used a "progressive rhetoric to obscure the continuation of traditional practices" without being aware that they were doing so. After their engagement in the action research program, the actual pedagogy of almost all teachers in Butler's 1993 study was more congruent with their educational philosophy. In other words, those who espoused more progressive beliefs taught more progressively, whereas those who held more traditional beliefs continued to teach more traditionally. If practitioners are offered the opportunity to engage with the curriculum—as Kirk (1993, p. 262) put it, "to learn from experience, to regenerate, and to imagine beyond experience—in a word, to be reflexive"—then goals can be linked with practice in a process that lies at the heart of the constructivist approach.

Discussion Questions

1. Compare and contrast the education priorities, philosophies, and methods of the TGfU curriculum model and other curriculum models used in physical education.

2. What underlying assumptions about society and education are supported by the TGfU curriculum model as compared to other curriculum models?

3. Develop and analyze a basic spiral curriculum for use in a middle or early high school program based on two classification groups. How could intertask and intratask transfer be optimized? Consider seasonal issues in this application.

4. In the implementation of a TGfU curriculum, how is a skill development best addressed?

5. Imagine that you are designing a physical education curriculum for grades 4 through 6. After determining what percentage games education should be present for each grade level, identify the concepts involved in one of the classifications and determine their progressions.

References

Allison, P.C., & Barrett, K.R. (2000). *Constructing children's physical education experiences.* Boston: Pearson Education.

Brooker, R., Kirk, D., Braiuka, S., & Bransgrove, A. (2000). Implementing a game sense approach to teaching junior high school basketball in a naturalistic setting. *European Physical Education Review, 6* (1), 7-26.

Brooks, J.G., & Brooks, M.G. (1999). *The case for constructivist classrooms.* Alexandria, VA: Association for Supervision and Curriculum Development.

Bruner, J. (1977). *The process of education.* Cambridge: Harvard University Press.

Bunker, D., & Thorpe, R. (1982). A model for the teaching of games in secondary schools. *Bulletin of Physical Education, 18,* 7-10.

Bunker, D., & Thorpe, R. (1986). Is there a need to reflect on our games teaching? In R. Thorpe, D. Bunker, & L. Almond (Eds.), *Rethinking games teaching* (pp. 25-34). Loughborough, England: University of Technology, Department of Physical Education and Sports Sciences.

Butler, J. (1993). Teacher change in sport education. *Dissertation Abstracts International, 54,* (02A), 0457. (UMI No. 9318198).

Butler, J.I. (1997). How would Socrates teach games: A constructivist approach to games teaching. *Journal of Physical Education, Recreation and Dance, 68* (9), 42-47.

Butler, J.I. (1998). Factory vs. village green. Two approaches in teaching games education. *Education for life.* Association Internationale des Ecoles Superieures d'Education Physique. World Convention Proceedings, New York.

Butler, J. (2002). Teaching games for understanding: A holistic alternative in games education. In B. Lombardo (Ed.), *Sport in the twenty-first century: Alternatives for the new millennium.* Boston: Pearson Education.

Collier, C.S., & Oslin, J., (2001). Achieving competency and proficiency in physical education. *Journal of Physical Education, Recreation and Dance, 72* (8), 20-22, 33.

Doolittle, S., & Fay, T. (2002). *Authentic assessment of physical activity for high school students.* Reston, VA: National Association Sport and Physical Education.

Ellis, M. (1983). *Similarities and differences in games: A system for classification.* Paper presented at the Association Internationale des Ecoles Superieures d'Education Physique Conference, Rome, Italy.

Ellis, M. (1986). Modification of games. In R. Thorpe, D. Bunker, & L. Almond (Eds.), *Rethinking games teaching* (pp. 61-65). Loughborough, England: University of Technology, Department of Physical Education and Sports Sciences.

Fleming, S. (1994). Understanding "understanding": Making sense of the cognitive approach to the teaching of games. *Physical Education Review, 17* (2), 90-96.

Griffin, L.L., Mitchell, S.A., & Oslin, J.L. (1997). *Teaching sport concepts and skills: A tactical games approach.* Champaign, IL: Human Kinetics.

Jackson, S., Jones, D., & Williamson, T. (1983). It's a different ball game: A critical look at the games curriculum. In L. Spackman (Ed.), *Teaching games for understanding* (pp. 21-24). Cheltenham, England: The College of St. Paul and St. Mary, Curriculum Development Center.

Jewett, A.E., Bain, L.L., & Ennis, C.D. (1995). *The curriculum process in physical education.* Dubuque, IA: WCB Brown & Benchmark.

Kirk, D. (1993). Curriculum work in physical education: Beyond the objectives approach. *Journal of Teaching in Physical Education, 12* (3), 244-265.

Kirk, D., & Tinning, R., (1992). *Physical education pedagogical work as praxis.* Paper presented at the annual meeting of the American Educational Research Association, San Francisco, CA.

Launder, A.L. (2001). *Play practice: The games approach to teaching and coaching sports.* Champaign, IL: Human Kinetics.

Laws, C.J. (1990). Individualism and teaching games: Contradiction of terms. *Research Supplement (8).*

Light, R., & Fawns, R. (2003). Knowing the game: Integrating speech and action in games teaching through TGfU. *Quest, 55,* 161-176.

Mauldon, E., & Redfern, H.B. (1981). *Games teaching: An approach to the primary school.* England: MacDonald and Evans.

Metzler, M. (2005). *Instructional models for physical education* (2nd ed). Tempe, AZ: Holcomb-Hathaway.

Ministry of Education, Singapore. (2003). *Desired outcomes of education.* Retrieved January 10, 2003, from http://www1.moe.edu.sg.

National Association for Sport and Physical Education. (1995). *Moving into the future: National standards for physical education.* Boston: McGraw-Hill.

National Curriculum Council. (1992). *Physical education in the national curriculum.* York, England: Author.

Piaget, J., & Inhelder, B. (1971). *Psychology of the child.* New York: Basic Books.

Rink, J. (2002). *Teaching physical education for learning.* New York: McGraw-Hill.

Thorpe, R. (1989). A changing focus in games teaching. In L. Almond (Ed.), *The place of physical education in schools* (pp. 42-71). London: Kogan Page.

Thorpe, R. (2001). Rod Thorpe on teaching games for understanding. In L. Kidman (Ed.), *Developing decision makers. An empowerment approach to coaching* (pp. 22-36). Christchurch, New Zealand: Innovative Print Communication.

Thorpe, R., Bunker, D., & Almond, L. (1984). *A change in focus for the teaching of games.* Paper presented at the Olympic Scientific Congress, Eugene, OR.

Turner, A., & Martinek, T.J. (1995). Teaching for understanding: A model for improving decision making during game play. *Quest, 47,* 44-63.

Tyler, R. (1949). *Basic principles of curriculum and instruction.* Chicago: University of Chicago Press.

Werner, P., & Almond, L. (1990). Models of games education. *Journal of Teaching in Physical Education, 61* (4), 23-27.

Werner, P., & Thorpe, R. (1996). Evolution of a model. *Journal of Teaching in Physical Education, 6* (11), 28-34.

chapter

4

Teaching and Learning Games at the Elementary Level

Steve Mitchell

Second-grade students enter the gymnasium for their physical education class in pairs. They collect their own equipment, set up their own small playing areas, and commence activity without intervention by the teacher. They are playing net games, and activity is purposeful with students engaged in solving problems posed by the game performance of opposing classmates. The teacher encourages problem solving through well-designed questions intended to foster critical thinking (for example: "If Matt is back there (deep in the court), where can Katie throw to make it harder for him to get the ball?"). After some thought Katie identifies an area of open space, and play continues with players trying to hit open spaces.

The previous scenario is very plausible but rare. Instead students more often enter the gymnasium and sit in a circle or on a spot while the teacher explains activities. This is particularly the case in games instruction.

Elementary physical education curricula typically introduce sport or games content at the second- or third-grade level. This introduction usually takes the form of teaching and learning manipulative skills through drill-type activities, which will lead eventually to game play. In fact, I have heard some physical educators express the opinion that children as young as second grade are not capable of game play and should be restricted to skill practice only. Needless to say, I disagree with this viewpoint and

Games can and should be played by children as young as second grade.

suggest that games can and should be played by children as young as second grade.

The purpose of this chapter is to provide a conceptual rationale for using the Teaching Games for Understanding (TGfU) model at the elementary level by reviewing some recent research, and to suggest strategies for the implementation of TGfU at the elementary level. I will suggest that the implementation of TGfU at the elementary level is best accomplished by taking a thematic approach to content development. A thematic approach involves taking the view that games have similar components (I will use the term *tactical problems*) that must be addressed for students to play successfully. Using the games classification system based on similarities of rules and tactics (Almond, 1986), I will argue for a thematic approach to content development by showing how teachers can develop scope and sequence for content selection. Examples of this process will be provided.

Having outlined a process for content development, I will address the potential trials and tribulations of implementing TGfU at the elementary level. Although TGfU is tried and tested at the secondary level, this is not the case at the elementary level, where teachers have legitimate concerns about strategies for enabling independent, small-sided game play among students. I will address possible pitfalls and realistic expectations for implementing TGfU in elementary schools. The chapter is divided into three sections that address the rationale for using TGfU in elementary schools, a thematic approach for elementary physical education, and the implementation of TGfU in elementary schools.

Rationale for TGfU in Elementary Physical Education

A rationale for using TGfU as an instructional model in elementary physical education can be derived from a combination of empirical and anecdotal evidence. This evidence suggests valuable outcomes in the cognitive and affective domains. Cognitive outcomes, particularly an *understanding* of games and game tactics, were critical to the initial conception of TGfU by Bunker and Thorpe (1982). They argued that novice learners would become more proficient games players and more knowledgeable spectators if they learned to understand the decisions to be made during game play and the impact of these decisions on the skills required for successful performance. This understanding, they argued, would aid game knowledge and performance regardless of successful implementation of required skills.

Research has confirmed the importance of cognitive outcomes. An early study by French and Thomas (1987) indicated that the cognitive components of knowledge and decision making were important determinants of effective game performance in 8- to 12-year-old basketball players. Subsequent research has supported the importance of cognitive factors in contributing to the game performances of elementary age children, particularly in the case of net games (McPherson & Thomas, 1989) and invasion games (Nevett, Rovegno, Babiarz, & McCaughtry, 2001), although findings related to knowledge in striking/fielding games have been less supportive because skill execution is considered a more important contributor to game performance (see Rovegno, Nevett, & Babiarz, 2001, for a review of this literature).

> **N**ovice learners would become more proficient games players and more knowledgeable spectators if they learned to understand the decisions to be made during game play and the impact of these decisions on the skills required for successful performance.

Again, with regard to cognitive outcomes, teachers suggest that learning the tactical components of one game can help with the learning of another tactically similar game. A teacher gave this example during the early stages of a second-grade invasion games unit in which students were playing a modified game of team handball. When a girl, whose play indicated a good understanding of supporting movements, was asked by the teacher, "How did you know that was a good place to move to?" she replied simply, "I play soccer!" (Mitchell, Oslin, & Griffin, 2003). This is a common finding among elementary physical educators, although one that has not been investigated empirically at the elementary level. Nevertheless, there is evidence of cognitive transfer at the secondary level, where Mitchell and Oslin (1999) found that an understanding of one net game transferred positively to another net game and aided in game performance.

> **W**hen a girl, whose play indicated a good understanding of supporting movements, was asked by the teacher, "How did you know that was a good place to move to?" she replied simply, "I play soccer!" (Mitchell, Oslin, & Griffin, 2003)

Affective outcomes are reported by elementary physical educators with experience in modifying game play and using TGfU at this level. These teachers like the approach for several reasons (Mitchell et al., 2003).

- The approach enables young students to see the links between the skills they practice and the application of those skills to game situations.
- Increased time spent in game play provides a more enjoyable and motivational experience for young students, and they will not need to ask the all-too-common question, When are we going to play a game?
- If the previous question is the most commonly asked by young games players, not far behind (and usually asked during skill-based lessons) is, Why are we doing this? In any given TGfU lesson, students learn to appreciate the value of skill practice, first through early game play and discussion, which demonstrates the need for skill practice, and second through later game play, which allows the application and performance of learned skills in the game. This lesson format makes for a more motivational environment during skill practice.

Thematic Approach for Elementary Physical Education

Given the cognitive and affective outcomes alluded to earlier, in this section I advocate not teaching discrete games, such as soccer, volleyball, or softball, but instead teaching units of invasion games, net games, and striking/fielding games centered on specified tactical problems. For the purposes of this discussion I will define a *tactical problem* as a situation arising during game play that must be solved by making decisions and executing skills, if the player is in possession of the ball, or through movements (offensive or defensive), if the player is not in possession of the ball.

When teaching invasion games, such as soccer, hockey, and basketball, teachers might teach young students to keep possession of a ball by passing, receiving, and supporting. The tactical problem to be understood in this example is related to keeping possession of a ball, a problem that players must solve to be successful in their performance. Simply put, if you don't have the ball, you cannot score! If players and teams cannot keep possession, they have a major problem. Depending on the length of the instructional unit, time spent on invasion games might also include learning shooting techniques in these games, addressing the tactical problem of attacking the goal. In this way, novice performers learn to address the tactical problems of all invasion games rather than looking only at the skills of a specific game in isolation. This approach should develop more knowledgeable and adaptable game players at the elementary level, players who can switch easily among different invasion games.

Similarly, in teaching net/wall games to second- or third-grade students, a teacher might first address the problem of maintaining a rally through the use of consistent throwing or striking techniques so that novice learners can keep the ball in play and progress to a competitive game. This problem can be addressed in game play both across a small net and off a wall, enabling players to see that the problem applies similarly to both types of games (Mitchell & Clemens, 2003). As players become more capable of maintaining a rally, game play will become more competitive with players naturally attempting to move each other around the court, whether playing over a net or against a wall. At this point teachers should address the tactical problems of creating and defending space within the court boundaries as a means of being able to win points against an opponent. Solving these problems will necessitate practice and the implementation of specific game-related skills and movements.

> *The development of instructional materials for such a thematic approach requires that teachers first identify the tactical problems to be addressed in elementary games teaching and then appropriately sequence instruction related to these tactical problems.*

The development of instructional materials for such a thematic approach requires that teachers first identify the tactical problems to be addressed in elementary games teaching and then appropriately sequence instruction related to these tactical problems. Our attempt to do this takes the form of tactical frameworks and levels of game complexity.

Developing Tactical Frameworks

In this section I will address the problem of breaking games down into tactical problems and identifying solutions to these problems. Solutions are in the form of decisions to be made, on-the-ball skills, and off-the-ball movements. These solutions represent the content of games instruction at the elementary level. I recommend the development of frameworks similar to that presented in table 4.1, which shows a tactical framework for net/wall games. This framework provides the "scope" of content for teaching net/wall games at the elementary level by breaking down this game category according to the problems associated with scoring and preventing scoring.

Table 4.1   Framework for Net/Wall Games for the Elementary Level

Tactical problems/ concepts	Decisions and movements	Skills
Offense/scoring		
Maintaining a rally	Boundaries and rules	Underhand throw
	Moving to catch/receive/strike	Underhand strike— forehand and backhand
Setting up an attack		Shots for depth—lob, drive, and clear
	Court spaces—long and short	Approach shot
	Opening up to teammates	Drop shot
		Service
		Passing and setting
Winning a point		Downward hitting—volley, smash, spike
	Where to attack	
	Power vs. accuracy	
Defense/preventing scoring		
Defending space	Base positioning	
	Covering the court as a team	
	Sliding	
Defending against attacks	Backing up teammates	Blocking downward hits
	Shifting to cover	

Table 4.1 provides an example of how elementary teachers might break down a game category into its fundamental tactical problems. The most basic problem for novice net/wall games players to solve is how to keep the ball inside the court boundaries to maintain a rally. A game cannot be played unless this can be accomplished. To solve the problem of maintaining a rally, students must first understand the court boundaries and the rules of the game (which will determine decisions made during play) and be able to throw or strike the ball within the designated boundaries (requiring a level of skill development). Having propelled the ball, players must then be able to move to position themselves in the best place to receive the partner's return. Increasing in complexity, and as players progress to competitive situations, the problem of setting up an attack becomes important in this example as a necessary prelude to winning points (although admittedly points can often be won because opponents fail to keep the ball in court). Depending on the net/wall game being played, setting up an attack might involve movements such as approaching the net in mini-tennis or pickleball or aiming for deep spaces on the court (this can even be done by second-

grade students in a "throw-tennis" type of game) (Mitchell & Clemens, 2003). Having set up an attack, net/wall games players can then attempt to win the point, usually by means of a downward strike such as a smash or spike, each of which can certainly be taught in upper elementary physical education if equipment is modified.

Defensive aspects of game playing can also be identified as tactical problems. Table 4.1 suggests two basic defensive problems to be over-come by novice net/wall games players. The first such problem is that of defending space, either on a player's own side of the net or within court boundaries (in the case of wall games). To defend space, players must first learn to return to a base position within the court, usually somewhere around the center of the court or the center of the baseline. Regardless of the exact position, defense of space is accomplished by returning to a position (between skill attempts) that covers the court to cut down available space for the opponent to hit into, and from which it will be easier to reach the subsequent shot to make a return. Having addressed the problem of defending space, players can then address the problem of defending against attack by returning the opponent's attempted winning shot.

Levels of Game Complexity

In this section I suggest ways of sequencing tactical content, such as that suggested in table 4.1, to make games instruction developmentally appropriate. I recommend identifying levels of game complexity for each games category. The levels of game complexity provided in table 4.2 provide an appropriate sequence for the content described earlier. Taken together, the framework and levels of game complexity provide developmentally appropriate *scope and sequence* of net/wall games content for elementary children. These levels will include the learning of concepts and skills across a variety of games.

At level I, students might learn to maintain a rally in a modified tennis game that involves throwing and catching rather than striking, which can easily be transferred to playing against a wall to help students understand the transfer of tactics and skills between net and wall games (Mitchell & Clemens, 2003). As players progress in game complexity, level II will be more sophisticated, involving greater creation and use of space as players develop the abilities to set up attacks with a variety of shots and defend space both individually and as a team. Table 4.2 indicates a clear progression of both tactical and technical requirements, with singles throw-catch games at level I, progressing to singles striking games (one-bounce) and team two-contact (throw-and-catch) games at level II, followed by singles (no-bounce) and two- to three-contact games such as volleyball at level III.

Table 4.2   Levels of Game Complexity for Net/Wall Games

Tactical problems/ concepts	Game complexity level I	Game complexity level II	Game complexity level III
Game progressions	One-bounce throw-and-catch games	a. One-bounce, striking with hand b. Two-contact, throw-and-catch, no-bounce	a. No- or one-bounce, striking with implement (badminton, pickleball, tennis) b. Two-contact, striking with hands (volleyball)
Offense/scoring			
Maintaining a rally	Boundaries and rules Moving to catch	Underhand striking—hand only (forehand)	Underhand striking—implement (forehand and backhand)
Setting up an attack	Court spaces—long and short	Shots for depth—lob, drive, clear Opening up	Clears Drop shots Service Passing and setting
Winning a point		Where to attack	Downward hitting—approach shot, volley, smash, spike, power vs. accuracy
Defense/ preventing scoring			
Defending space	Base positioning	Covering the court as a team Sliding	Backing up teammates Shifting to cover
Defending against attacks			Blocking downward hits

Table 4.2 suggests three possible levels of game complexity on which the development of unit and lesson plans can be based. The depth of tactical understanding required progresses from simple to more complex as do the solutions to tactical problems required for successful performance. The key to this approach is that by addressing concepts of increasing complexity, students will more quickly understand what they need to do to play net/wall games successfully.

Implementing TGfU
in Elementary Physical Education

Teachers must recognize the need to prepare young learners to learn within a new framework. A tactical approach requires that elementary students be able to engage in simultaneous game play, independently and in small groups; this represents a different way of learning for most elementary students. An additional concern for most elementary teachers is available time. Many elementary physical education teachers have back-to-back classes of approximately 30 to 40 minutes' duration. When one class is finished, the next class is already lined up at the door ready to enter the gymnasium, a scenario familiar to many who teach in elementary schools. An added complication is that a first-grade class might be followed by a fourth-grade class and then a third-grade class, making it virtually impossible to set up equipment and leave it for three classes in a row. These and other practical problems are addressed in the remainder of the chapter.

> **A** tactical approach requires that elementary students be able to engage in simultaneous game play, independently and in small groups; this represents a different way of learning for most elementary students.

Training Students to Play Small-Sided Games

This section outlines procedures for training elementary students, as young as second grade, to play small-sided games independently. In particular, young learners need to learn simple rule structures and to respect the game play of other games on adjacent courts or fields, particularly when a ball enters the wrong court. Elementary students at the second-grade level can adhere to two simple rules:

1. When your ball rolls into another game, wait at the edge of that court or field for the ball to be returned (move around the outside of the gymnasium if necessary).

2. When a ball rolls into your game from another game, stop the ball and roll it back to that game, or to the nearest sideline if the other game is too far away.

Simple though they seem, these rules must be taught and reinforced in the early stages of games teaching when multiple games are being played. Teachers at the elementary level have found young learners more than able to restrain themselves from rushing onto another court to retrieve a ball and also able to resist the temptation to kick or throw a ball that has come into their game from another game. An additional challenge lies in enabling elementary students to learn and understand the court or field boundaries. Assigning students to permanent courts or fields will aid in this learning (see Mitchell et al., 2003, for examples).

Teaching Appropriate Sport Behavior

Several children in most second- or third-grade classes will have gained youth sport experience through programs run by the local parks and recreation department or perhaps by the YMCA or YWCA. These programs are administered and coached by adults, often with lower coach-to-player ratios than the 1-to-20 or 1-to-30 ratios facing the physical education teacher every day. Additionally, these programs often facilitate large-sided games controlled by an adult, alleviating the need for the players to be responsible for the conduct of the game.

The small-sided nature of TGfU, combined with the higher number of students per teacher, requires students to learn to organize their own game play cooperatively so that they are able to play a purposeful game in which teams try to score against each other. The organization of permanent teams and "home courts," and the assignment of simple student roles and responsibilities, can facilitate learning game play and appropriate sport behavior. A model such as Sport Education (Siedentop, 1994) can provide mechanisms for team, equipment, and game organization, as well as a means of developing appropriate sport behaviors.

Teaching Rules and Routines

Simple rules and routines are critical in enabling TGfU to run smoothly within the short time frame (30 to 40 minutes) available to the elementary physical education teacher. These should include routines for entry into the gymnasium and equipment management. Routines have an enormous impact on the effective use of time in physical education. Many classes begin with the students sitting in squads, on spots or in a circle, so the teacher can take attendance, explain what will happen, and distribute equipment. Alternative routines can allow for a more active start to a lesson in which students enter the gymnasium and begin activity immediately, organizing their own equipment.

Consider, for example, a second-grade class of 24 students involved in net games play. They are learning the tactics and skills of a modified net game against an opponent (singles play) in a designated playing area. Rather than using a net in the early stages of play, they are playing a simple throw-and-catch game across a line (or perhaps a jump rope laid flat on the floor). This enables the students to work on the tactical aspects of play without having to worry about having to clear the height of a net. The game also uses a mandatory "one bounce within the boundary" rule (i.e., the ball *must* bounce once). Assuming that equipment is not left out following the previous class (because the previous class might have been kindergarten or fifth-grade students learning something different), the teacher's first task involves setting up 12 playing areas and getting play started as quickly as possible. Obviously, it is not time efficient for the teacher to set up all the playing areas; she needs a simple system for the students to follow so they can set up their own playing areas. Using the available gymnasium floor lines (which are present in every gymnasium we have ever used or visited), it is easy for the students to set up playing areas such as those in figure 4.1. Students enter the gymnasium and, in their established pairs, set up the court by taking cones from a

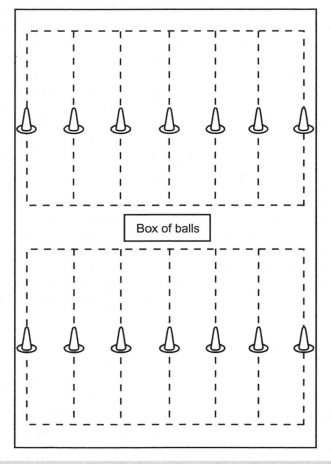

Figure 4.1 Playing areas for net games.

predetermined location and placing them in the appropriate place. *Small pieces of colored floor tape should be used to guide students to place the cones in the right position.* Court setup can be accomplished independently by one player while the opponent collects the ball to be used. Play can begin immediately once the court is set up.

Restart Rules

In addition to learning how to initiate their own game play, students must also learn how to restart play when a natural break occurs, such as when the ball goes out of bounds or into the net. It may seem obvious that when one team causes a ball to go out of bounds in an invasion game, the game is restarted at the sideline by the other team. However, teachers need to teach this rule to young players, and to provide frequent reminders until players understand the rule. Restart rules that increase the likelihood that a team passing the ball into play can do so successfully without the ball going immediately out of bounds again are particularly helpful. For example, the teacher might stipulate that any defender must be at least one arm's length back from the player taking the in-bounds pass. The teacher may use a rule that says the first pass into play is "free" (i.e., cannot be intercepted), but it must go backwards (i.e., toward the passer's own goal). In a game such as soccer, in which a ball is thrown into play and must be controlled with the feet, use of a free "kick in" on the ground would help the receiving player control the ball.

Options for restarting after a goal is scored can also vary from a restart at the center (as in soccer) to a restart from the goal line (as in basketball). The advantage of using the latter in all invasion games teaching is that it speeds up play because players will learn to restart more quickly and make an effective transition from defense to offense before the opposing team recovers. The advantage of a restart at the center of the court or field is that it enables a team that has conceded a goal to restart from farther up the court or field.

Similarly, some sensible principles will help with efficient restarts in net games. First, in the early stages of learning net games, all starts and restarts (i.e., "service") should take the form of an underhand toss. By providing an easier ball for the opponent to receive, players increase the likelihood of a longer rally or point score. Second, service should alternate after every point so that no single player can dominate a game (or be dominated) by having a strong (or weak) service. Third, in games in which rules state that scoring is only done by the serving player or team, as in badminton or volleyball (or elementary modifications thereof), a "rally scoring" system can be used in which points can be scored on either serve. Again, this provides more scoring opportunities for novice learners.

Defense Rules

The intensity of defense, particularly in invasion games, is often a hindrance to offensive performance. Although high-intensity defense is necessary for effective game play, it can impede the development of decision-making capacity and motor skill performance. We recommend a graded system of defense, beginning with "cold" defense and moving through "warm" and "hot" defense. Cold defense is obviously the easiest type of defense to play against. In skill practice and game situations, this amounts to defenders simply acting as obstacles for players to have to pass or move around. Defenders can neither intercept passes nor knock balls from opponents' hands when playing cold defense, making it somewhat inappropriate for game play situations. On the other hand, warm defense is ideal for game play situations with novice players because it allows players to intercept passes without knocking the ball out of an opponent's hands or tackling an opponent. In warm defense, a defender must stay one arm's length away from the player in possession of the ball, providing some space and time for decision making and skill execution. Warm defense also provides an appropriate extension of skill practice tasks that begin with cold defense. Hot defense is recommended as a progression once players have shown some mastery of decision making and skill execution. Players are permitted to intercept passes and to tackle in hot defense, the latter having implications for the teaching of appropriate sport behavior as outlined previously.

Conclusion

In this chapter I have outlined a conceptual rationale for the use of TGfU at the elementary level, where it has been implemented much less than at the secondary level. Elementary teachers report that the model can be adapted suitably to provide a games-based format for the teaching of games in elementary schools. Moreover, more readily available resources (e.g., Mitchell, Oslin, & Griffin, 2003) increase the likelihood that elementary physical education teachers will experience success with this approach. Again, teachers report the following benefits:

- Modified game play provides a developmentally appropriate environment for student learning. Changes to equipment, playing areas, and rules enable young children to play games that have been modified to suit their needs.
- Increased time spent in game play provides a more enjoyable and motivational experience for young learners.

- Young learners can see the links between the skills they practice and the application of those skills to game situations.
- In any given lesson, students learn to appreciate the value of skill practice, first through early game play and discussion, which demonstrate the need for skill practice, and second through later game play, which allows the application and performance of learned skills in the game.
- Learning the tactical components of one game can help with the learning of another, tactically similar game.

The scenario provided as an introduction to this chapter is a realistic possibility for teachers who seek to maximize student engagement, encourage student thinking, and foster student responsibility. Nevertheless, games teaching at the elementary level does not come without issues related to student ability and encouraging competition at an early stage within the elementary physical education curriculum. The discussion questions that follow address these issues.

Discussion Questions

1. What are the abilities of elementary students relative to competitive game play?
2. What issues does TGfU playing bring to the curriculum? Can you resolve any of these issues?
3. Compare and contrast different approaches to games teaching that you have seen in elementary physical education.
4. How might an invasion games tactical framework be different from the net/wall games framework?
5. How can TGfU in elementary physical education be combined with TGfU in secondary physical education to create a comprehensive games education curriculum?

References

Almond, L. (1986). Reflecting on themes: A games classification. In R. Thorpe, D. Bunker, and L. Almond (Eds.), *Rethinking games teaching* (pp. 71-72). Loughborough, England: University of Technology, Department of Physical Education and Sports Science.

Bunker, D., & Thorpe, R. (1982). A model for the teaching of games in secondary schools. *Bulletin of Physical Education, 19,* 5-8.

French, K., & Thomas, J. (1987). The relation of knowledge development to children's basketball performance. *Journal of Sport Psychology, 9,* 15-32.

McPherson, S., & Thomas, J.R. (1989). Relation of knowledge and performance in boys' tennis: Age and expertise. *Journal of Experimental Child Psychology, 48,* 190-211.

Mitchell, S., & Clemens, L. (2003). Introducing game play in elementary physical education: A net/wall games example. *Teaching Elementary Physical Education, 14* (1), 12-15.

Mitchell, S., & Oslin, J. (1999). An investigation of tactical understanding in net games. *European Journal of Physical Education, 4,* 162-172.

Mitchell, S., Oslin, J., & Griffin, L. (2003). *Sport foundations for elementary physical education: A tactical games approach.* Champaign, IL: Human Kinetics.

Nevett, M., Rovegno, I., Babiarz, M., & McCaughtry, N. (2001). Changes in basic tactics and motor skills in an invasion-type game after a 12-lesson unit of instruction. *Journal of Teaching in Physical Education, 20,* 352-369.

Rovegno, I., Nevitt, M., & Babiarz, M. (2001). Learning and teaching invasion-game tactics in 4th grade: Introduction and theoretical perspective. *Journal of Teaching in Physical Education, 20,* 341-351.

Siedentop, D. (1994). *Sport education: Quality PE through positive sport experiences.* Champaign, IL: Human Kinetics.

Teaching and Learning Games at the Secondary Level

Adrian P. Turner

J im Larson has just finished teaching a unit of field hockey to his sixth-grade class. During the unit he focused on teaching the basic skills of the game (e.g., dribbling, passing and receiving, tackling, and shooting). The majority of his learning tasks were structured drills, and the students were given a chance to play some games at the conclusion of the unit. Jim noticed that many of the students who had done so well during the practice drills performed poorly during games.

Turner & Martinek, 1995, p. 42.

The preceding vignette illustrates the frustration of secondary teachers concerning their students' inability to transfer skills meticulously taught in practice sessions to game play. The "skills first, game second" approach (Turner & Martinek, 1995) has been widely used, but has been problematic for both teachers and learners. The Teaching Games for Understanding (TGfU) model evolved from this concern as an approach to teaching and learning that fostered tactical understanding in conjunction with skill development to better facilitate participants' playing, understanding, and enjoyment of games.

This chapter addresses the implementation of the TGfU model at the secondary level and includes the following:

- A rationale for using TGfU and highlights of some of the research support for the model
- A discussion of some of the misconceptions about TGfU that have led preservice and in-service teachers to be reticent about using the approach
- A tactical framework that will provide secondary teachers with adequate knowledge to start using this approach
- An abbreviated TGfU unit plan based on the tactical components of invasion games to illustrate content progression in STXBALL (modified lacrosse)
- An explanation of the four component parts of TGfU (game form, game-related practice, skill practice, and modified game/full game)
- A list of pedagogical tools that will assist teachers with their instruction using the TGfU model
- A discussion of some managerial issues instructors need to consider to teach effectively with the TGfU model

The Games Problem

Playing games is about solving tactical problems; skills are used to overcome these problems. When teaching games, teachers should help students make the optimal decision and subsequent execution based on the game situation and their ability. To do this, teachers usually begin each TGfU lesson with a modified game. Students (aided by the teacher) learn to understand the tactical aim of what they are trying to do in the game. Once they are aware of their tactical problem, they can learn skills that are potentially useful to them to help solve this problem in practice situations that combine the interdependent tactical and technical elements of game play. The students can then return to their initial game, or a modified version of it, to try out their tactical solutions and begin to investigate the next problem they encounter. Students recognize the need for developing an understanding of tactics and appropriate skills because they are frequently playing the game. This notion represents a constructivist learning orientation (discussed in chapter 2) in which students are making new meaning from prior knowledge and experience as they attempt to improve their subsequent understanding and performance (Prawat, 1999). Constructivism is a prime tenet of the TGfU approach.

Several experimental studies have shown the advantage of TGfU teaching over technique-based teaching for improving student decision making in games such as field hockey (Turner, 1996; Turner & Martinek, 1999). Other studies have also found TGfU advantageous for developing off-the-ball player movements in soccer game play (Mitchell, Griffin, & Oslin, 1995) and passing effectiveness during field hockey games (Turner & Martinek, 1999). Research has also shown significant gains in student game knowledge for TGfU groups versus technique groups in field hockey and volleyball (Griffin, Oslin, & Mitchell, 1995; Turner, 1996). Other studies have produced more equivocal findings (Rink, French, & Graham, 1996), but there is little doubt that, from a research perspective, TGfU does offer a viable alternative for teaching students to play games (Metzler, 2000).

Misconceptions About TGfU in Secondary Teaching

At its most simplistic level, the TGfU approach could be interpreted as little more than "game-practice-game." In reality, teaching with this model requires considerable pedagogical skill. Tactics and skills specific to various game forms (invasion, net/wall, fielding/run-scoring, and target) must be understood first by the teacher and then introduced to students through modified games that pose tactical and strategic problems. The teacher has to have some knowledge of the game, or game form, to be able to do this and to teach about what is happening in the game. At first, teaching from the context of the game is much less predictable for the teacher than planning a series of technique drills with little regard for how the students are actually performing in their modified games. Because TGfU is less predictable, teaching using this method is more of a challenge; but the outcomes of games are also unpredictable. In most games, to be a successful participant, or even a coach, a person has to be able to react and change his thinking and execution. The same is true when a teacher first employs the TGfU approach (see Barrett & Turner, 2000, and Berkowitz, 1996, for examples of experienced teachers attempting to undertake this shift in thinking about teaching games).

A common misconception is that a teacher needs to know all of the intricacies (technical and tactical) of each game to teach it to students using the TGfU approach. Werner and Almond's (1990) categorization of games (invasion, net/wall, fielding/run-scoring, and target) suggests that a number of tactical concepts are transferable within any games category (i.e., between basketball and soccer within the invasion games category). This principle of game sampling (Thorpe, Bunker, & Almond, 1984) shows similarities between games that can lead to an improved understanding of games for all participants (students and teachers). Teachers can take solace in the fact that some tactical knowledge of one game in a category can help them immensely to teach another game in that same category using the TGfU approach. That does not solve the problem of knowing about the specific skills for every game, but it has been apparent for many years that teachers prefer to equip themselves with material to teach techniques because they have tended to assume that these are more predictable and easier to teach than tactics. In the TGfU approach, teachers still have to be prepared to teach skills, but within an overarching tactical framework and in a more contextual setting, once they have recognized the tactical and technical deficiencies in the game.

> *T*eachers can take solace in the fact that some tactical knowledge of one game in a category can help them immensely to teach another game in that same category using the TGfU approach.

When starting to use the TGfU approach, teachers may be comfortable teaching a game they are familiar with. Teaching games playing is also about teaching students to take appropriate risks, so some teachers may want to be adventurous and try a novel game first. Consider Sandy, a veteran teacher attempting to come to terms with the interplay of tactics and skills when teaching a novel game for the first time (see Barrett and Turner, 2000). "Sandy's Challenge" was to think differently about teaching games having previously based games instruction on the development of specific techniques. A series of fictional e-mails were used in this study to examine an experienced practitioner's journey into teaching an invasion game (STXBALL, or modified lacrosse) from the perspective that tactics could be the initial focus of lessons and that skills are subsequently varied in modified game situations. The use of a tactical framework may help alleviate some of the fears of teachers like Sandy about TGfU.

Getting Started With a Tactical Framework

Invasion games can be the most strategically complex, followed by fielding/run-scoring, net/wall, and target games. If a teacher can develop an understanding of a framework for teaching invasion games using TGfU, then teaching in another category with less tactical complexity should be fairly straightforward. The two basic problems in all invasion games are to score and prevent the opponents from scoring. On offense, individual or collective ball or object movement is used to retain possession and to advance in order to score. On defense, attempts are made to prevent scoring and player or ball advancement and ultimately to regain possession. In any invasion game, players assume one of only four roles:

on-the-ball attacker, off-the-ball attacker, on-the-ball-defender, and off-the-ball-defender (Wilson, 2002). With the basic objectives and participant roles defined, four generic tactical action principles of attack (mobility, advancement, width, and depth/retaining possession) and four action principles for defense (engagement/restraint, depth, contraction, and expansion) are used to overcome most of the major tactical problems in invasion games. The tactical principles do not represent an exhaustive list but a suggested starting point for teachers beginning to teach with a tactical focus.

Teachers who can comprehend these concepts have the basic tactical premise for beginning to teach TGfU in most invasion sports. Other games categories have similar overarching tactical frameworks (see Griffin, Mitchell, & Oslin, 1997, for an overview of tactical problems in net/wall, fielding/run-scoring, and target games). Once teachers have a basic understanding of a tactical framework, they are ready to examine the specific components of teaching TGfU. The majority of examples in this chapter will be applied to teaching invasion games at the secondary level.

TGfU Model Components

An overview of a TGfU unit for STXBALL (modified lacrosse) based on four offensive and four defensive tactical principles common to invasion sports (Wilson, 2002) is presented in table 5.1. Specific examples of the TGfU model components (game form, game-related practice, skill practice, and modified game/full game) are provided for each tactical problem in the unit.

- *Game form.* The initial game will normally be a version of the full game. It will typically include two essential characteristics: *representation* and *exaggeration* (Thorpe, Bunker, & Almond, 1984). The game should be *representative* of the full game and retain some of its strategic complexity, but should be modified to accommodate the technical and physical limitations of the participants. For example, in STXBALL (modified lacrosse), lightweight sticks can be used to play small-sided (3v3) games, with one-meter goals, but without goalkeepers. The keeper strap on the stick enables the student to retain possession of the ball and move about the field, throwing and catching without requiring the sophisticated technical competence of the cradle—a technique that is fundamental to the adult game of lacrosse. In the same game, the tactical problem of mobility in attack can also be exaggerated by specifying a rule that the ball must be passed across the halfway line—not run across (see table 5.1, column 2, row 1). This exaggerates to the students the need to pass the ball forward and move into space to create a scoring opportunity. It reduces

Table 5.1 TGfU STXBALL Unit

1. Offensive action principle/tactical problem	2. Game form	3. Game-related practice (tactical focus)	4. Skill practice (technique focus)	5. Modified game/full game
Mobility (exploiting and creating space via player and ball movement)	3v3 STXBALL (on 30-m × 20-m field with 1-m goals) Rules: ball passed, not run, over halfway line; both hands on stick; no body/stick contact	Mobility (3v1 in 20-m × 10-m grid with 1-m goal) Three consecutive passes prior to shot on goal; move to space to receive pass; question students regarding timing of pass and angles of support	Teach catching with stick because students are dropping ball (in 20-m × 10-m grid) Select from practices (static or dynamic): self-toss and catch; catching partner-tossed ball; 1 with 1(pass and catch); 3v1/2v1 (keep away)	3v3 STXBALL (on 30-m × 20-m field with 1-m goals) Rules: ball passed, not run, over halfway line; both hands on stick; no body/stick contact Game condition: three consecutive passes prior to shot on goal
Advancement (player or ball penetration to attack opponents' goal line)	3v3 STXBALL (on 30-m × 20-m field with 1-m goals) Rules: ball passed, not run, over halfway line; both hands on stick; no body/stick contact; player with ball must run (5 s maximum prior to passing)	Penetration (1v1 in 10-m × 10-m grid—defender without stick) Offensive player must reach goal line to score; defender touches opponent's stick to stop; offensive player protects ball by trying to cradle, reaches goal line by changing speed, faking, spinning, dodging, etc.	Teach cradle to carry ball (in 20-m × 10-m grid) Select practices (static/dynamic): jog and cradle (no ball, add ball); self-toss, catch, and cradle; 1 with 1 + sticks (pass, catch, cradle); 2v1 (cradle, then "give-and-go," or offensive player keeps ball); 2v2 "endball" (use cradle when running with ball)	3v3 STXBALL (on 30-m × 20-m field with 1-m goals) Rules: player with ball must run (5 s maximum prior to passing) Game condition: players must cradle or they turn over ball; remove keeper strap from stick for more skilled players

Width (player/ball dispersal to provide lateral support on the flanks)	4v4 STXBALL (on 30-m × 25-m field with 1-m goals) Rules: ball passed, not run, over halfway line; both hands on stick; no body/stick contact; 2-m channel for offensive player only to enter on either flank inside sidelines.	Use of width (4v0-3 in 20-m × 25-m grid 3 players attacking 1-m goal, 1 player in channel) Wide offensive player uses "give-and-go" to move down channel and across halfway line; supporting offensive players attack near and far post of goal; receive throw, cradle, and attempt to score; teach timing of runs, crossover tactic for supporting players	Teach passing (throwing) to facilitate width (in 20-m × 25-m field with 1-m goal) Select practices (static/dynamic): throw to wall; throw to partner, high arc; pass with partner to stick target on partner's right then left (resembles reception from wide player); 4v2 (half-court practice), before scoring attempt at goal, must throw ball from one flank to other to change point of attack	4v4 STXBALL (on 35-m × 25-m grid with 1-m goals) Rules: ball passed, not run, over halfway line; both hands on stick; no body/stick contact; 2-m channel for offensive player only to enter on either side of field Game condition: before attempt on goal, player must switch ball into both channels on flanks
Depth/retaining possession (supporting players' contributions from behind the ball)	4v4/5v5 STXBALL (on 35-m × 20-m field with 1-m goals) Rules: ball passed over halfway line to target player; target player must stay in offensive half of field; both hands on stick; no body/stick contact	Support for target player (3v2 in 30-m × 20-m grid with 1-m goal) Ball thrown to target player, marked by defensive player; ball is delivered to additional support player behind ball by target player because target player cannot go forward with the ball; additional offensive player moves to space square of support player to assist the play	2v1—throw to target player marked by defender (in 20-m × 15-m grid with 1-m goal) Target player lays ball off for support player who shoots at goal from distance (can also use target player behind goal); teach shooting like throw/pass with follow-through to low part of goal	4v4/5v5 STXBALL (on 30-m × 20-m field with 1-m goals) Rules: ball passed over halfway line to target player; defensive player cannot front target player; target player must lay ball back to support player Game condition: no shot at goal unless previous pass was backwards

(continued)

Table 5.1 *(continued)*

1. Offensive action principle/tactical problem	2. Game form	3. Game-related practice (tactical focus)	4. Skill practice (technique focus)	5. Modified game/full game
Engagement/restraint (challenging the opponents' progression and regaining possession)	4v4/5v5 STXBALL (on 30-m × 20-m field with 1-m goals) Rules: ball passed over halfway line; both hands on stick; no body/stick contact; 3 s maximum in possession of ball; person-to-person defense; dropped ball, first player to cover with stick earns restart	2 attackers vs. 1 defender and shot to goal—throw to target player marked by defender (in 20-m × 10-m field with 1-m goal) Defender attempts interception if ball contact is certain; if not, defender positions (marks) to prevent forward pass/shot, attempts to force offensive player to flank or pass back to support player; attacker has only 3 s to decide action or a turnover occurs	2v2 STXBALL (on 20-m × 10-m field with 1-m goals) As in previous tactical practice but add second defender who pressures support player after pass; pressure will now cause offense to drop ball frequently; ball on ground must be recovered by pickup/scoop; teach pickup from ground and then cradle, self-rolled ball and scoop; 1v1— players chase rolled ball for pickup	4v4/5v5 STXBALL (on 30-m × 20-m field with 1-m goals) Rules: ball passed over halfway line; both hands on stick; no body/stick contact; 3 s maximum in possession of ball; person-to-person defense Game condition: ball dropped is scooped up only; no covering ball to regain possession
Depth (positioning of supporting defensive players in relation to the challenging defender)	4v4/5v5 STXBALL (on 35-m × 20-m field with 1-m goals) Rules: ball passed over halfway line; both hands on stick; no body/stick contact	2 defenders vs. 1 attacker (in 20-m × 10-m grid with 1-m goal on inside corner of grid) First defender shepherds offensive player to sideline staying between ball handler and target, attempts to prevent shot at goal from good angle; second defender covers first defender	2 defenders vs. 1 attacker (in 20-m × 10-m grid with 1-m goal) First defender moves quickly to ball handler but slows approach in last few meters; second defender positions just inside first defender between ball and goal; covering defender communicates with first defender to force attacker to flank, steps to ball carrier if defender evaded	4v4/5v5 STXBALL (on 35-m × 20-m field with 1-m goals) Rules: ball passed over halfway line; both hands on stick; no body/stick contact Game condition: in half-court defense, closest player to the ball should move to challenge ball carrier; covering players communicate with first defender to channel opponent

Contraction (movement of defensive players to protect the target area)	4v4/5v5 STXBALL (on 35-m × 25-m field with 1-m goals) Rules: ball passed over halfway line; both hands on stick; no body/stick contact Game condition: offense must pass ball long into attacking third	4v4 zone coverage (on 35-m × 25-m field with 1-m goals) Every player covers the opponent in his/her zone; in 4v4, defense is organized at least two lines deep; challenge opponent with ball only in zone and occupy space on goal side of ball	4 attackers vs. 2 defenders and 2 recovering defenders (in 30-m × 20-m grid with 1-m goal) Initial 2 defenders retreat slowly without committing to the ball carrier; 2 recovering defenders (start initially behind offense) and move rapidly to be goal side of ball to challenge ball carrier or occupy space	4v4/5v5 STXBALL (on 35-m × 25-m field with 1-m goals) Rules: ball passed over halfway line; both hands on stick; no body/stick contact; focus on quick retreat Game condition: zone defense
Expansion (defensive players move in relation to movements of specific attackers to regain possession)	4v4/5v5 STXBALL (on 35-m × 25-m field with 1-m goals) Rules: 3 s maximum in possession of ball; both hands on stick; no body/stick contact; person-to-person defense	3 attackers vs. 4 defenders (in 35-m × 25-m grid with 1-m goals) Attackers must use short pass from own goal line to begin play each time; no pass over 8 m, defense attacks ball carrier and supporting players (pressing); use of "double team" or "3-point trap"	4 attackers vs. 4 defenders (in 35-m × 25-m grid with 1-m goals) Defenders keep on goal side of opponents while tracking runs, keep ball and opponent in view; defender attempts interception or marks to prevent forward pass/shot	4v4/5v5 STXBALL (on 35-m × 25-m field with 1-m goals) Rules: 3 s maximum in possession of ball; both hands on stick; no body/stick contact Game condition: person-to-person defense

Several exemplar skill practices (column 4) were modified from *Teaching Materials for STXBALL-LACROSSE*, by K.R. Barrett and S. Collie, 1997. Copyright 1997, STX, Inc. & U.S. Lacrosse, Inc.

the focus on an on-the-ball runner's penetration from a deep position—a tactic that could subsequently be introduced under the advancement action principle.

■ *Game-related practice (tactical focus)*. From the initial game, the teacher can derive some of the tactical weaknesses from the students via a questioning protocol (to be discussed later in this chapter). A typical problem in the STXBALL game will be the failure of students to move into space to receive a pass from the ball carrier. At this point, the teacher can help to focus play on the problem at hand (lack of mobility) and facilitate a solution—three consecutive passes must be made prior to the shot on goal in a 3v1 situation. This would be a suitable game-related practice to help amend the tactical (mobility) predicament of moving to space to receive the pass (see table 5.1, column 3, row 1).

■ *Skill practice (technical focus—if necessary)*. In the previous example, the students will almost certainly need to work on their STXBALL throwing and catching skills. When it is evident that techniques and not tactics are restricting the students' participation, a combination of static or dynamic (throwing and catching) practices might be used to promote skill development. The teacher's discretion is crucial to deciding the level that students may need to work at (1 with 1, 3v1, 2v1, etc.). Different types of practices in the same class might be provided to cater to individual students' needs (see table 5.1, column 4, row 1).

■ *Modified game/full game*. Students should then return to the initial game form, sometimes with a new condition or rule added. In this instance, three consecutive passes must be made prior to the shot on goal in the 3v3 games (see table 5.1, column 5, row 1). This condition could subsequently be lifted when the teacher perceives that the players' mobility is no longer an issue. Subsequently, it will be necessary to leave the game again to work on additional tactics or skills.

In the STXBALL unit, the smallest number of participants is used in the game form or practice to permit maximal practice opportunities for the students while retaining the tactical complexity of the adult game. As student understanding and skill progress, closer approximations to the full-sided game or practice can be implemented over time. The unit would be presented

The smallest number of participants is used in the game form or practice to permit maximal practice opportunities for the students while retaining the tactical complexity of the adult game. As student understanding and skill progress, closer approximations to the full-sided game or practice can be implemented over time.

lesson by lesson using the following proposed structure (Turner & Martinek, 1995):

1. Game form setup
2. Observation of play
3. Investigation of tactical problems and potential solutions in a game-related practice (teacher and students)
4. Observation of play
5. Intervention to promote skill (skill practice if necessary)
6. Observation of the modified game and intervention to teach tactics or skills based on the emerging game problem

Within the game form, game-related practice, skill practice, and modified game/full game, instructors will at first likely need some methods to facilitate teaching for understanding.

Pedagogical Tools to Teach TGfU

In this section I have provided some pedagogical tools that will assist teachers with their instruction using the TGfU model. These pedagogical tools focus specifically on designing and tailoring games.

■ *Game conditions.* Exaggerating the game or practice via specific game conditions, for example, can develop tactical appreciation. In many invasion games, beginners typically gravitate to the ball around the center of the field, the so-called beehive phenomenon. To encourage the use of width in attack, a condition can be made that one player from each team must stay within 2 yards (1.8 meters) of the opposing sidelines to create more space. The ball must reach the player on the sideline at least once before an attempt can be made on goal by the offensive team. Specific conditions can also be stipulated for players of different skill levels. For example, in soccer a highly skilled player can be restricted to passing and shooting with her nonpreferred foot. This condition could improve the high-skilled player's performance and also facilitate more equality during game play.

■ *Rule and equipment modifications.* Changing specific rules to promote tactical understanding is another way to modify games. In invasion games, a rule can be made that players in possession of the ball are not allowed to walk; they must either run or stand still. This encourages runners to either penetrate or pass the ball. As a result, defensive players have to reposition rapidly. Alternatively, in games such as rugby, soccer, and basketball, a no-contact rule can be in effect. When body contact is virtually eliminated, defensive players must learn positioning and funneling to create pressure on offensive players and to force them away from their target areas. Lightweight equipment will also be more developmentally appropriate in many instances and permit safer and more skillful participation among beginners.

■ *Changing spatial arrangements to vary the difficulty of the game or practice.* In most invasion games, a larger space will help offensive players to function well tactically and technically. The skill is put under less pressure; as Launder (2001) suggested "space = time = skill (good decisions and good execution)" (p. 59). In other games categories, varying the size of the space can also have tactical implications. In net games such as badminton, playing on a narrow court encourages the use of drop shots and clears to attack court space close to and far away from the net. In fielding/run-scoring games such as cricket, batters can be rewarded with differentiated scoring for striking the ball into specific target areas of the field (Turner, 2004); for example, short-pitched deliveries from the bowler should be hit square of the wicket on either side using either a "pull" or "cut" stroke.

■ *Loading the practice (offense–defense ratio).* When skill is a restricting factor, the offensive ratio can be increased to permit achievement of the tactical objective. In most invasion games, destroying defensively is easier than creating offensively when students' game understanding and skills are still developing. An overload of players for the offense will help facilitate tactical success. In many instances, a one-player advantage (for example 3v2 in basketball) appears to be adequate, but for many secondary school students, a 3v2 soccer game will still present a considerable challenge for the offense. In some cases, a two- to three-player advantage may be necessary to secure offensive success, particularly when players' techniques are still developing. The overload situations also frequently occur as microsituations in the full versions of the game. Defenders can often find themselves outnumbered by several players in games such as soccer, field hockey, and basketball. Another tool to facilitate offensive success is the use of a neutral player who becomes an extra player for whichever team is on offense.

Students should be encouraged to learn to read the game. The use of a questioning protocol (what? where? when? why? with whom? how?) is a key pedagogical tool in TGfU.

■ *Developing a questioning protocol.* One of the notions behind TGfU is that instructors are trying to teach performers to understand in a game context. Students should be encouraged to learn to read the game. The use of a questioning protocol (what? where? when? why? with whom? how?) is a key pedagogical tool in TGfU.

In virtually every game or practice, teachers need to look at the scenario and ask students the following questions:

1. What is going wrong?
2. Where does the problem occur?
3. When does the problem occur?
4. Why does the problem occur?
5. Who owns the problem?
6. How can it be fixed?

Consider the following example of a game-related practice in a STX-BALL lesson: three attackers versus one defender in a 20-yard × 10-yard (18-meter × 9-meter) grid. Attackers score by running the ball over the goal line. The offense is having trouble with this task.

Q. What does the ball carrier need to do?

A. The ball carrier needs to attack the defender by moving toward the goal line.

Q: Where does the problem occur in the game area?

A. Where the ball carrier approaches the defender.

Q. When should the ball carrier pass the ball?

A. When the defensive player is committed to the ball. The decision about when to pass (timing of the pass) will be crucial.

Q. Why does the problem occur?

A1. If the pass is too early, the defender has time to get across to the receiver.

A2. If the pass is too late, the defender will cut off the passing lane.

Q. Who owns the problem?

A. The offensive off-the-ball players and the on-the-ball player.

Q. How can the problem be fixed?

A. Teammates can move wide to position in space. They need to support the ball carrier. (The teacher can talk about angles of support, positioning square of the passer, or penetrating past the defender to receive a pass closer to the goal line).

Q. How can the ball carrier help after passing?

A. Cut to space behind, or in front of, the defender after the pass.

The question cycle can subsequently be developed for the technique aspects of the task.

Q: What are the components of good passing?

A: Timing, accuracy, pace/weight, and disguise.

■ *Examining option scenarios.* One of the keys to students' learning to play games effectively is the ability to use skills tactically based on the information-rich aspects of the game. In TGfU, teachers need to assist participants in recognizing specific cues that are crucial to a particular scenario in the game and the specific tactics to overcome the problem (Kirk & MacPhail, 2002). For example, when faced with a 3v1 break in the prior STXBALL situation, the defensive player has to make some decisions about whether to attack the opponent with the ball or to wait for the offensive players to make their moves. A number of factors will govern the defensive player's tactical decision making, including the respective distance of the players to the goal line, the position of another defensive player (if any), the speed of the offensive players, the level of passing and running ability of the ball handler, the position of the off-the-ball attackers and their catching abilities, and the angle for the pass by the offensive ball handler. Linking game conditions with refined condition-dependent responses connected to game tactics is characteristic of an advanced level of knowledge related to game understanding (McPherson, 1994). In TGfU, instructors can suggest potential game scenarios and discuss the alternatives that a player could select, or examine the implications of students' actions during game play (Turner, Allison, & Pissanos, 2001). This can occur by having students provide insights pertaining to game vignettes before the scenario is played out, while the activity is taking place, or after the play has occurred (Gréhaigne, Godbout, & Bouthier, 2001). Several techniques have been suggested for teachers to intervene in game tasks (Metzler, 1990), and these are particularly pertinent in a TGfU setting at the secondary level.

• *Walk-through.* Players demonstrate their anticipated movements on the playing area prior to the action in a slowed-down version of the play. For example, offensive players can show their movement in a 3v3 basketball game to illustrate how they would run a "pass and pick away" from the top of the key and balance the floor if the "pick" was unsuccessful. The play could first be illustrated without defensive players and then subsequently could include defensive players on the court.

• *Situations.* In this approach, the teacher stops or freezes the play at a teachable moment and uses a questioning protocol similar to the one previously described to facilitate students' tactical understanding. In some instances, there may be no simple criterion for determining whether a single choice during game play is correct. The students' responses to the questioning may be based on a choice of tactics with specific risks. Participants examine the risk or reward of each action with the teacher's assistance. For example, in 5v5 soccer, when the ball is played into a target player (with his back to goal) closely guarded by a defender on the edge of the penalty area, the target player has several options: turn and shoot, pass the ball to a supporting attacker, or try to dribble past the defender (similar to the triple threat in basketball).

▪ *Instant replay.* When an alternative response might have been used, the teacher resets the play and allows the scenario to be played out again. The teacher may encourage one or several of the players to try a different option. For example, in a 3v3 "touch" rugby game, the defensive player approaching the ball handler is overplaying the pass and looking for an interception. The offensive player in possession of the ball could be encouraged to either fake the pass and run by the defensive player or chip/grubber kick the ball into space and accelerate past the rapidly approaching defender to recover the ball.

▪ *Player-coach.* The teacher can become a participant in the game to manipulate a tactical component. For example, the teacher perceives that the field hockey game would be improved if a central midfield player controlled the tempo of the game by holding the ball longer and not making such rapid decisions before passing short (under 10 yards, or 9 meters) to teammates. The teacher participates in the game to illustrate this point.

▪ *Television analyst.* The teacher encourages the remainder of the class to analyze a small-sided game for several minutes and then reflect on what has taken place. Why was team X successful in the soccer game? What made it easy for them to maintain possession of the ball? How could team Y put more defensive pressure on their opponents and attempt to win the ball?

▪ *Video analysis.* Recent studies have attempted to use videotape to examine option scenarios (Shutler, Turner, & Allison, 2001). After experiencing the game form, and prior to engaging in a game-related practice, participants viewed a videotape of a staged tactical concept performed in a controlled setting. The use of I-movie and computer-based simulations also provide an opportunity to examine students' game option scenarios in physical education. The use of examples between sports, such as the sweeper in soccer and the free safety in football, offers students an opportunity to grasp tactical similarities between player roles in digital formats.

Managing TGfU

In addition to tools for content development, teachers need to comprehend managerial issues in TGfU. Class management is particularly important because there are often many small-sided games taking place simultaneously.

- *Appropriate use of space.* In general, lack of space is a problem when attempting to teach using small-sided games in TGfU. For this reason, teachers need to select games units within the confines of their specific facilities. A large outdoor space is required for sport units such as soccer and flag football that require multiple minigames. Other games can operate within a confined space. Small-sided games of volleyball, pickleball, and badminton can include a relatively high number of students in a restricted gymnasium space. The use of modified equipment also helps in organizing several games in a small instructional area. For example, minigames of softball and cricket can take place in a gymnasium using plastic bats and either Nerf or Whiffle balls. By slowing the speed of the ball, realistic game experiences that promote an understanding of the tactical nuances of games can take place in restricted space settings.

- *Supervising multiple games.* In TGfU, once teachers have the game form, practice, or modified game running, they need to scan quickly across the activity area, noting the performances of the students in all of the minigames. Teachers must be patient and prepared to stand back and watch for a few minutes, allowing the play to develop. Effective teachers are good observers of the tactical components of game play. If the same problem is occurring in all the minigames or practices, the teacher should provide feedback to the whole class without bringing the students in for a specific demonstration. Alternatively, the students can be assembled around a demonstration area in an L formation, and the game intervention techniques mentioned previously can be used for more detailed concept explanations.

> *Teachers must be patient and prepared to stand back and watch for a few minutes, allowing the play to develop. Effective teachers are good observers of the tactical components of game play.*

- *Instructional layout and transitions.* Before multiple games and practices take place, the boundaries for the game and practice areas need to be clearly marked. Teachers have used cones for years, but now plastic markers can be used to superimpose practice areas on game markings. Students are simply asked to switch their attention from one set of markers to another when moving from game to practice or vice versa. Color-coding with the markers can make visualizing the specific instructional area even easier. There is no doubt that this requires preparation prior to a class, but the process will facilitate rapid transitions (game-practice-practice-game) for students and will maximize learning time during a lesson. Clock management is also critical to the success of a TGfU lesson. A major issue for teachers when they first use the TGfU format is learning to devote an appropriate amount of time to each of the sections in a lesson. Many teachers tend to spend too long in the initial game and subsequent practice and fail to allow enough time to return to the modified game at the end. Teachers should recognize that games serve as the motivation to practice; this is a strength of the TGfU approach that is tantamount to its instructional success.

Conclusion

Jim Larson's teaching scenario at the start of this chapter illustrates the frustration that many physical education teachers and coaches have experienced in their attempts to teach games to children. They have taught techniques and put them into game situations hoping that the application of those techniques would emerge as game skill. Sadly, only a few players are ever effectively able to make the transition to skillful game performance. In contrast, the TGfU approach allows students to show what they are able to do in a game context and what they need to learn to play the game more effectively. They participate in practices, usually designed by the teacher, to discover what tactics and skills will help them to improve their game performances. The game contexts allow students to experiment with their solutions. By varying the game context, the teacher can challenge students to find new ways to solve the tactical problems they encounter during game play and can also pose additional problems to the students.

This chapter has attempted to facilitate the use of TGfU at the secondary level by examining some of the misconceptions about the model, emphasizing the importance of adopting a tactical framework, and focusing on tactical principles as the basis for a TGfU games unit. Each of the TGfU model components (game form, game-related practice, skill practice, and modified game/full game) was briefly described as a basis for individual lesson development. Pedagogical tools and managerial considerations were also provided to enhance practitioner delivery of the TGfU approach.

Discussion Questions

1. How is the TGfU approach indicative of your values as a student or teacher?
2. What are the major strengths of using TGfU in secondary teaching or learning, and what do you consider to be the major challenges in using this approach?

3. To what extent does teaching experience and a strong sport knowledge base (perhaps from coaching) assist instructors when attempting to teach using TGfU?

4. Suggest how you would plan a lesson on an invasion game of your choice based on an offensive/defensive tactical problem (suggested in the games unit in this chapter) using the game form, game-related practice, skill practice, and modified game/full game components of the TGfU model. What pedagogical tools would you use in your lesson to develop the content? (Now try a similar activity for a complete unit of the invasion game that you selected, or try it for a unit in a different category such as net/wall, striking/fielding, or target).

5. TGfU focuses on students solving problems in games, but do you think it can produce better players compared to other instructional models? Please explain your response.

References

Barrett, K.R., & Collie, S. (1997). *Teaching materials for STXBALL-LACROSSE.* STX, Inc. & U.S. Lacrosse, Inc.

Barrett, K.R., & Turner, A.P. (2000). Sandy's challenge: New game, new paradigm a correspondence. *Journal of Teaching in Physical Education, 19,* 162-181.

Berkowitz, R.J. (1996). A practitioner's journey from skill to tactics. *Journal of Physical Education, Recreation and Dance, 67* (4), 44-45.

Gréhaigne, J.-F., Godbout, P., & Bouthier, D. (2001). The teaching and learning of decision making in team sports. *Quest, 53,* 59-76.

Griffin, L.L., Mitchell, S.A., & Oslin, J.L. (1997). *Teaching sport concepts and skills: A tactical games approach.* Champaign, IL: Human Kinetics.

Griffin, L.L., Oslin, J.L., & Mitchell, S.A. (1995). An analysis of two instructional approaches to teaching net games. *Research Quarterly for Exercise and Sport, 66* (Suppl. 1), A-64.

Kirk, D., & MacPhail, A. (2002). Teaching games for understanding and situated learning: Rethinking the Bunker-Thorpe model. *Journal of Teaching in Physical Education, 21,* 177-192.

Launder, A.G. (2001). *Play practice: The games approach to teaching and coaching sports.* Champaign, IL: Human Kinetics.

McPherson, S. (1994). The development of sport expertise: Mapping the tactical domain. *Quest, 46,* 223-240.

Metzler, M.W. (1990). Teaching in competitive games—Not just playin' around. *Journal of Physical Education, Recreation and Dance, 61* (8), 57-61.

Metzler, M.W. (2000). *Instructional models for physical education.* Boston: Allyn & Bacon.

Mitchell, S.A., Griffin, L.L., & Oslin, J.L. (1995). The effects of two instructional approaches on game performance. *Pedagogy in Practice: Teaching and Coaching in Physical Education and Sports, 1* (1), 36-48.

Prawat, R.S. (1999). Dewey, Pierce and the learning paradox. *American Educational Research Journal, 36,* 47-76.

Rink, J.E., French, K.E., & Graham, K.C. (1996). Implications for practice and research. *Journal of Teaching in Physical Education, 15,* 490-502.

Shutler, C.C., Turner, A.P., & Allison, P.C. (2001). Teaching basketball tactics to students with disabilities using the games for understanding model. *Research Quarterly for Exercise and Sport, 72* (Suppl. 1), A-104.

Thorpe, R.D., Bunker, D.J., & Almond, L. (1984). A change in focus for the teaching of games. In M. Pieron & G. Graham (Eds.), *Sport pedagogy: Olympic Scientific Congress proceedings,* vol. 6 (pp. 163-169). Champaign, IL: Human Kinetics.

Turner, A.P. (1996). Teaching for understanding: Myth or reality? *Journal of Physical Education, Recreation and Dance, 67* (4), 46-48, 55.

Turner, A.P. (2004). Teaching striking/fielding concepts in cricket. *Teaching Elementary Physical Education, 15* (4), 10-14.

Turner, A.P., & Martinek, T.J. (1995). Teaching for understanding: A model for improving decision making during game play. *Quest, 47,* 44-63.

Turner, A.P., & Martinek, T.J. (1999). An investigation into teaching games for understanding: Effects on skill, knowledge and game play. *Research Quarterly for Exercise and Sport, 70,* 286-296.

Turner, A.P., Allison, P.C., & Pissanos, B.W. (2001). Constructing a concept of skillfulness in invasion games within a games for understanding context. *European Journal of Physical Education, 6,* 38-54.

Werner, P., & Almond, L. (1990). Models of games education. *Journal of Physical Education, Recreation and Dance, 61* (4), 23-27.

Wilson, G.E. (2002). A framework for teaching tactical game knowledge. *Journal of Physical Education, Recreation and Dance, 73* (1), 20-26, 56.

chapter

6

Introducing the Teaching Games for Understanding Model in Teacher Education Programs

Kath Howarth

Good theories are workable for practitioners, make sense, can be applied to the real world of classrooms and schools, and are generalizable to the greatest number of real situations.

Waxman & Walberg, 1991, p. 64

One of the greatest challenges for teacher education is helping preservice teachers connect educational theories and ideals to the challenges they will face in the classroom. For an instructional model to work for preservice teachers, the model needs to be relevant to their limited experience and their own immediate future as teachers.

In this chapter I address the attractions and barriers faced by preservice teachers when introduced to the Teaching Games for Understanding (TGfU) model. I will also show how the assimilation of the model into their teaching arsenal can be stimulating, demanding, and informing, both for them and for the teacher educators who teach and work with them.

Educators should take three important considerations into account when introducing an instructional model to preservice teachers. First, the model must be appropriate for the subject matter. Second, the model must provide preservice teachers with a realistic, alternative way to teach the subject matter. Finally, because instructional models embody different philosophies of teaching and learning, it is unlikely that one model

For an instructional model to work for preservice teachers, the model needs to be relevant to their limited experience and their own immediate future as teachers.

will fit all teachers in all contexts. The question is how best to represent the TGfU model, or the Tactical Games model, in teacher education programs so that preservice teachers perceive it as a viable model for them to use and so that they understand more clearly the content and structure of sport. According to Metzler (2000), an instructional model has six components:

1. Foundations
2. Teaching and learning features
3. Teacher expertise and contextual needs
4. Teaching the TGfU course
5. Assessment of learning
6. Contextual modifications

This theoretical framework for an instructional model and anecdotal reports from preservice and in-service teachers will be used to establish the implications of teaching the TGfU model to preservice teachers.

Foundations: The Internal Logic of a Game

The focus of the TGfU model is the game, and this is both a problem and an attraction to the inexperienced teacher. Although knowledge of the game as a whole is a crucial ingredient, teachers need skills of observation and analysis, questioning, and probing to successfully use their tactical knowledge. These skills are more likely to be found in the expert teacher or coach than in preservice teachers, no matter how deep their knowledge of the game may be. Even if correct observations are made and tactical knowledge is assured, preservice teachers may lack skill in posing questions and guiding players through the cognitive processes required for them to play with greater tactical awareness. The lesson may include game play, but it may not include the required manipulation of situations to facilitate decision making and the framing of tactical opportunities to help players develop tactical awareness.

Even prior to using these skills of observation, analysis, questioning, and probing, the teacher should assess what players need to learn by judging what they are ready to learn tactically and technically. From this assessment, the teacher can select appropriate game forms and designs so that the required tactical complexity is introduced to students without requiring overly demanding technical skills.

Making the game the central focus for learning and teaching, or using the "game as problem" approach, is nevertheless attractive to preservice teachers because they know from their own experience that playing games is highly motivating. The affective aspects of focusing on game tactics and strategy are apparent to preservice teachers. Players want to play the game and are less enthusiastic about skill acquisition, particularly as they move into high school. Students can perceive skill acquisition as both less authentic and more frustrating than the game. The attraction of a game, however, is soon lost if the game experience is not conducive to success. If the game size, level of difficulty, tactical emphasis, or skill requirements is inappropriate, students will lose their motivation to participate.

The format of the "game as problem" approach is also attractive to preservice teachers because they can involve the players immediately in game competition and social interaction.

The format of the "game as problem" approach is also attractive to preservice teachers because they can involve the players immediately in game competition and social interaction. The typical format of playing a game, followed by skills practice, and then returning to the game provides motivation for all students. However, using the game as a "laboratory" to address the emerging tactical understanding of players and to identify the tactical and technical learning to be addressed in the skills portion of the lesson can be overwhelming for a preservice teacher. The danger is that this type of lesson becomes, or is at least seen to become, just another "roll out the ball" lesson because it lacks sufficient interaction between teacher and players on both a cognitive and technical level.

The first step in designing a game form is to determine the internal logic of the game and how it affects the way preservice teachers are introduced to the model.

In the TGfU model, the focus for teachers is game form design. Therefore, the first step in designing a game form is to determine the internal logic of the game and how it affects the way preservice teachers are introduced to the model. Gréhaigne, Godbout, and Bouthier (1999) suggested that four elements appear in team games in varying strengths and complexity: opposition, cooperation, attack, and defense. They explain that "the idea for each player is to cooperate with partners in order to better oppose the opponents either while attacking (keeping one's defense in mind) or while defending (getting ready to attack)" (p. 163). These deceptively simple and obvious descriptions belie the complexity of either teaching or performing in team games. This becomes

Table 6.1   Four Elements of Team Games Broken Down by Strategy and Tactics

	Opposition	Cooperation	Attack	Defense
Strategy (pre-game planning)	• Offensive and defensive plan • Assessment of opposition	• Individual role and team plan • Assessment of own and team's strengths and weaknesses	Plan of attack (with the opposing defense in mind)	Plan of defense (with the opposing offense in mind)
Tactics (in-game response)	Application and adjustment of game plan relative to changing game situation	Individual and team response relative to the actual team performance	Attacking in response to own offense and opponents' play	Defending in response to own defense and opponents' play

apparent when the elements are broken down into more detail as in table 6.1.

Gréhaigne and Godbout (1995) described tactics as "knowledge in action" and identified three categories of knowledge: action rules, play organization, and motor capacities. For example, when responding to a game situation, players need to understand individual rules of efficient action, such as how to protect the ball. These action rules, however, must also be seen in the context of what each side wants to achieve as a *principle of action,* such as maintaining possession in attack or regaining possession in defense. Such actions and principles are tied closely to motor skill. For example, how a player protects the ball in lacrosse (an action rule) as part of a principle (maintaining possession) is determined by the player's stick skills and body control. Also closely related are "play organization rules" (Gréhaigne & Godbout, 1995, p. 498) governed by space, player positioning, and roles. Thus, the fact that in lacrosse the space behind the goal is available will influence which systems of play are adopted prior to the game (strategy) and how movement of the ball and players is maintained in offense (tactics).

The fact that the game provides ever-changing problems to be solved

> *The fact that the game provides ever-changing problems to be solved means that the form of the game needs to be carefully selected to accent the particular tactical problem the teacher wants to introduce.*

means that the form of the game needs to be carefully selected to accent the particular tactical problem the teacher wants to introduce. It also means that players have to make decisions that are strongly influenced by external events and conditions. The choice of game form will be crucial to player success. However, players will not succeed if there is a mismatch between their knowledge of the game (such as rules, positions, and roles) and their skills and ability to respond appropriately to game situations. Indeed, the ability to perform correctly based on decision-making and technical skills is one of the hallmarks of the expert (Turner & Martinek, 1995).

Teaching and Learning Features: The Active Teacher and Learner

The trend for some time in education has been to create curricula in which the learner is active rather than passive in the learning process. This is often described as a constructivist approach and has been developed intermittently in physical education for many years through instructional models such as Movement Education, TGfU, and Sport Education. Despite the variety of ideological perspectives represented in constructivist theory (Kirk & Macdonald, 1998), the common elements are the active involvement of the learner, who constructs knowledge and meaning within a task, and the recognition that learning occurs within, and is influenced by, social and cultural contexts.

Kirk and Macdonald (1998) attempted to synthesize these perspectives for physical education pedagogy by citing one constructivist approach, situated learning. They suggested that "the key concepts in Lave and Wenger's theory of situated learning are the notions of legitimate peripheral participation in communities of practice" (p. 380). A *community of practice* refers to the accepted shared structure and practices of a group and the ways they influence an individual. One example of a community of practice is sport. Participation in a community gives meaning to what an individual does and learns.

Because the school setting is itself a community of practice, it tends to mediate between the outside world of sport, recreation, and physical fitness and what happens in physical education. There is no doubt, however, that the aims and goals of physical education have focused on authentic, lifelong participation as a way to give meaning to the curriculum. These goals emphasize the authentic sport experience for young people, and have paved the way for the reemergence of the TGfU, Teaching Personal and Social Responsibility, and Sport Education models (Hellison, 1995; Siedentop, 1994).

This focus on meaning, authenticity, and the learner as active participant can be a problem for preservice teachers who lack experience in content and in how to relate to and motivate students. Expert teachers know more about content, are better able to gauge learner ability levels and problems, and are more comfortable and excited about teaching their subject than are preservice teachers (Schempp, Manioss, Tan, & Fincher, 1998).

In the TGfU model, teachers must not only be knowledgeable about the game but also able to make appropriate cognitive demands on learners to encourage them to be active in the development of tactical understanding. Deductive questioning and high levels of verbal interaction with students go hand in hand with game designs based on student levels of motor skill and tactical understanding. The teacher must design the right questions to help students construct a knowledge base about how to play the game. Many preservice teachers have had little or no experience in using the deductive method, either as students or teachers in physical education settings. This lack of questioning and probing skills can be stultifying, even for those with considerable knowledge of the game. This complex combination of required knowledge and skills for teaching the TGfU model is presented in table 6.2.

> *This focus on meaning, authenticity, and the learner as active participant can be a problem for preservice teachers who lack experience in content and in how to relate to and motivate students.*

Table 6.2   Knowledge and Skill Requirements for the Preservice Teacher

Knowledge		Observation skills	Teaching skills	
Game	*Development*	*Student ability*	*Planning*	*Questioning*
Rules and roles	Motor ability	Psychomotor skill	Game design	Deductive
Technique	Affective	Cognitive response	Tactical level	Use of probes
Tactics	Cognitive	Game performance	Requisite skill	Age appropriate
Strategy				

Teacher Expertise and Contextual Needs: Attractions and Obstacles to Teaching the Model

To gather evidence for this section, I conducted a semistructured interview with a small group of preservice teachers and gave a questionnaire to preservice, in-service, and university teachers based on the six components of the TGfU model identified by Metzler (2000). Pseudonyms are used when quoting from any of these sources.

When asked how useful the Tactical Games, or Teaching Games for Understanding, model was for them at their stage of teaching preparation, preservice teachers had similar responses. They understood the demands of the model in terms of the games knowledge and the teaching expertise required of them as teachers. Those who took a tactical concepts class described the model in the following ways:

> *Jack:* It's like the strategies involved in the game—more what to do without the ball, I guess, because that is where most of the time is spent by most of the players. . . . Tactical presents more of a cognitive association to the game also rather than just the skills of the game.

> *Brendan:* When I think of tactical, I think of what goes into the game in order to play it correctly. . . . We would play and then we would come back out, and we would actually go over what we had to do to perform better inside that game . . . breaking the whole game down into parts.

> *Jim:* Tactical—how you think or how you react, anticipate what's going to happen. It's not as physical as it's mental. You can think before it happens, you can anticipate, and you may be correct or not in your anticipation. It's how you respond to that.

When asked what attracted them to the TGfU model, the preservice teachers responded as follows:

> *Deirdre:* I like the TGfU style of teaching because it allows all students to participate in game play or activity. This format eliminates the time spent on classroom management and allows for more physical activity and more opportunities for students to be on task. I like the fact that teachers can use live on-/off-the-ball skills, teach concepts and skills in a real gamelike setting. The students remain engaged and are having fun.

Elise: TGfU, I believe, stimulates the creative minds of children and makes activities more challenging for the mind. This model is also a lot more fun for the teacher and student.

Brendan described his field experience in a lacrosse unit in clear contrast to the tactical concepts class he was taking:

Probably a better model than we are used to. I'm thinking about [field experience]. . . . I was . . . teaching them lacrosse, and I'm only there on Tuesdays, so I don't know what [the teacher] does on Thursdays. All I know is that we had three days of passing and catching, standing in a line. Then he had one day showing them . . . fake dodges. We got them into the game and there were like seven kids standing in the middle of the goal and I just wanted to stop the game and tell them what to do . . . particularly as it was after I'd done . . . creating space and tactics, and I was sitting there thinking, I could really teach these kids something. The model would really work with these kids.

All preservice teachers recognized that they needed to have strong content knowledge about the game and that learner characteristics such as cognitive ability, learning preference, and decision making were key to this approach. They all recognized the cognitive focus. For example, Chris listed three important things for the teacher to know:

Know the concept they want the children to learn

Know what games can be used for the concept

Know how to draw the concept from the children without telling them

The preservice teachers also realized the complexities of analyzing their students' learning abilities and preferences. When asked what they found difficult about the TGfU model, the teachers mentioned similar problems:

Deirdre: Being new to the style, I am still learning. I find it hard to analyze tactical problems—how to modify a game so that it works on what we are trying to achieve. Until last year I have never heard of this model.

Chris: Asking questions that draw the knowledge from the students.

Elise: Planning creatively. Thinking of ways to teach children skills/game . . . as well as making it fun and interesting.

> *Julia:* Analyzing tactical problems was what I found most difficult when using this model.

When preservice teachers were interviewed after a course in which there was a group project to plan a lesson for peer teaching, they mentioned other problems that consistently arose about the use of questioning and whether planning for questioning before the lesson was possible.

> *Jim:* We talked together in our group when we met about how to not tell [students] everything. And we said, "We've got to concentrate," and we laughed about it, saying, "It's going to be difficult. We want to tell them everything!" . . . I found myself answering a couple of questions and giving them a couple of answers I shouldn't have, but I picked up on it pretty fast. I realized that's not the idea; the idea is to open up discussion, and after that (that was after like the first sentence), it felt much easier. I understood the whole idea.

> *Brendan:* Actually I was watching [the students], and I didn't remember the questions! We wrote out an outline, but I didn't remember anything we wrote down! I knew the drill because I made them up . . . but the questions! When I asked them, it was basically on what they were doing. I looked at what they were doing.

> *Jack:* I think I gave a little too much instructing and not enough guiding for this style of teaching. . . . I forgot to present the questions on how does the overlap work and where is the side of the field you need to push the ball to gain a tactical advantage. I had the questions and I reverted back. . . . I think it's something that would take getting used to and practice doing to avoid that exact situation.

When asked what was going on in his mind when he was teaching, John said,

> Basically all the questions I could ask! I mean I knew all the questions I wanted to ask. I just wanted to watch their game to see if I could pick up something that I saw there.

When queried on whether he asked the players questions, he laughed.

> No, I told them what they had to do! . . . It's just a reaction, because you're not used to asking kids the questions. You're just used to telling them the answers and giving them the

answers of how to do it. But you never ask the kids the questions and see if they understand why. Most classes, I think teachers will tell you how to correct it or what the answer is, but they don't let—they don't give—the kids the opportunity to think about it—maybe come up with the answers themselves.

When thinking about the model, several preservice teachers believed that time and lack of experience were critical issues for them in school. Others who had some coaching experience believed that they might start the model in coaching first because they could see it helping them with team play.

Teaching the TGfU Course

One clear message from all college instructors who were asked about their involvement with the model was that preservice teachers who lack sufficient knowledge of the basic structure and strategies of games as performers would find the model problematic and frustrating. If preservice teachers do not understand the internal logic of a game, they will be unlikely to be able to present that game successfully to their students.

Teaching the Basic Concepts of Games

When teaching activity classes to preservice teachers, an instructor generally has the problem of balancing content and method. For example, experienced coaches may have excellent presentation of content, but may leave discussions of how to teach the sport to varying age levels to other classes, specifically methods classes. This dichotomy of form and content can create serious problems for preservice teachers. Because they may have little background knowledge of the skill levels and developmental stages of their future students, when they copy the styles and expectations of their activity teachers, they may adopt approaches that are inappropriate in schools. Teacher education programs have addressed this issue in various ways. Some adopt one model, such as the TGfU model, which is then used in most or all activity classes. Others adopt several models that are exemplified through a variety of activities. The assumption, however, is that the model, or models, adopted provide a strong cognitive content to

The model becomes the medium for teaching about the nature of games regardless of which instructional model the preservice teacher eventually chooses to use when teaching sport-related games.

activity classes. The model becomes the medium for teaching about the nature of games regardless of which instructional model the preservice teacher eventually chooses to use when teaching sport-related games.

Value of the Model

When asked about the value of teaching the TGfU model to preservice teachers, teacher educators and activity instructors conveyed similar reactions. The first value was described as contextual because this approach focuses on the game and gives meaning to what students are learning. The second value was affective because learners had to work together and show patience in playing to their own skill levels and those of their teammates. Third, learners felt competent and motivated because they were involved in authentic game situations. Finally, a hidden advantage was that the model helped preservice teachers understand more explicitly the similarities of sport-related games so they could approach a new activity with more understanding when they

> *F*inally, a hidden advantage was that the model helped preservice teachers understand more explicitly the similarities of sport-related games so they could approach a new activity with more understanding when they began teaching.

began teaching. For example, preservice teachers can be encouraged to see the similarities between soccer and field hockey in terms of tactics while being aware of the differences imposed by rules and equipment.

Time Problems Presented by the Model

The major problems for preservice teachers using the TGfU model were described as planning, questioning, observing and analyzing, facilitating skills, and a lack of content knowledge. The TGfU model presents some challenges with regard to the time demands of observing and working through teachable moments during the games to structure learners' knowledge of game tactics. Teachers and coaches who teach using this model accept that this model is "out of the box" for most preservice teachers and embrace the special challenges. Yet, teacher educators seem to find it a very satisfying model to teach. Those who try to present it are fully committed and excited to see some of their students adopt it as a meaningful teaching model for them. Teacher educators comment that they wish they had more time to teach sport content and innovative instructional models such as TGfU. Given this dual focus of teaching both the content of the sport and also the model through which to teach that content, it can be difficult to equalize the knowledge base for those pre-service teachers who start at different levels of tactical understanding. However, it can increase teachers' ability to suggest a variety of tactical solutions to a particular problem (Howarth & Walkuski, 2001).

Cognitive Dissonance

Teaching the TGfU model requires a broad perspective and a willingness to change. Because one of the virtues of the model has been that tactical concepts can be generalized to other similar games, the content of many games needs to be analyzed. Preservice teachers should practice the "game–practice–game" pattern to plan and present the model effectively. Teachers also have to practice asking questions and eliciting answers based on observing particular tactical situations. Again, this is different from the typical teaching format used by teachers (i.e., preservice and in-service) and coaches. College instructors have to be fully committed to the model if they are to try to encourage change in preservice teach-ers' ways of understanding, planning, and presenting different ways of teaching sport. When faced with the need to change from long experience of the teacher as expert to becoming the teacher as questioner, preser-vice teachers can feel a disconcerting level of cognitive dissonance until they become more comfortable with this new solution to the teaching of games.

On the other hand, the perceived difficulty of teaching this model could also be seen as its strength. Above all, the TGfU approach is cognitively engaging for both teachers and students. However, the affective obstacles to introducing an alternative method to preservice teachers should not be ignored. Teacher educators will have to encourage and support preservice teachers in taking the risk to try the model in schools because (1) it may make more visible their limited content knowledge and (2) they may be met with resistance from the teachers in those schools. Textbooks that give specific examples of lessons based on the TGfU, or Tactical Games, model are a great start (Griffin, Mitchell, & Oslin, 1997; Mitchell, Oslin, & Griffin, 2003). Lesson planning and small-group peer teaching are good ways for preservice teachers to get their feet wet. It enables them to see the model in action, to try it out in a relatively safe environment, and to learn from one another's struggles and successes.

Connecting to the Real World of Teaching and Learning

In the real-world setting, preservice and in-service teachers should choose the sport they know best so that they start teaching the model with a depth of content knowledge. They should also start to practice the model with just one class. Team teaching a unit can also help establish confidence in the TGfU model because one of the elements of this approach is the use of small-group games that the teacher observes and uses as a base for questioning and building tactical knowledge. Having more than one pair of eyes helps teachers avoid discipline problems and learn from each other as they comment and question the groups. Simple strategies such as counting 10 seconds and then blowing the whistle to stop the game force inexperienced teachers to "freeze" the game and ask players questions about the tactical emphasis. Planning a series of "start-up" questions also helps to change the teaching style from information giving to information getting.

Assessment as a Learning Tool

Assessment tools such as the Game Performance Assessment Instrument (GPAI) (Griffin, Mitchell, & Oslin, 1997) and the Tactical Concepts Knowledge Rubric (Howarth & Walkuski, 2001) not only assess student performance in the game, but also help teachers learn more about their teaching skills and about the games they are teaching. When preservice teachers design and use assessment tools, they soon realize their own shortcomings in terms of both knowledge of and performance in tactical situations in the game. Such tools focus attention on the use of observation and recording. Teachers can design their own, more basic assessment instruments using these tools as guides.

The Context for TGfU

Probably the first context preservice teachers identify as ideal for the application of the TGfU model is in their coaching. They recognize that their knowledge of the sport will make it easier for them to design and plan tactical problems. From that vantage point, the preservice teachers can move toward a broader view of the implementation of the model in physical education using a variety of sports. Seeing the model in action with their peers helps them to see that it is not only the athlete who can benefit from this approach. In fact, they see many less able players showing a good cognitive grasp of how to solve tactical problems. Preservice teachers also see it as a fresh approach to a traditional part of the physical education curriculum, particularly at the secondary level make connections with other similar models such as Sport Education where students practice the many different roles within the sport context.

Conclusion

Is the TGfU model workable for teachers? Can it be used successfully by beginning teachers in authentic school settings? Is it a good theory (Waxman & Walberg, 1991)? TGfU is very attractive to knowledgeable players, coaches, and teachers (i.e., preservice and in-service). It capitalizes on their deep or emerging knowledge and expertise of what is involved in playing sport. TGfU can also complement the Sport Education model, which also uses the authentic sport setting as the focus for the teacher. Both models consider sport as a social, affective, and cognitive endeavor, not just the performance of skills. Both models offer multiple opportunities for social interaction, active involvement, and problem solving. These connections can be motivating for faculty involved in teacher education programs. The major challenge, however, is to develop ways of teaching the model so that teachers and coaches believe that TGfU is a viable model for enhancing students' sport-related games learning.

Discussion Questions

1. What were the pros and cons of learning to teach using the TGfU model that the preservice teachers quoted in this chapter shared?
2. Explain what you understand by the author's reference to the game as a "problem" or a "laboratory."
3. Using table 6.2, analyze your own readiness to teach the TGfU model using a sport and a class of students of your own choice.

References

Gréhaigne, J.-F., & Godbout, P. (1995). Tactical knowledge in team sports from a constructivist and cognitivist perspective. *Quest, 47,* 490-505.

Gréhaigne, J.-F., Godbout, P., & Bouthier, D. (1999). The foundations of tactics and strategy in team sports. *Journal of Teaching in Physical Education, 18,* 159-174.

Griffin, L.L., Mitchell, S.A., & Oslin, J.L. (1997). *Teaching sport concepts and skills: A tactical games approach.* Champaign, IL: Human Kinetics.

Hellison, D. (1995). *Teaching responsibility through physical activity.* Champaign, IL: Human Kinetics.

Howarth, K., & Walkuski, J. (2001, August). *Teaching tactical concepts in the college setting: Utility or futility?* Paper presented at the AIESEP International meeting, Waterville Valley, NH.

Kirk, D., & Macdonald, D. (1998). Situated learning in physical education. *Journal of Teaching in Physical Education, 17,* 376-387.

Metzler, M.W. (2000). *Instructional models for physical education.* Boston: Allyn & Bacon.

Mitchell, S.A., Oslin, J.L., & Griffin, L.L. (2003). *Sport foundations for elementary physical education: A tactical games approach.* Champaign, IL: Human Kinetics.

Schempp, P.G., Manioss, D., Tan, S.K.S., & Fincher, M.D. (1998). Subject expertise and teachers' knowledge. *Journal of Teaching in Physical Education, 17,* 342-356.

Siedentop, D. (1994). *Sport education: Quality PE through positive sport experience.* Champaign, IL: Human Kinetics.

Turner, A., & Martinek, T.J. (1995). Teaching for understanding: A model for improving decision making during game play. *Quest, 47,* 44-63.

Waxman, H.C., & Walberg, H.J. (1991). *Effective teaching: Current research.* Berkeley, CA: McCutchan.

chapter

7

Implementing Teaching Games for Understanding: Stories of Change

Steven Tan

I think that at the end of the day, the choice whether to use the TGfU approach or not is entirely a personal one. TGfU allows me to do something different apart from what these children are experiencing as "free play" in their other PE classes. If they have an opportunity to be in my class, they would at least be able to experience a TGfU lesson. These kids can get to be excited and be interested in PE, and at the same time be learning. In this sense, I am very much motivated, and I believe that I should not shortchange the kids.

Benjamin (physical education specialist)

Over the past decade, physical education has been inundated with different change initiatives worldwide. These efforts to initiate curriculum change in our schools stem from broad-scale, centralized government legislation and reports to school-based, decentralized formulation and decision making by teachers and individual schools (Sparkes, 1991a; Ward & Doutis, 1999). Encouraging school-based educational planning and innovation would open up new horizons for more teacher initiative and participation to meet individual schools' needs and characteristics. This type of school-based planning allows for greater autonomy, participation, control, flexibility, and accountability, and recognizes the teacher as central in the curriculum change process. However, despite calls for reform and efforts to bring about change at the school level, top-down government mandates, initiatives, and policy making still permeate curriculum decision making (Levin, 1998).

In the current model of educational reform efforts, people external to the schools usually control the agenda and make the key decisions regarding the nature of planned educational change. The source of the innovation tends to lie with small groups of experts based in government agencies. Likewise, the development of new curricula is the responsibility of central agency experts, who then disseminate the policies, standards, strategies, and instructional packages to schools for adoption and implementation (Sparkes, 1991a). Subsequently, although teachers may be involved in some decision-making processes, they are mainly restricted to providing feedback to these central bodies on existing curricula.

In this chapter I will discuss how teachers made sense of and experienced change as they attempted to successfully negotiate a new initiative mandated by a central government agency. The first section will provide a brief explanation of the adoption and implementation of the curriculum. It is followed by a description of the context of change, the research study, and individual and school characteristics related to the teachers' implementation of the new curriculum. The unique stories of four teachers, which include their beliefs, rationales, decisions, and actions during the change process, are the major focus of this chapter. The chapter concludes with recommendations for school administrators, teacher education institutions, and practitioners regarding the successful implementation of future external change initiatives.

After reading this chapter, the reader should be able to do the following:

- Clarify the relationship between the adoption and implementation of a curriculum innovation

- Articulate the influence of physical education teachers' own lived experiences and philosophical orientation toward engagement in a new teaching approach

- Recognize that successful innovative reform creates a necessity for personal commitment and costs

- Understand the significance of positive student learning outcomes in sustaining personal satisfaction and motivation during the change process

- Provide suggestions for schools to create the necessary conditions and support for teachers to develop new competencies

Adoption and Implementation of a Curriculum Innovation

A major assumption related to external change initiatives is that schools and teachers will wholeheartedly adopt and implement the policies and intentions of the official curriculum. However, this is usually not true; many educational change efforts have been met with resistance or low levels of implementation (Curtner-Smith, 1999; Morris, 1995).

An educational initiative might not be implemented in schools for one of two reasons: reluctance to adopt it or an inability to implement it once it is adopted. The adoption of a new, mandated curriculum, for example, merely represents a decision by a school to accept or use the curriculum; it does not ensure that the curriculum will be implemented in the way it was originally intended. Implementation implies a process over time in which individuals, circumstances, and available resources influence how the curriculum will ultimately be used. Furthermore, there is no guarantee that worthwhile policies and innovative practices will either be adopted or implemented in schools (McLaughlin, 1998; Morris, 1995).

> **A**n educational initiative might not be implemented in schools for one of two reasons: reluctance to adopt it or an inability to implement it once it is adopted.

The literature on educational reform has identified numerous factors critical for the successful adoption and implementation of innovations in schools. These include teacher expertise, school leadership, teachers' beliefs and values, costs and rewards, systematic support, school environment and climate, financial resources, curriculum materials and technologies, assessment, and teaching strategies (Faucette & Graham, 1986; Fullan, 1991, 1993; Fullan & Hargreaves, 1996; Kirk, 1988; Sparkes, 1991b). Despite the fact that many change initiatives are frequently implemented unsuccessfully (numerous research studies have documented the frustrations and failure of teachers as they attempted to implement educational reforms in their schools), some schools have had success with curriculum changes (e.g., McKenzie, Sallis, Faucette, Roby, & Kolody, 1993; Rovegno & Bandhauer, 1997). This chapter examines the experiences of these teachers and schools as they underwent the change process.

Context

In 1998, Singapore's Ministry of Education (MOE; 1998) embarked on a comprehensive Curriculum Review Masterplan for all content areas. The purpose was to shift the emphasis of the education system away from the mastery of content toward the acquisition of thinking and learning skills that would stay with students throughout their lives. The most significant impact of this revision on the physical education curriculum has been the introduction of a new syllabus for all grade levels (Singapore Ministry of Education, 1999). A major change in this new syllabus was the creation of a framework specifying the different grade levels at which various concepts and games from the three games categories—territorial, net/wall, and striking/fielding—are to be introduced to pupils (see table 7.1). Depending on factors such as school culture, teacher expertise, facilities, student interest, and equipment, the school's physical education

Table 7.1   Grade Level Requirements for the Teaching of Different Categories of Games

Grade level	Concepts, skills, and game requirements
Primary 3	Teach net/wall and territorial game concepts using various fundamental skills applied in modified games
Primary 4	Teach net/wall, territorial, and striking/fielding* game concepts using fundamental skills applied in modified games
Primary 5	Select one game each from the net/wall and striking/fielding categories and two games from the territorial category
Primary 6	Select one new game each from the net/wall and striking/fielding categories and two new games from the territorial category
Secondary 1	Review net/wall and territorial game concepts using one game from each category
Secondary 2	Review striking/fielding and territorial game concepts using one game from each category
Secondary 3	Review or introduce one new game from the striking/fielding category and two new games each from both the net/wall and territorial game categories
Secondary 4	Review game concepts using three previously introduced or new games from any two game categories
Pre-university 1	Teach six games (revisit or new) selected from the three game categories with a minimum of one game from each category
Pre-university 2	Teach five games (revisit or new) of which two must be from the three different game categories

* The category *target games* is not included as a content in the physical education syllabus.

Adapted from *Revised physical education syllabus for primary, secondary, and pre-university levels*, by the Curriculum Planning and Development Division, Singapore Ministry of Education, 1999, pp. 22, 43, 44.

department would select appropriate sample games from the categories. Corollary to this content framework is the promotion of the Teaching Games for Understanding[1] (TGfU) pedagogy, which is considered most appropriate for achieving the stated aims and objectives identified in the new curriculum.

Since the curriculum revision, the MOE's Physical Education Curriculum Unit has been actively training facilitators, organizing workshops, and publishing resources to introduce the new curriculum framework and TGfU approach to Singapore's physical education teachers. Begun in 2000, the National Institute of Education (NIE) has also revised its physical education teacher education programs to prepare physical education teachers for this initiative, both at the initial and continuing education levels (Tan & Wong, 2001; Tan, Wright, McNeill, Fry, & Tan, 2002). Implementation of the new curriculum and pedagogy for the teaching of games in schools began in 2000.

Since this physical education initiative was introduced into Singapore schools in 2000, a gap appears to exist between the MOE's intended curriculum and pedagogy and the actual achievements of schools and teachers. Tan and colleagues (McNeill et al., 2004; Tan & Tan, 2001; Tan et al., 2002; Wright, Tan, McNeill, Fry, & Tan, 2001) identified high expectations of teachers' competencies, little intrinsic motivation, unavailability of teaching resources, lack of appropriate equipment and facilities, insufficient instructional time, and new roles for students as several reasons practicing physical education teachers are not, or are incapable of, implementing the teaching of games curriculum innovation in Singapore schools.

Despite little evidence to suggest that the majority of schools and practitioners in both elementary and high schools have used the TGfU approach and have implemented the new curriculum, some teachers have attempted to promote substantial educational change in their classes. Where TGfU has been implemented, it's more a case of single teachers plowing away rather than the whole department or school being involved. This chapter is therefore about four teachers who are plowing away in their own schools against constraints and challenges. I hope these stories will help inform the experiences and practice of others who endeavor to bring about change in their own practice to improve student learning and achievement.

The Study and the Teachers

This chapter represents the outcome of a research study whose goal was to capture and portray four teachers' experiences during the implementation of TGfU and their attempts to make sense of distinct changes that occurred. All teachers were in their first year of curriculum change.

MOE-sponsored districtwide workshops and NIE in-service courses for professional development by their school leaders. In all cases, the teachers' involvement with the TGfU initiative presented them with the opportunity to clarify their views and concerns about implementing the initiative. Learning about and understanding the nuances and subtleties of any innovation is always difficult and daunting, as expressed by Katherin:

> Before I attended the course, I was actually still very fuzzy about TGfU. I was unsettled and had questions like, How to teach it? Are you sure the children can do it? I was skeptical. I was doubtful because I was not sure what TGfU was all about. . . . We know that we should play like this . . . but playing like this does not mean that we can teach like this. Actually, before I attended the course, I was really lost. The instructor made it clearer. Attending the course helped me very much.

What helped these teachers adopt this approach, however, were changes in their philosophy regarding the instruction of physical education and games in schools and how they defined the notion of skillfulness in their personal lives. Reflecting on his own experiences with sports while growing up, Benjamin best expressed the sentiments of the group after knowing about TGfU:

> Personally, I had the skills, but somehow in a game, I could not play fully. People were always playing better than I was, even those who were less skilled. So something else must be missing. When I was exposed to the games concept, I realized that *that* [italics added] was the missing thing. Through all these years, I have been taught skills, but not the concepts. . . . I wish that somebody had managed to explain to me the concepts. Then I would have been able to play sports at a higher level. With this understanding, I am beginning to see or play certain sports in a way that I was not able to do in the past.

These teachers were clearly convinced of the usefulness of TGfU for both teaching and learning games, and they were eager to bring about changes in their practices to meet the demands for educational change. However, they still had to contend with the practical challenges of implementing this approach in their respective schools.

Adaptations During the Change Process

Like most curriculum reforms that require teaching resources (Fullan, 1991), the TGfU approach places some additional demands on teachers and schools during the implementation process. The four teachers maintained that, undeniably, some commitment was expected in the initial stage of implementing TGfU. This commitment could take the form of time and effort needed to design new instructional plans, to acquire appropriate equipment, or to adapt and organize available facilities to suit the innovation. As Benjamin stated, "You need to invest time if you really want to think about doing it well. But as with any new thing, it's just the teething problems that you have to experience. You just have to get yourself to do it."

In general, teachers do not use particular instructional skills simply because they can. Rather, they make critical judgments based on the fit between the suitability of pedagogy and the demands, constraints, and opportunities of the working environment (Fullan, 1991; Tan & Tan, 2001). For the teachers in this study, the flexibility in their schools' physical education programs was seen as an advantage as they considered the operability of the initiative and their abilities to implement the changes. This was true for Danny; his response illustrates some of the adaptive decisions of these teachers:

> *In general, teachers do not use particular instructional skills simply because they can. Rather, they make critical judgments based on the fit between the suitability of pedagogy and the demands, constraints, and opportunities of the working environment.*

> I think it is very important for us to be happy and to be able to understand what we can control and what we can't control. I realized that nobody was using the [school] hall. I was thinking to myself, How can I have a PE lesson in the hall? rather than, Because I like pickleball, I should use the hall. If that's the reason, then I should be demanding the basketball courts or the soccer field because I want to play basketball or soccer. I looked at what spaces were underutilized, and I just came up with this idea of pickleball.

Danny's decision to implement TGfU using a pickleball unit for grade 8 students was not without further practical constraints. Even though adequate space was available in the school hall for pickleball for 40 students, the school didn't have pickleball equipment. Danny had to dedicate time, money, and energy to solve this problem creatively:

> The school didn't budget for pickleball. But I wanted to have pickleball in my PE lesson. I asked the technical teachers to require the secondary two [students] to make pickleball bats.

Then I went to buy the pickleballs myself. I was therefore able to keep the pupils happy for one whole term. They had four to five weeks of skills and concept development, followed by another three weeks of round-robin competition.

Similarly, Benjamin did not follow the school's recommended curriculum and decided to teach territorial game concepts by introducing ultimate Frisbee to his grade 4 and 6 classes instead. This was a conscious decision because he was aware that ultimate Frisbee is not on the recommended list of territorial[4] games for primary schools. Furthermore, the school did not have any Frisbees. He explained his rationale for his adaptation:

If you pick soccer or basketball, you may have something that the girls may not like. Basically, ultimate Frisbee is something that is very new to all of them. It evens the playing field. And, furthermore, I like to try new things. . . . I borrowed some [Frisbees] and I bought some.

Besides making curricular adaptations, the teachers also had to constantly modify or compromise their instructional practice because of their lack of experience and uncertainty about using the TGfU approach. Despite having acquired some theoretical knowledge and pedagogical skills from their teacher education programs, workshops, or in-service courses, these adaptations were necessary because TGfU is complex and a considerable amount of time is needed to learn to teach well. All of the teachers used some adaptations as they began to institute changes in their own classes. Debra explained:

I was using [the TGfU approach], but not strictly following the prescribed structure. The TGfU structure is to play first, discuss the concept behind it, and then [students] play again. However, I taught them a bit of the game plus skills first; then they got into the game. This was then followed by some discussion. . . . I allowed them to interpret the game themselves. I tried not to restrict them. I allowed them to go ahead and try before I commented or told them something. . . . Sometimes I did ask them, "What do you think is the mistake?" but most of the time, in my haste, I would say, "Look, she is making a big mistake." I should rather ask them to think about what they need to do to make it better.

In their own special ways, these teachers displayed an overall tendency to moderate their personal commitment and costs during the implementation of TGfU. Regardless of the costs they incurred, the rewards in student learning were definitely worthwhile.

Perceptions of Change in Student Learning

What originally attracted these teachers to TGfU was the promise that this approach would enhance their effectiveness in promoting student learning outcomes. Whether it was a field-based component structured into the TGfU module, a student teaching experience, or required practice for the in-service courses, these learning experiences provided the teachers with numerous success stories. Benjamin recalled:

> During my teaching practice I was taking a primary 3 class and I let them play Captain's ball. I found that they knew how to pass. But after passing, they didn't move. They didn't know the game concept of running into space. So I started explaining and teaching them about moving into space. Later when they were playing soccer, they were able to transfer this understanding of moving into space to another game. It made the teaching of [soccer] easier and made me believe in TGfU. . . . It was only after teaching practice that there was the realization that it works. The teaching practice helped to reinforce my belief that it works.

For all teachers, positive changes in students' behaviors were evident following the implementation phase of this instructional innovation. Benjamin was pleased with the improvement in student performance during game play after his Frisbee unit during his first year of teaching. He proudly asserted:

> In the initial phase, you will be surprised that the pupils will just stand there, not knowing what to do. At the end we had a tournament and I watched them play . . . they were moving forward well. They knew what they had to do. When their teammate had the Frisbee, they knew they had to invade and increase their space. When the other team had the Frisbee, they needed to defend. This was after several sessions of me using the TGfU. I saw the success as the kids managed to understand what they needed to do.

Katherin also shared the encouraging responses of her students with TGfU:

> They found it very challenging, particularly the games concept dimension. You ask me, "Are they able to understand what they needed to know to make decisions in [hockey]?" I have to say, "They can!" They have learned it from TGfU. "We [the students] did not run into space enough and that's why we were crowding around." I asked them, and they could tell me.

As Debra became more comfortable in her practice of TGfU, her students were also adapting to new learning expectations and behaviors. After one semester of trying TGfU, Debra was pleased that students benefited from her questioning. "Even my quiet ones were answering my questions." Besides the students' verbal responses, they were also keen to apply that cognitive understanding in their games. This was despite their lack of skills and ability. Cognitively, the students knew what needed to be done, but physically, they lacked the motor skills to perform successfully. Despite this, Debra was encouraged by their dedication:

> Some of my students, to the extent of understanding the concepts, know what to do. They wanted to carry on. They wanted to continue; whether it was successful or not, it didn't matter. They wanted to move into space. They understood the concept.

However, more cogent than changes in students' behavior were changes in their attitudes and motivations for participation in games voluntarily. Students, on their own initiative, would choose to play ultimate Frisbee using their personal equipment and on their own time or to be involved in a pickleball game. Danny was very satisfied to witness changes in his students' attitudes and desire to participate voluntarily in both organized and free play activities. In a sense, it was a testimony that TGfU had worked for him:

> In the last four sessions, I put them into a round-robin competition to look for a class champion. All the pupils took part. I mean, if they didn't like it, they wouldn't have wanted to win every point. . . . There are certain situations where you have to let them play a free game. Some of the students will choose to play pickleball, even after one whole term of pickleball. So I take that as a compliment.

For these teachers, the positive results they observed in their students were significant as they strived to continue with this initiative effort. This confidence allowed them to move forward with the change process while reflecting on future implications of the TGfU innovation in their schools.

Visions of Future Challenges

These four teachers responded to the change process differently depending on the extent of their training in TGfU. Katherin and Debra had limited opportunities to experiment with TGfU and to be involved with curriculum planning in detail because of the short duration of their workshops and in-service programs. As such, during the course of curriculum implementation, they relied heavily on the help and support of fellow colleagues in the schools who were either familiar with the approach or were enrolled in the same workshop and course.

For both Katherin and Debra, collegiality and collaboration among teachers in their schools increased, and the school leadership saw that as an important means of fostering staff development and as an effective way to promote TGfU. Katherin shared her principal's future expectations and challenge: "She wanted us to conduct the course for the other teachers at the end of the year. She wanted us to work together with the other teachers and to get them comfortable with it."

For Katherin and Debra, the desire and potential was there for them to keep up the momentum and to continue the change process by working collaboratively with other teachers. The main focus of this collaboration appears to be related to revising and planning curricula and lessons that are more aligned to TGfU, and finding the time and opportunity to achieve that. As Debra articulated, "I was hoping to find the time with my colleagues to do more curriculum planning. We need to identify the linkages between concepts and activities so as to reinforce TGfU in our teaching."

Benjamin and Danny, however, had extensive exposure to TGfU instruction, unit and lesson planning, and guided practice in different school environments, all of which were structured holistically within their teacher education programs. Therefore, they appeared very confident and comfortable and had no anxiety working independently while implementing TGfU in their schools. In adapting the school syllabus to suit the students' needs and constraints, they chose to work either alone or in limited partnership with a few others. As a result, their perceptions of future challenges tended to focus on issues of instruction and learning rather than on curriculum development. Benjamin revealed his intentions for the future:

> I would like to try and experiment with TGfU with primary 2. With the primary 4, I've already realized that at that level, they were able to understand the concepts. I was thinking, How will this be compared to the younger ones? Will TGfU work? I'm just curious to know. How will it work? What will be the kind of results I can expect to see? That will be interesting to find out.

These teachers' curriculum change stories reveal to some extent how they managed a large-scale reform within the context of their own schools. The teachers' stories explain how they think about TGfU, what levels of sacrifice they are prepared to undertake, how they perceive changes in their students, and how they envision their future obligations to keep this initiative going.

Helping Teachers Initiate Change

The new physical education national curriculum has led to excitement and activity, as well as to changes and challenges posed to the prevailing culture of teaching games in Singapore schools. These changes and challenges include (1) publishing teaching resources, (2) improving initial and in-service teacher development programs, (3) purchasing new equipment, (4) organizing districtwide sharing sessions and workshops, and (5) developing new schemes of work. However, Schwarz and Alberts (1998) reminded us that "surface changes can be legislated, but lasting changes in how teachers view and do their work, in how they think and feel, must happen on a deeper level, teacher by teacher, community by community" (p. 153). At the heart of school reform and improvement are the teachers who are the key agents of educational change (Fullan, 1993; Fullan & Hargreaves, 1996). This, a truth as expressed in the opening quote by Benjamin, clearly reflects how teachers alone decide whether an innovation is to be implemented wholeheartedly in schools. Teachers like Benjamin who are motivated and committed to doing what is best for students must be prepared well and supported adequately in their endeavor. This section will address what professional development leaders and principals can learn from the experiences of these four teachers that will help prepare other teachers to be effective change agents for their schools.

One responsibility of professional development programs (courses and workshops) should be to help teachers reexamine their philosophies and goals related to the new physical education curriculum (Butler, 1996). These four teachers underwent fundamental philosophical adjustments that helped them develop, define, and interpret the TGfU initiative. On the one hand, these teachers really wanted to implement the approach because of a deep commitment to what they deemed to be best for their students. On the other hand, they sought to relish the successes and accomplishments that would result from their efforts. All four teachers cited examples of student learning and change as a source of pride and as a sense of accomplishment. This change is critical because it moves the teachers beyond the attraction of a new product to a serious examination of the *real* reason for change and the more important issues of teaching and learning.

Recognizing the need for change, teachers who want to implement new initiatives need to master new knowledge, to learn something new in place of something old. The stories in this chapter indicate that these teachers' professional knowledge base had been challenged; they had to learn different processes and develop new competencies. Therefore, another responsibility of preservice training, workshops, and in-service activities is to carefully structure sufficient knowledge with "practical and teacher-ori-

Recognizing the need for change, teachers who want to implement new initiatives need to master new knowledge, to learn something new in place of something old.

ented experiences" (Butler, 1996, p. 20) so that teachers can begin to feel comfortable. Development programs that fail to provide specific and practical ideas that deal directly with the pragmatic actions of the instructional innovation are unlikely to succeed.

Even as teachers begin to believe in the innovation and attempt to exercise some form of personal discretion, initiative, and creativity, they still need to address some practical issues. A lack of structured administrative support, professional guidance, facilities, resources, and time (Doutis & Ward, 1999; Tan & Tan, 2001) tends to distract teachers from their goals. Although Benjamin and Danny managed to overcome equipment and space constraints in their schools, other teachers may not be willing or able to do likewise. Katherin and Debra yearned for structured time during which colleagues could get together for discussion, planning, and sharing. Hargreaves (1994) stated that "scarcity of time makes it difficult to plan more thoroughly, to commit oneself to the effort of innovation, to get together with colleagues, or to sit back and reflect on one's purposes and progress" (p. 15). Schools, therefore, need to create the appropriate conditions and provide support that will help strengthen and encourage teachers in their capacity and desires for change.

Both Debra's and Katherin's collegial experiences seem to indicate that when teachers collaborate in implementing new initiatives, the risk of failure decreases and their confidence for experimentation increases. The new initiative opens up new opportunities for teachers to communicate. Specifically, the collegial support and sharing of expertise, as well as of frustrations, help sustain teachers' sense of efficacy, resulting in a committed professional obligation to continuous improvement (Hargreaves, 1994). For schools to be successful in mandating change, they need to identify and support a core of teacher volunteers, first within individual schools and then across school districts. Through smaller, more intimate professional development workshops and activities, the needs, concerns, and expectations of these teachers can be served and addressed. Bennett (1996) argued that "sending individuals on courses to bring back the good news is much less successful a strategy than sending out a small group together or incrementally in order to create a critical mass of committed individuals and provide a support group for each other" (p. 46).

Conclusion

The teachers in this chapter are committed to doing their best for the children in their care. I hope their stories of change will provide an insightful understanding of what living through change efforts means for some teachers, as these teachers themselves begin to understand their own desires for and actions of change in the process of implementing TGfU in a new physical education curriculum.

Discussion Questions

1. What are your views about the purpose of physical education and how games teaching should be approached in schools? What implications do these have for your decision to adopt and implement the TGfU approach?

2. If you were to implement the TGfU approach in your present school, what possible constraints and challenges would you have to confront? What adaptations would be necessary for you to implement the approach successfully? Suppose you had total freedom and flexibility in implementation. Can you think of any disadvantages?

3. Measuring and assessing student game performance (e.g., decision making and tactical play) resulting from a TGfU approach is more difficult than simply observing changes in students' specific skills. How can a teacher evaluate how much students have learned to demonstrate the outcomes of learning through the TGfU approach?

4. As an approach to teaching games, how does the TGfU approach make the best use of time and resources to help children understand and play games effectively?

5. Describe any feelings of anxiety or excitement you have about the TGfU approach you plan to adopt and implement in your school. What can you do to overcome any feelings of anxiety? How can you channel your excitement toward overcoming the challenges of implementation?

Endnotes

1. The Ministry of Education has adopted the terminology *Games Concept Approach* to teaching games. This approach is akin to the Tactical Games approach presented by Griffin, Mitchell, and Oslin (1997) in the United States. The theoretical basis to this approach is similar to that of the Teaching Games for Understanding (TGfU) approach

in the United Kingdom (Thorpe, Bunker, & Almond, 1986). However, to be consistent with international recognition, the term *Teaching Games for Understanding* was used in this chapter rather than *Games Concept Approach.*

2. Government schools in Singapore are equivalent to public schools in the United States. Government-aided schools are schools historically established mainly by different religious orders and Chinese clans and organizations. Both types of schools receive funding from the government and follow a national curriculum and national examinations.

3. The Singapore education system includes six years of primary (the U.S. equivalent of grades 1 through 6), four years of secondary (grades 7 through 10), and two years of postsecondary (grades 11 through 12) education.

4. Listed under the territorial games category for primary schools are minibasketball, minihockey, netball, Singa rugby, and soccer.

References

Bennett, H. (1996). The need to cope with change. In V. McClelland & V. Varma (Eds.), *The needs of teachers* (pp. 43-66). London: Cassell.

Butler, J. (1996). Teacher responses to teaching games for understanding. *Journal of Physical Education, Recreation and Dance, 67* (9), 17-20.

Curtner-Smith, M.D. (1999). The more things change the more they stay the same: Factors influencing teachers' interpretations and delivery of national curriculum physical education. *Sport, Education, and Society, 4,* 75-97.

Doutis, P., & Ward, P. (1999). Teachers' and administrators' perceptions of the Saber-tooth project reform and of their changing workplace conditions. In P. Ward (Ed.), The Saber-Tooth Project: Curriculum and workplace reform in middle school physical education [Monograph]. *Journal of Teaching in Physical Education, 18,* 417-427.

Faucette, N., & Graham, G. (1986). The impact of principals on teachers during inservice education: A qualitative study. *Journal of Teaching in Physical Education, 5,* 79-90.

Fullan, M. (1991). *The new meaning of educational change* (2nd ed.). New York: Teachers College Press.

Fullan, M. (1993). Why teachers must become change agents. *Educational Leadership, 50* (6), 12-17.

Fullan, M., & Hargreaves, A. (1996). *What's worth fighting for in your school* (2nd ed.). New York: Teachers College Press.

Griffin, L.L., Mitchell, S.A., & Oslin, J.L. (1997). *Teaching sport concepts and skills: A tactical games approach.* Champaign, IL: Human Kinetics.

Hargreaves, A. (1994). *Changing teachers, changing times: Teachers' work and culture in the postmodern age.* New York: Teachers College Press.

Kirk, D. (1988). Ideology and school-centered innovation: A case study and a critique. *Journal of Curriculum Studies, 20,* 449-464.

Levin, B. (1998). An epidemic of education policy: (What) can we learn from each other? *Comparative Education, 34,* 131-141.

McKenzie, T.L., Sallis, J.F., Faucette, N., Roby, J.J., & Kolody, B. (1993). Effects of a curriculum and inservice program on the quantity and quality of elementary physical education class. *Research Quarterly for Exercise and Sport, 64,* 178-187.

McLaughlin, M.W. (1998). Listening and learning from the field: Tales of policy implementation and situated practice. In A. Hargreaves, A. Lieberman, M. Fullan, & D. Hopkins (Eds.), *International handbook of educational change* (pp. 70-84). London: Kluwer Academic.

McNeill, M.C., Fry, J.M., Wright, S.C., Tan, W.K.C., Tan, K.S.S., & Schempp, P.G. (2004). 'In the local context': Singaporean challenges to teaching games on practicum. *Sport, Education and Society, 9* (1), 3-32.

Morris, P. (1995). *The Hong Kong school curriculum: Development, issues and policies.* Hong Kong: Hong Kong University Press.

Rovegno, I., & Bandhauer, D. (1997). Norms of the school culture that facilitated teacher adoption and learning of a constructivist approach to physical education. *Journal of Teaching in Physical Education, 16,* 401-425.

Schwarz, G., & Alberts, J. (Eds.). (1998). *Teacher lore and professional development for school reform.* Westport, CT: Bergin & Garvey.

Singapore Ministry of Education. (1998). *Curriculum Review Report.* Singapore: Author.

Singapore Ministry of Education, Curriculum Planning and Development Division (CPDD). (1999). *Revised physical education syllabus for primary, secondary, and pre-university levels.* Singapore: Author.

Sparkes, A.C. (1991a). Curriculum change: On gaining a sense of perspective. In N. Armstrong & A. Sparkes (Eds.), *Issues in physical education* (pp. 1-19). London: Cassell.

Sparkes, A.C. (1991b). Exploring the subjective dimension of curriculum change. In N. Armstrong & A. Sparkes (Eds.), *Issues in physical education* (pp. 20-35). London: Cassell.

Tan, S.K.S., & Tan, H.E.K. (2001). Managing change within the physical education curriculum: Issues, opportunities and challenges. In J. Tan, S. Gopinathan, & W.K. Ho (Eds.), *Challenges facing the Singapore education system today* (pp. 50-70). Singapore: Prentice Hall.

Tan, S., & Wong, L.H. (2001, August). The games concept approach: Reflections on an innovation. *Physical Education Newsletter, 12,* 2-3.

Tan, S., Wright, S., McNeill, M., Fry, J., & Tan, C. (2002). Implementation of the games concept approach in Singapore schools: A preliminary report. *Review of Educational Research and Advances for Classroom Teachers,* Singapore, *21* (1), 77-84.

Thorpe, R., Bunker, D., & Almond, L. (Eds.) (1986). *Rethinking games teaching.* Department of Physical Education and Sports Science. Loughborough, England: University of Technology.

Ward, P., & Doutis, P. (1999). Towards a consolidation of the knowledge base for reform in physical education. In P. Ward (Ed.), The Saber-Tooth Project: Curriculum and workplace reform in middle school physical education [Monograph]. *Journal of Teaching in Physical Education, 18,* 382-402.

Wright, S., Tan, S., McNeill, M., Fry, J., & Tan, C. (2001, December). *An investigation of a curricular innovation in physical education.* Paper presented at the Australian Association for Research in Education International Education Research Conference, Fremantle, Australia.

8

The Role of Assessment in Teaching Games for Understanding

Judith L. Oslin

The role of assessment in TGfU is that it ensures that students develop the skillfulness, competence, and confidence needed to play games.

As a teacher and teacher educator, I have been constantly challenged to find resources for designing games, practice drills, and assessments that are aligned with the Teaching Games for Understanding (TGfU) approach. Most texts are aligned with a more technical or skill-based approach and focus primarily on skill development, often separate from the game context. The purpose of this chapter is to describe components or aspects of games that ought to be considered when selecting and designing student assessments. The intent here is not to describe how to assess, because resources are available to do this, but rather to discuss what ought to be assessed and why. The chapter will begin with a discussion about the importance of assessment and some issues related to traditional methods of assessing skills.

I would like to begin by stating that I believe games are worth teaching and learning. I have experienced the excitement of many students who, for perhaps the very first time in their lives, are competently and confidently participating in a game. I believe in the value of games as vehicles for promoting healthy, active lifestyles and social change. However, this can only come about if we are intentional about how we teach games and if we consider what we want students to understand about games and game play.

Importance of Assessment

I recently had the privilege of discussing assessment with one of my colleagues, who is considered by many to be an expert on assessment, Dr. Deborah Tannehill. (She was one of the authors of the Standards for Physical Education used in the United States, and coordinator of the National Association of Sport and Physical Education Assessment Series). She stated, "If it's worth teaching and learning, it's worth assessing." If we choose to teach via TGfU, our methods of assessment must be aligned with what we teach and how we teach it. According to Dr. Tannehill, teachers should

> Tell students what they are going to learn and why it is important. Teach them what you told them they would learn, and assess them on what you taught them and what they've been practicing, and that [helps students] make the whole connection. (personal communication, July 26, 2001)

If we want students to learn how to play games, we must assess game performance. Unfortunately, most of what we know about assessment comes in the form of skill tests, which tend to measure only one component of game play—skill execution. In addition, we often use product measures from skill tests to measure or to infer the degree to which students can play the game. Hence, the recurring question from students when performing skill drills and skill tests: Why are we doing this? If students are asking this question, they obviously have not made the connection between what they are doing and what the teacher wants them to learn or do (i.e., play a game).

"If it's worth teaching and learning, it's worth assessing."

"If we want students to learn how to play games, we must assess game performance."

Problems With Assessment

Much of the difficulty in converting our teaching and assessing from a technical or skill-based approach to a TGfU approach, I believe, lies in many of the faulty assumptions we have made about skill and skill development. As most K-12 curricula suggest, we have assumed that we can teach—and children can learn—the 150 or more sport skills needed to play, on average, 30 to 40 different games, in classes that are scheduled once per week for 30 minutes, with 25 to 30 children per class. Even if you are lucky enough to teach physical education daily for 45 minutes, this is a daunting and impossible task, especially when considering how long it takes to develop skills and the depth and breadth of experiences needed to do so.

Another problem in converting teachers' practice relates to the form of the game we expect students to learn. Is it necessary to teach or learn 5v5 basketball, 6v6 volleyball, 11v11 soccer, and so on? If we consider recreation leagues, both public and private, we see 3v3 basketball, 2v2 volleyball, 5v5 indoor softball, and 7v7 indoor soccer to accommodate smaller numbers of players as well as to adjust to the available facilities. Many of our current practices have evolved from the notion that physical education is a "feeder" or training camp for school athletic teams. However, if our goal in physical education is to develop lifelong participants, we should reconsider the types of games and activities we believe are best for our students to learn as well as the constraints of our K-12 curricula.

Many physical educators also adhere to the assumption that you cannot play the game until you learn the skills. As a recreational participant in an unofficial golf league and softball "D-league," I can assure you that we do not always have the skills, but we play the game nonetheless. This assumption implies not only that an optimum level of skill is necessary to play a game, but also that the development of skill can and should occur outside of "the game."

I believe it is faulty to assume that students can learn "the skill" outside of game play and that skills performed in drills somehow transfer to the game. We are constrained here, and I mean no offense, by our motor development mentality. We have an image of what "the skill" should look like at the various stages of development, but we fail to consider that "form follows function."[1] That is, the form the skill takes is dependent on the goal, or function, of the task.

> **I** believe it is faulty to assume that students can learn "the skill" outside of game play and that skills performed in drills somehow transfer to the game.

Developing Skillfulness

When a player or student uses a skill in a game, she modifies the skill to accommodate the particular game situation. Allison, Pissanos, and Turner (2000) referred to this as skillfulness. The form of the movement shifts as the game shifts, as the opponent changes, and as conditions change. This does not mean we should let children play the elite form of the game, but rather we should design games children can play. By doing so, we allow them to develop skillfulness and confidence in their ability

TGfU situates skill within the context of the game, where it is shaped and reshaped depending on a number of factors related to the game or task, the learner, and the context.

to be successful games players. This is the basic premise of TGfU (Bunker & Thorpe, 1982). TGfU situates skill within the context of the game, where it is shaped and reshaped depending on a number of factors related to the game or task, the learner, and the context.

Because the game is the focal point of TGfU, it is important to look at the game, the nature of games, or both, to better understand not only how to teach games but how to assess them. First, let us consider how a forearm pass in volleyball is generally taught. After the teacher reviews the important elements of the skill, students typically perform one or two practice tasks, such as a forearm pass to self. To successfully perform this task, the student must position his body in an upright posture and contact the ball at about shoulder or eye level. During a forearm pass in a game, the body position is low, bent at the waist; contact is below the waist and ahead of the knees, and requires very little if any arm movement. This is a very different movement than the one required in the forearm pass to self, meaning that a pass to self is not likely to transfer to game play as effectively as a forearm pass to a partner in a gamelike context. To develop skillfulness in students, teachers should select or design tasks, games, and assessments that require the same form of the movement needed to be successful in game play. Skillfulness goes beyond the execution of a particular skill within the game; it includes other components that relate to game play, such as support, movement off the ball, defensive actions, and decision making.

To develop skillfulness in students, teachers should select or design tasks, games, and assessments that require the same form of the movement needed to be successful in game play.

Considering Contextual Elements

Outside of the performance elements of game play, the teacher should also consider contextual elements because these can make assessing game performance difficult. First, games are socially constructed. Men have constructed most of the games that hold prominence in our society, and as others (particularly women and children) play them, they modify rules and equipment to accommodate their own characteristics and interests. Games are constructed and reconstructed all the time. Consider baseball, for example, as it is played in a league versus at a family picnic or neighborhood pickup game. Or, consider just one kid pitching a ball to a wall in a schoolyard, with game events and highlights running through his head as he pitches a nine-inning game. The point here is that physical educators need to better understand the impact that the social context has on game play if they want to design and assess games that are meaningful for all students.

Games are competitive by design, intended to test one's physical abilities against another's. Of course, this also involves a contest of cognitive abilities, such as tactical maneuvering, which is as important as physical ability or prowess. Tactics and strategy are important elements of games; they dictate how and when we use skill and what skills we use in the game. Tactical awareness can give one player an advantage over another, even another considered more skilled. Physical educators ought to consider the nature of competition and competitors, the place of competition within physical education, and the capacity of competitive environments to motivate some to play and to deter others from playing altogether.

> *Tactics and strategy are important elements of games; they dictate how and when we use skill and what skills we use in the game.*

Games are interactive. Interactions occur among teammates, opponents, officials, and even sometimes spectators. These interactions have implications for both skill and game performance. Consider, for example, a game between the first- and second-place team, with heightened anxiety and motivation to win, as well as with the spirited banter and hype that often accompanies such games. The interactions among players in this situation will likely be much more intense than that in a game between the first- and last-place teams.

Games are governed by rules. Rules not only regulate game play, but also dictate or define the skills needed to play the game. We often consider only the regulatory function of rules, but rules do much more. According to Torres (2000), "Rules . . . specify what has to be achieved as well as the spatio-temporal limitations under which the goal has to be pursued, the required equipment, and the evaluation system that converts achievements to a score" (p. 82). For example, specific rules define how to move the ball between players and how to shoot on goal. Thus, the rules of the game not only regulate play, court dimensions, ball size, and so on, but also dictate the skills needed to play the game. These aspects of games, and others, influence the game and the form the skills take within game contexts.

Same Class, Different Games

In physical education classes, the same game is commonly interpreted differently by different groups of children. For example, during a recent visit to a middle school, I observed a lesson in which the children were instructed to play a half-court game of basketball. The players in one game restarted play from half-court, enforced violations, and frequently shot off the pass. In a game on the adjacent court, players chose to restart play from the baseline, did not call fouls or violations, and frequently shot off the dribble. As a teacher observing these games, I would ask myself whether the rule changes constrained or accommodated the goal or objective of the lesson, and then, if necessary, I would change or add conditions to help students achieve the lesson objective. In the example of the students who chose to shoot off the dribble, I could take away the dribble because its use discouraged movement off the ball.

In the basketball example, the game and lesson modifications imposed by the students, whether intentional or unintentional, compromised the lesson objectives. This emphasizes the need to hold students accountable for performing tasks as directed. As teachers, we need to be as intentional about monitoring tasks (Hastie, 2000; Schuldheisz & van der Mars, 2001) as we are about designing games. Experts on effective teaching (e.g., Graham, Holt-Hale, & Parker, 2001; Siedentop & Tannehill, 2000) have recommended a number of strategies for holding students accountable for completing tasks as directed by the teacher. For example, as the game is being played or as an assessment task is being performed, students should be closely monitored to ensure that they are working to achieve the goal of the assigned task.

Question-and-answer segments can also be used to assess what students understand about a task, but the questions must be aligned with the goal of the task or game if they are to be effective (Mitchell, Oslin, & Griffin, 2003). Questions should focus on what is happening, what should happen in a particular situation, or why students are doing what they are doing. These focused questions help the teacher determine the degree to which students are appropriately engaged, are able to achieve lesson objectives, and view tasks and assessments as relevant. Teachers should also "check for understanding" (Graham, 2000) following an instructional segment to determine whether students understand the practice, game, or assessment task. In addition, at the end of the lesson, closure provides the

> *Questions should focus on what is happening, what should happen in a particular situation, or why students are doing what they are doing.*

teacher and students the opportunity to review task and lesson objectives (Siedentop & Tannehill, 2000).

Formal Methods of Assessment

Besides informal methods, there are formal methods of assessing both individual and team performance. For example, the Game Performance Assessment Instrument (GPAI; Oslin, Mitchell, & Griffin, 1998; Mitchell & Oslin, 1999) and the Team Sport Assessment Procedure (TSAP; Gréhaigne, Godbout, & Bouthier, 1997, 2000) allow for formal assessment of various components of game play. Both instruments have been shown to provide valid and reliable measures of game performance.

The GPAI contains seven basic components (see table 8.1) that apply across all categories of game play (i.e., invasion, net/wall, striking/fielding, and target). For example, the first five components apply to softball, with *base* referring to the starting position of each player before the ball is pitched, and *adjust* being a shift in that base position, such as when the outfield shifts for a left-handed batter. The last five components relate more specifically to invasion games. Each component can be assessed independently or in combination with other components. For example, decision making (i.e., the choice to shoot, pass, or dribble) can be assessed while also assessing skill execution (i.e., shooting form or outcome). The scores of each component (e.g., total frequency of appropriate decisions, appropriate support moves, or efficient skill execution) can

Table 8.1   GPAI Components of Game Play

Components	Definitions
Base	Appropriate return of performer to a "home" or "recovery" position between skill attempts
Adjust	Movement of performer, either offensively or defensively, as required by the flow of the game
Decisions made	Making appropriate choices about what to do with the ball (or object) during the game
Skill execution	Efficient performance of selected skills
Support	Off-the-ball movement to a position to receive a pass (or throw)
Cover	Defensive support for player making a play on the ball, or moving to the ball (or object)
Guard/mark	Defending an opponent who may or may not have the ball (or object)

Table 8.2   Formulas for Calculating GPAI Outcome Variables

Outcome variables	Calculation
Game involvement	(Total appropriate responses) + (number of efficient skill executions) + (number of inefficient skill executions) + (number of inappropriate decisions made)
Decisions made index (DMI)	(Number of appropriate decisions made) / (number of inappropriate decisions made)
Skill execution index (SEI)	(Number of efficient skill executions) / (number of inefficient skill executions)
Support index (SI)	(Number of appropriate supporting movements) / (number of inappropriate supporting movements)
Game performance	(DMI + SEI + SI) / 3

Measuring a variety of game performance components, beyond skill performance, provides an objective measure of participation, rewarding students who engage in game play both on and off the ball.

also be used to calculate particular game performance indicators, such as a game involvement score, decisions made index, skill execution index, support index, and an overall game performance score (see table 8.2).

The TSAP focuses on two fundamental aspects of game play: (1) gaining possession of the ball (conquering [tackling/intercepting] the ball, receiving a pass from a teammate in the course of play) and (2) disposing of the ball once the player has possession (passing the ball off, playing an offensive ball [an assist, for example], or taking a shot on goal). The TSAP combines volume of play and the efficiency index to compute team performance (see tables 8.3 and 8.4)—or what the authors (Gréhaigne, Godbout, & Bouthier, 1997) referred to as "rapport of strength."

Measuring a variety of game performance components, beyond skill performance, provides an objective measure of participation, rewarding students who engage in game play both on and off the ball. Students who have not had many opportunities to develop skill can be rewarded for moving into position to receive a pass (support play), making good decisions (when to pass, when to shoot), or appropriately marking a player to keep her from scoring or gaining possession of the ball.

Besides the GPAI and TSAP, other measures can be useful for assessing player and team performance during game play. Player and team statistics are frequently used in elite and professional sport as a way of describing

Table 8.3 TSAP Components of Game Play

Components	Definitions
Gaining possession of the ball	
-Conquering the ball (CB)	Intercepting, stealing the ball from the opponent, or recapturing the ball after an unsuccessful shot on goal or near-loss to the other team
-Receiving the ball (RB)	Receiving the ball from a partner and not immediately losing control of it
Disposing of the ball	
-Playing a neutral ball (NB)	Passing the ball to a partner, or any pass that does not put the other team in jeopardy
-Losing the ball (LB)	Losing the ball to the other team without having scored a goal
-Playing an offensive ball (OB)	Passing the ball to a partner, thus pressuring the other team, which most often leads to a shot on goal
-Executing a successful shot (SS)	Scoring or maintaining possession of the ball following the execution of a shot

Modified from Grehaigne, Godbout, & Bouthier, 1997.

Table 8.4 Formulas for Calculating TSAP Outcome Variables

Outcome variables	Calculation
Number of attack balls (AB)	(Total number of OB) + (total number of SS)
Volume of play (PB)	(Total number of CB) + (total number of RB)
Efficiency index (EI)	$(CB + AB) / (10 + LB)$ or $(CB + OB + SS) / (10 + LB)$
Performance score (PS)	Determined via a "nomogram," which uses the EI scale, VP scale, and PS scale (see Grehaigne, Godbout, & Bouthier, 1997)

OB = Playing an offensive ball, SS = Executing a successful shot, CB = Conquering the ball, RB = Receiving the ball, LB = Losing the ball, VP = Volume of play

the success of a player or team, such as batting averages, fielding percentages and assists. Various combinations of measures can be used to assign student grades. For example, some or all of the components of the GPAI or TSAP, a variety of player and team stats, short one-minute quizzes (Griffin & Oslin, 1990), and perhaps a formal examination can be useful for assessing students and subsequently assigning grades. A combination of peer, self-, and teacher assessments are useful for determining individual and team performance as well as assigning student grades.

Conclusion

Formal measures, combined with informal measures, allow for ongoing assessment and can help the teacher provide a clear message that the intent of physical education is to improve performance. Physical educators are "architects" of task design. They must create conditioned games and assessments that drive the skills and competencies they know students should learn to be successful games players. The role of assessment in TGfU is that it ensures that students develop the skillfulness and the competence and confidence needed to play games—games that are worth learning and worth playing long after students leave physical education programs.

Discussion Questions

1. How have we come to believe that we can't play the game until we have the skill? What are the implications of this belief on games teaching in physical education?
2. What components of game play, besides skills, could be considered when assessing game performance? What would be the value of using multiple performance measures for the purposes of assigning student grades?
3. How does teaching for skillfulness differ from teaching for skill development?
4. How might a game involvement score serve as a measure of student participation?

Endnote

1. Louis H. Sullivan served as mentor to Frank Lloyd Wright and was credited for coining the phrase "form ever follows function" (Sullivan & Wright, 1956).

Acknowledgments

This was modified from a keynote presentation at the Teaching Games for Understanding Conference, Waterville Valley, New Hampshire, August 2001. It is a privilege to have this opportunity to share some of my perspectives on assessing game performance, and I would like to thank Joy

Butler and Linda Griffin for this opportunity. The conference provided us TGfU enthusiasts an occasion to confer and share our passion for teaching children to enjoy and play games.

References

Allison, P.C., Pissanos, B.W., & Turner, A.P. (2000). Preservice physical educators' epistemologies of skillfulness. *Journal of Teaching in Physical Education, 19,* 141-161.

Bunker, D., & Thorpe, R. (1982). A model for the teaching of games in secondary schools. *Bulletin of Physical Education, 18,* 5-8.

Graham, G. (2000). *Teaching children physical education: Becoming a master teacher* (2nd ed.). Champaign, IL: Human Kinetics.

Graham, G., Holt-Hale, S., & Parker, M. (2001). *Children moving: A reflective approach to teaching physical education* (5th ed.). Mountain View, CA: Mayfield.

Gréhaigne, J.-F., Godbout, P., & Bouthier, D. (1997). Performance assessment in team sports. *Journal of Teaching in Physical Education, 16,* 500-516.

Gréhaigne, J.-F., Godbout, P., & Bouthier, D. (2000). Students' precision and interobserver reliability of performance assessment in team sports. *Research Quarterly for Exercise & Sport, 71,* 85-91.

Griffin L.L., & Oslin, J.L. (1990). Take a minute: Knowledge testing in physical education. *Strategies: A Journal for Physical Education and Sport Educators, 4,* 7, 23.

Hastie, P.A. (2000). An ecological analysis of a Sport Education season. *Journal of Teaching in Physical Education, 19,* 355-373.

Mitchell, S.A., Oslin, J.L., & Griffin, L.L. (2003). *Teaching sport concepts and skills in elementary physical education.* Champaign, IL: Human Kinetics.

Mitchell, S.A., & Oslin, J.L. (1999). *Authentic assessment in games teaching: The Game Performance Assessment Instrument (NASPE Assessment Series).* Reston, VA: NASPE.

Oslin, J.L., Mitchell, S.A., & Griffin, L.L. (1998). The Game Performance Assessment Instrument (GPAI): Development and preliminary validation. *Journal of Teaching in Physical Education, 2,* 231-243.

Schuldheisz, J.M., & van der Mars, H. (2001). Active supervision and students' physical activity in middle school physical education. *Journal of Teaching in Physical Education, 21,* 75-90.

Siedentop, D., & Tannehill, D. (2000). *Developing teaching skills in physical education* (4th ed.) Mountain View, CA: Mayfield.

Torres, C.R. (2000). What counts as part of a game? A look at skills. *Journal of the Philosophy of Sport, XXVIII,* 81-92.

Sullivan, L.H., & Wright, R.M. (1956). *Autobiography of an idea* (rev. ed.). New York: Dover.

9

Integrating
Tactical Games and
Sport Education Models

Connie S. Collier

Teamwork divides the task and doubles the success.

Anonymous

The purpose of this chapter is to describe and analyze the processes and questions surrounding the integration of the Tactical Games model (TGM; Griffin, Mitchell, & Oslin, 1997; Mitchell, Oslin, & Griffin, 2003) and the Sport Education model (SEM; Siedentop, 1994). Integrating curriculum approaches that have complementary features affords teachers an opportunity to enhance the learning outcomes for students. As you read this chapter, think of SEM and TGM as teammates on a curriculum team. If the task of integration is thoughtful and purposeful, the likelihood of doubling the success of our physical education students is probable. In this chapter I will describe the following:

- Methods for determining the compatibility of SEM and TGM
- Key similarities and differences between SEM and TGM
- Benefits and challenges associated with the integration of SEM and TGM
- Considerations of how to integrate SEM and TGM using a volleyball season

Determining Compatibility

The first step in determining compatibility involves assessing the viability of players as teammates. This process begins by examining each player's background, a type of teammate chemistry analysis if you will. The primary goals of SEM, according to Siedentop (1994), include becoming (1) a competent sportsperson who has sufficient skills to participate in games, is knowledgeable and understands the game, and can execute strategies appropriate to game complexities; (2) a literate sportsperson who values the rules, rituals, and traditions of sports and can distinguish between good and bad sporting practice; and (3) an enthusiastic sportsperson who participates in ways that preserve and capture the essence of the sporting culture. Mitchell, Oslin, and Griffin (2003) maintained that TGM teaching leads to improved knowledge of games and better game performance. They suggested that this model promotes high degrees of student engagement because students (1) spend plenty of time in game play, (2) see the value of skill practice before engaging in it, and (3) discover tactical similarities between different games (Mitchell, Oslin, & Griffin, 2003).

Although both models contribute significantly to the psychomotor domain by focusing on skillful performance, they also possess a strong cognitive component in the form of tactical awareness and skillful decision making. The intent of these models is to better serve all children by providing developmentally appropriate sport and game experiences. Turning children and youth onto game play is fundamental to motivating them to continue to play and be active before, during, and after school. As a result, these models emphasize developing a sufficient level of skillfulness so that students experience the joy and pleasure of games that will perhaps afford them both the motivation and the competence to continue playing for a lifetime.

Role of Play Theory

When you examine the theoretical underpinnings of TGM and SEM, play theory evolves as a common element. Siedentop (2002) established play theory as the foundation for SEM. He promoted a "play education curriculum" in his early writings when he suggested that physically active play is central to a shared culture (Siedentop, 1968). Siedentop (2002) also cited Huizinga's (1955) argument that although play is not serious, it absorbs players "intensely and utterly" (p. 12). Further, Siedentop encouraged us to revisit the role of play as it relates to student engagement. He believes play theory may be key in helping teachers and teacher educators better understand how to use physical education as a bridge for engaging students in lifelong physical activity.

Although Mitchell, Oslin, and Griffin (2003) made inferences about the role of play in their approach to games teaching, earlier writings on games teaching by Mauldon and Redfern (1969) made strong connections to Piaget and rule-governed play. Mauldon and Redfern's primary argument for including games in the school curriculum hinged on the natural appeal of games to children and how this interest quite often leads to competitive play involving rules and point scoring whether against oneself or others. Mauldon and Redfern described the role of games teaching as having potential benefits for the physical aspects of education but also the intellectual, social, and moral aspects. They promoted a version of games teaching that would be an extension of children's experience, which is profitable for all (Mauldon & Redfern, 1969, p. 5). Mauldon and Redfern upheld the sentiment that unless games have educational value for all children, they should be relegated to after-school programs, which complements Siedentop's SEM (1994) endorsement of "sport for all."

Healthy Competition

Another facet of the Sport Education model and Tactical Games models is that the game is a central organizing feature for both models. In a typical SEM season, a competitive schedule of games is made up of scrimmages, regular season games, and tournament play. In the TGM approach, students also participate regularly in games from the initial lesson and do not wait until the final week of a unit to play, as is the case with a traditional, skill-based unit. TGM is known for the game-practice-game lesson format, which accommodates the competition schedule of SEM very easily. An example of how to layer the game-practice-game format in a competitive schedule is provided in table 9.1.

Competitive game play is the foundation on which TGM and SEM are built. Although much criticism surrounds the role of competition in physical education in general and in elementary physical education in particular, SEM and TGM

Competitive game play is the foundation on which TGM and SEM are built. Although much criticism surrounds the role of competition in physical education in general and in elementary physical education in particular, SEM and TGM emphasize ways to celebrate the healthy challenges associated with game play and instruct students about the cooperative behaviors that are essential to fair play.

Table 9.1 Volleyball Season Integrating TGM and SEM

Day	Tactical focus	Roles and rituals	Competition and festivities
1	Winning point (attacking, spike) Skill execution	Team formation Identifying roles Selecting roles	Selecting team name Team pictures Game play
2	Winning point (spike) Off-the-ball movement (transition)	Warm-up (athletic trainer) Equipment setup (equipment manager)	First game: intrasquad scrimmage Final game: 2v2 ladder tournament Coin flip and handshake
3	Setting up attack (pass) Skill execution	Line calls (officials) Team logo design (sport information director)	First game: intrasquad scrimmage Final game: 2v2 ladder tournament Coin flip and handshake
4	Setting up attack (pass) Support play (communication and opening up)	Illegal contacts (officials) First aid procedures (athletic trainer)	First game: intrasquad scrimmage Final game: 2v2 ladder tournament
5	Setting up attack Forearm pass Overhead set Combination	Run first practice (coach) Record scores, switch sides of court (sport information director)	First game: intrasquad scrimmage Final game: 2v2 ladder tournament
6	Attacking as a team Serve reception Base	Overlapping (officials) GPAI on team serve reception (statistician)	3v3 round-robin mixed Team huddles and cheers
7	Winning the point Serving (skill execution)	Design own practice (coach) Service stats (statistician)	3v3 round-robin Mixed-ability teams
8	Defending space Free ball Base and transition	Care of equipment; net and volleyball inspection (equipment manager)	3v3 round-robin Mixed-ability teams
9	Setting up to attack Winning point Pass, set, hit combinations	Conditioning issues (athletic trainer)	3v3 round-robin Mixed-ability teams
10	Defending space Digging (skill execution)	Team building (coaching clinic)	3v3 round-robin Mixed-ability teams

11	Defending space Pursuit and save	Midseason stats (statistician)	3v3 round-robin Mixed-ability teams
12	Defending space (solo blocks)	Identify play of the day (sport information director)	Midseason news release 3v3 round-robin Ability-grouped teams
13	Attacking to win Points, tips, and downballs	Fair play—yellow card definitions (officials)	3v3 round-robin Ability-grouped teams
14	Defending as a team	Cues on skill execution for defense (coaching clinic)	3v3 round-robin Ability-grouped teams
15	Attacking as a team Attack coverage	Pregame nutrition and hydration (athletic trainer)	3v3 round-robin Ability-grouped teams
16	Defending as a team Double blocks Block coverage	Review scorekeeping procedures (officials)	3v3 round-robin Ability-grouped teams
17	Offensive and defensive team practice	Officiating game play Substitution rules (officials)	National anthem Starters announced 6v6 double elimination
18	Offensive and defensive team practice	Brackets and court organization (equipment manager)	6v6 double elimination
19	Offensive and defensive team practice	Design awards for finals (sport information director)	6v6 double elimination
20	Team practice Final day	Prepare team speeches (coach) Prepare final team and individual profiles (statistician)	Tournament finals and awards banquet

emphasize ways to celebrate the healthy challenges associated with game play and instruct students about the cooperative behaviors that are essential to fair play. Both of these curriculum innovations rely heavily on healthy competition. Siedentop (1994) promoted the use of educationally appropriate competition that honors the opponent, emphasizes festivities, and provides a means to educate students about playing hard and playing fair. TGM also has developmentally appropriate competition at its foundation. Mitchell, Oslin, and Griffin, (2003) defined a game as "a competitive situation where there are two approximately equal teams, each of which has an opportunity to score" (p. 8).

Authentic Learning Experiences

Both TGM and SEM use learning experiences or games that represent authentic sport and game experiences. In recent writings, Kirk and MacPhail (2002) and Kirk and MacDonald (1998) contended that both models are representative of situated learning theory. Kirk and MacPhail (2002) made a case for using situated learning theory as a way to enhance the underdeveloped aspects of games teaching by better understanding why and how teachers can design and teach games that are more meaningful for children. Siedentop (2002) recognized that Sport Education may fit well with the situated learning perspective, but did not consider SEM an application of situated learning through sport. Rather, Siedentop explained that SEM provides students with opportunities to learn sport in a meaningful context.

Designing developmentally appropriate games and sport experiences is critical to the success of both TGM and SEM. Both models depend on the teacher's sound understanding of the content, the learner, and the context. The use of small-sided teams in both models lays the foundation for developmentally appropriate play and allows students numerous opportunities to respond during games. When teachers understand the nuances of the sport or game, they are able to design developmentally appropriate games that preserve the integrity and authenticity of the sport. When students are engaged to this extent, they stop asking, When are we going to play the *real* game? This authentic game experience is one feature that sets SEM and TGM apart from what others refer to as "lead-up" games (Pangrazi, 2001). Holt, Strean, and Bengoechea (2002) referred to this concept as "modification representation," whereby the adult game is modified to suit children, but the tactical structure of the game remains intact.

> *When teachers understand the nuances of the sport or game, they are able to design developmentally appropriate games that preserve the integrity and authenticity of the sport. When students are engaged to this extent, they stop asking, When are we going to play the real game? This authentic game experience is one feature that sets SEM and TGM apart from what others refer to as "lead-up" games (Pangrazi, 2001). Holt, Strean, and Bengoechea (2002) referred to this concept as "modification representation," whereby the adult game is modified to suit children, but the tactical structure of the game remains intact.*

The decisions that teachers have to make regarding the design of games and sporting experiences must take into account the developmental appropriateness of the psychomotor aspects of the games as well as the cognitive and moral issues involved. The cognitive components of decision making and tactical awareness required to be a successful games player need careful consideration. Both texts on the tactical approach to games (Griffin, Mitchell, & Oslin, 1997; Mitchell, Oslin, & Griffin, 2003) provide numerous lesson examples that exemplify developmentally appropriate practice. Guidelines for elementary and secondary SEM curricula are available in the text *Sport Education: Quality PE Through Positive Sport Experiences* (Siedentop, 1994). Mohr, Bulger, and Townsend (2001), in a recent publication, also provided a nice example of how to integrate the content of games in a seasonal SEM planning format.

Outlining the similarities between the models sets the stage for discussing why teachers of sport and games may consider integrating the models and what challenges and complexities may be involved in the integration process. I will use a seasonal plan for a volleyball segment of a university-based course. The course is focused on the development and analysis of game performance skills in net and wall games as a means of exemplifying the integration of TGM and SEM.

Team Building

After closer examination, TGM and SEM clearly have enough in common to begin the team-building process. With that said, the merger of these two models takes a good measure of analysis and expertise to create a team, particularly if that team is intent on successfully enhancing student learning. There is no quick fix for changing the face of physical education. However, if we hope to counter the frequent criticisms of physical education as a place where only the good get better and the low skilled are alienated, intentional planning and quality pedagogy are essential ingredients to creating and sustaining quality sport and game experiences. These models provide only the framework for change.

To be successful at integrating TGM and SEM, teachers need to contemplate one fundamental question: Am I willing to think differently about my teaching? In short, both models require a range of teaching styles. The direct, guided discovery, task, and peer teaching approaches inherent in these models are vastly different from the approaches commonly observed in the command style of teaching. Teachers using this integrated model must be willing to think differently about the teaching and learning process.

Table 9.1 presents Tactical Games content and assessment and Sport Education roles, responsibilities, competition schedules, and festivities. This seasonal plan represents the gradual development of student roles and a shift of responsibility for instruction from teacher to student.

Sample roles used in this season include coach, official, equipment manager, athletic trainer, statistician, and sport information director. This plan also shows ways to use teams of six players in a variety of competitive formats and exemplifies the use of rituals and festivities common to volleyball.

Benefits of Integration

In my own experience, combining several components of these two models results in sporting experiences that are richer than what the individual models could provide in isolation. These benefits include (1) creating longer units or seasons organized according to tactical categories; (2) highlighting festivities, which enrich the game playing experience; (3) using the Game Performance Assessment Instrument (GPAI; Mitchell & Oslin, 1999; Oslin, Mitchell, & Griffin, 1998) to educate coaches and teams about game performance; (4) using team affiliations to maintain consistent team membership for games instruction; and (5) structuring team practices around focused tactical problems.

■ *Using tactical categories as organizing features for seasons.* Teaching games across a tactical category helps to preserve the longer unit philosophy of Sport Education. Clearly, deliberate practice is essential to improved skill execution, and the length of the season plays a critical role in accommodating this desired practice (Grant, 1992). Gréhaigne, Godbout, and Bouthier (2001) suggested that decision making and tactical awareness require deliberate practice to develop, and learning when to use a skill in response to a game situation requires considerable time. By organizing seasons according to tactical categories (Almond, 1986), the teacher can build on students' prior knowledge of tactical problems with similar tactical solutions. Mitchell, Oslin, and Griffin (2003) described it as a thematic approach to teaching games and suggested that it is particularly useful at the elementary level for enhancing transfer.

■ *Festivities and sporting rituals.* The festivities, which are characteristic of the celebrations in SEM, make explicit the cultural flavor of games often assumed in TGM. Highlighting certain rituals, such as a coin flip as a means of determining first service or structuring the warm-up for tournament play so that it emulates Olympic volleyball, enriches the student experience. These types of festivities bring out the celebratory nature of sport and provide roles for students to play that represent a more inclusive form of sport that goes beyond the focus of performing on the field or court. Students may choose roles that represent professional life in a sporting culture such as sport information director, sports announcer, or sport commissioner.

- *The Game Performance Assessment Instrument* (GPAI; Mitchell & Oslin, 1999; Oslin, Mitchell, & Griffin, 1998). The GPAI is a well-suited teammate for the record-keeping feature in SEM. The GPAI is an assessment instrument that provides teachers and students with a means for assessing not only skill execution but also students' support and decision-making strategies, elements that traditional psychomotor assessments tend to overlook.

- *Team affiliation.* Use of persisting groups (Siedentop, 2002) is a primary characteristic of SEM. Although TGM uses small-sided team play, SEM emphasizes team affiliation; in other words, team membership remains consistent throughout an entire season. SEM's notion of team affiliation is of tremendous benefit when using TGM. Encouraging competitive game play and thoughtful decision making within game play is extremely difficult without a sense of trust and reliance on teammates, which only evolves from the use of persisting groups (Siedentop, 2002).

- *Strengthening team practices using exaggeration modification.* TGM promotes the use of conditioned games with rules that highlight a tactical problem to be solved. This characteristic of games teaching is called exaggeration modification (Holt, Strean, & Bengoechea, 2002). My many years of experience with SEM suggest that the team practices in a Sport Education season tend to lack intensity and focus, particularly when directed by students. By engaging TGM's use of exaggeration modification, the likelihood that the skills used in practices will be representative of those required in game situations increases, thereby resulting in more productive game play.

Preserving the Integrity of the Individual Models

As any coach will suggest, building a productive team requires substantial work. Despite the similarities of the two models, perfect team chemistry is rarely possible. One of the keys to avoiding a breakdown in teamwork is to determine which features of the respective models cannot be compromised to preserve their individual integrity. Too many times, losing seasons are the result of individuals on teams, or in this case the models, losing their own identity and failing to see their own contribution recognized.

One area that is sometimes compromised when implementing SEM is the process for determining student roles and responsibilities. Teachers sometimes settle for letting students act as uniformed teaching assistants rather than being intentional and explicit about each of the roles assigned.

To maximize the potential of student roles, teachers must ensure that students learn how to officiate just as they would learn the nuances of the skills and game rules. To assume that students know how to officiate the various ranges of sporting experiences is to disregard the integrity of SEM. Other teachers have trouble relinquishing control of any of these duties to students and therefore choose to control the game environment by neglecting the notion of student responsibility. The opposite effect occurs when teachers become overly passive and dump unrealistic responsibilities onto the students without appropriate instruction or preparation, resulting in little more than a roll-out-the-ball curriculum. Teachers who take the time to fully develop tasks that engage students in meaningful learning experiences reap the rewards of challenging students. If teachers are not intentional, this misinterpreted aspect of Sport Education tends to contaminate the intentions of both SEM and TGM.

Another issue deserving careful scrutiny is the use of students as coaches. Teaching students how to coach takes thoughtful tutoring. The one area that tends to break down in using SEM, particularly with younger students, is the team practice. When allowing students to run this practice, the use of questioning by the teacher, as suggested in TGM, can get lost in the efforts to involve the students. Although teachers eventually shift from the role of instructor to facilitator in both models, this shift is much more difficult to achieve than it appears at first glance. Knowing when to relinquish the duties to students, and knowing how ready they are to handle these duties, takes careful contemplation. The role of questions is central to TGM. Teachers who hope to maintain a tactical focus to their practice sessions must find ways to gradually shift the questioning to student coaches. Task cards or posters, as well as coaching homework assignments, can be used as prompts for student coaches.

As an instructor of a college-level activity course, I have integrated TGM and SEM. I have also mentored preservice teachers in their attempts to "merge" these two models during their student teaching experiences. This experience has provided me with a unique perspective of how to merge the models and how to assist beginning teachers as they work in combining the most practical aspects of these two models. Although the seasonal plan in table 9.1 provides ways to extensively integrate the models, my experience with beginning teachers suggests that implementing SEM and TGM separately before considering them as partners on an integrated team may be helpful.

Conclusion

The creation of a successful team requires a coach to first determine whether players will be good teammates. Successful coaches understand the capacities and limitations of each player and are able to maximize the strengths of individuals on their teams. A sport curriculum using both SEM and TGM, as teammates, has great potential to double the success for students in physical education. To create a successful team with SEM and TGM as players, teachers, in addition to analyzing the strengths and weaknesses of the models, must consider their own capacity for teaching differently. The recommendation is to start with a simple process of sharing a lesson format using the game practice suggestion in TGM (Mitchell, Griffin, & Oslin, 1997), which easily allows teachers to accommodate the competitive schedule of SEM (Siedentop, 1994). The other features requiring serious consideration are the use of student roles and maintaining the length of season recommendations in SEM so that students have adequate opportunities to develop into successful sport and games players. The benefits of TGM and SEM as teammates are many as long as teachers thoughtfully consider the integrity of each of the players in the process of integration.

Discussion Questions

1. Formulate three to five essential questions teachers must ask themselves before integrating SEM and TGM.
2. In debating the value of integrating SEM and TGM, what do you consider to be the primary benefits and the most significant challenges?
3. To what degree are the principles of student-centered learning represented in these curriculum models, and what are the inherent challenges associated with these principles?
4. If you were to act as a curriculum consultant, what process would you use with beginning teachers who are interested in integrating SEM and TGM?

Acknowledgments

I would like to respectfully recognize the origin of TGM as an extension of the Teaching Games for Understanding model (TGfU; Bunker & Thorpe, 1982). I have learned a great deal teaching games using TGM (Griffin, Mitchell, & Oslin, 1997) alongside my colleagues, Steve Mitchell and Judy Oslin, as well as attending the Teaching Games for Understanding Conference in Waterville Valley, New Hampshire, in the summer of 2001. Both my teaching experience and the conference have played significant roles in my development as a teacher of games. I would be remiss not to mention the text, *Games Teaching: A New Approach for the Primary School* by Mauldon and Redfern (1969) as also being helpful in my understanding of games education and a good reminder that games teaching isn't new but has resurfaced with renewed enthusiasm.

References

Almond. L. (1986). Reflecting on themes: A games classification. In R. Thorpe, D. Bunker, and L. Almond (Eds.), *Rethinking games teaching* (pp. 71-72). Loughborough, England: University of Technology, Department of Physical Education and Sports Science.

Bunker, D., & Thorpe, R. (1982). A model for the teaching of games in secondary schools. *Bulletin of Physical Education, 18* (1), 5-8.

Grant, B. (1992). Integrating sport education into physical education curriculum in New Zealand secondary schools. *Quest, 44,* 304-316.

Gréhaigne, J.-F., Godbout, P., & Bouthier, D. (2001). The teaching and learning of decision-making in team sports. *Quest, 53,* 59-76.

Griffin, L.L., Mitchell, S.A., & Oslin, J.L. (1997) *Teaching sport concepts and skills: A tactical games approach.* Champaign, IL: Human Kinetics.

Holt, N.L., Strean, W.B., & Bengoechea, E.G. (2002). Expanding the Teaching Games for Understanding model: New avenues for future research and practice. *Journal of Teaching in Physical Education, 21,* 162-176.

Huizinga, J. (1955). *Homo ludens: A study of the play-element in culture.* Boston: Beacon Press.

Kirk, D., & MacDonald, D. (1998). Situated learning in physical education. *Journal of Teaching in Physical Education, 17,* 376-387.

Kirk, D., & MacPhail, A. (2002). Teaching games for understanding and situated learning: Rethinking the Bunker-Thorpe model. *Journal of Teaching in Physical Education, 21* (2), 177-192.

Mauldon, E., & Redfern, H.B. (1969). *Games teaching: A new approach for the primary school.* London: MacDonald & Evans.

Mitchell, S.A., & Oslin, J.L. (1999). *Assessment series K-12 physical education series: Assessment in games teaching.* Reston, VA: National Association of Sport and Physical Education.

Mitchell, S.A., Oslin, J.L., & Griffin, L.L. (2003). *Sport foundations for elementary physical education: A tactical games approach.* Champaign, IL: Human Kinetics.

Mohr, D.J., Bulger, S.M., & Townsend, J.S. (2001). A pedagogical approach to sport education season planning. *Journal of Physical Education, Recreation and Dance, 72* (9), 37-46.

Oslin, J.L., Mitchell, S.A., & Griffin, L.L. (1998). The Game Performance Assessment Instrument (GPAI): Development and preliminary validation. *Journal of Teaching in Physical Education, 2,* 231-243.

Pangrazi, R. (2001). *Dynamic physical education for elementary school children* (13th ed.). Boston: Allyn & Bacon.

Siedentop, D. (1968). A theory for programs of physical education in schools. *Dissertation Abstracts International, 30* (03), 1006A. (University Microfilms No. AAT6913888)

Siedentop, D. (1994). *Sport education: Quality PE through positive sport experiences.* Champaign, IL: Human Kinetics.

Siedentop, D. (2002). Sport education: A retrospective. *Journal of Teaching in Physical Education, 21* (4), 409-418.

chapter 10

Integrating Cooperative Learning and Tactical Games Models: Focusing on Social Interactions and Decision Making

Ben Dyson

When I lived in New Hampshire, I was in a location that was conducive to learning to kayak, and I had friends there to teach me that skill. Without the location (opportunity) and the friends (social interdependence), I would not have kayaked as much and would not have developed kayaking skills. I was positively interdependent on friends to take me kayaking, and without them I would not have gone. In rough water, if you do not paddle your kayak, you will fall out. So by the very nature of the task, I was held accountable for paddling my kayak—that is, if I didn't want to swim in the cold ocean water. With Cooperative Learning, if the task is set up appropriately, the students "sink or swim together."

Sport-related games, as content in physical education, provide countless opportunities for social interactions and decision making. Integrating a Cooperative Learning model with the Tactical Games model provides a structure for foregrounding the cooperative dimension in games teaching and learning. Cooperative learning (CL) and Tactical Games (TG) share several pedagogical principles. First, the learning is student centered. Second, students work in small groups or teams and rely on each other to complete the learning activities. Third, the teacher facilitates learning by shifting the majority of responsibility to the students. Fourth, learning activities are authentic. Finally, learning activities have the potential to include social, physical, and cognitive development. These models also have as an inherent focus the use of modified games to better situate learning within the context of the game and to enable students to experience meaningful play. By integrating CL and TG, the teacher can potentially better highlight social interaction, problem-solving skills (i.e., decision making), and cognitive understanding.

The purpose of this chapter is to do the following:

- Provide an overview of CL as an instructional model
- Review the research on CL in physical education
- Make theoretical connections between CL and TG
- Emphasize the pedagogical integration of the models
- Provide practical examples of the integration of TG and CL (Griffin, Mitchell, & Oslin, 1997; Mitchell, Oslin, & Griffin, 2003)

TG is considered an extension of the original Teaching Games for Understanding model (TGfU) (Bunker & Thorpe, 1982). TG has been elaborated on throughout this text and will not be explained in this chapter.

Overview of Cooperative Learning As an Instructional Model

CL emerged as a response to the early educational reform in cognitive psychology (Deutsch, 1949; Dewey, 1924). Early progressive educators created a foundation of research and literature that led to CL being aligned with social constructivism (Antil, Jenkins, Wayne, & Vadasy, 1998; Cohen & Lotan, 1997; Perkins, 1999). CL is an instructional model that shifts the focus of learning to the student. Each student becomes a meaningful participant in learning. Students work together in structured, small, heterogeneous groups to master the content. The students are responsible not only for learning the material, but also for helping their group-mates learn (Antil et al., 1998; Putnam, 1998).

Students work together in structured, small, heterogeneous groups to master the content.

Five main elements of CL have emerged from research and teaching:

- *Positive interdependence.* Each group member learns to depend on the rest of the group while working together to complete the task.
- *Individual accountability.* Teachers establish and maintain student responsibility for appropriate conduct, task involvement, and outcomes (Siedentop & Tannehill, 2000).

- *Face-to-face interaction.* Group members have head-to-head discussions in close proximity to one another.
- *Interpersonal and small-group skills.* These include listening, shared decision making, taking responsibility, learning to give and receive feedback, and learning to encourage each other.
- *Group processing.* Time is allocated to discuss how well the group members achieved their goals and maintained effective working relationships. Group processing is similar to the processing or debriefing that takes place in adventure education experiences. This form of verbal reflection during or after a lesson serves as an opportunity for students to express themselves and for the teacher to provide specific and relevant feedback to the students, and can act as a form of accountability.

The four major approaches to CL, which were developed and researched by advocates of the model, emphasize the elements of CL to varying degrees (Antil et al., 1998; Cohen, 1994b; Putnam, 1998). The approaches (and their developers) are as follows: conceptual (Johnson, Johnson, & Johnson-Holubec, 1998), structural (Kagan, 1992), curricular (Slavin, 1996), and complex instruction (Cohen, 1994b).

- *Conceptual approach.* The conceptual approach, designed by Johnson and Johnson (1989), is based on the premise that teachers can learn the key elements of structuring effective CL activities. Teachers are taught to plan, implement, and assess CL activities to match their own curriculum needs. Generic or content-free forms of CL are used in a variety of subjects and at different grade levels. Johnson, Johnson, and Johnson-Holubec (1998) suggested that the five elements of CL are necessary for authentic implementation of CL.
- *Structural approach.* Kagan's (1992) structural approach to CL is based on different strategies that Kagan (1990) referred to as structures, such as Think-Share-Perform, Jigsaw, and Learning Teams. To ensure success when using the structural approach, Kagan (1992) highlighted two main elements, positive interdependence and individual accountability. The effective design of a CL lesson requires teachers to use a variety of different structures, each chosen for the cognitive, physical, and social goals it best accomplishes within a given teaching situation or context.
- *Curricular approach.* Slavin's (1990) curricular approach shifts away from the content-free structural approach to grade-level-specific and subject-specific curricula. In Slavin's (1996) highly structured approach, he defined group goals as students working together to earn recognition, grades, rewards and other indicators of group success. Slavin (1996) found that CL can be an effective means of increasing student achievement,

but only if the essential elements of specific group goals and individual accountability are integrated into the CL methodology.

■ *Complex instruction approach.* Cohen's (1994a) complex instruction approach focuses on group work as a strategy for enhancing student social and academic development. Complex instruction is a method of small-group learning that features open-ended discovery or a conceptual task that emphasizes higher order thinking skills. Of the four approaches, Cohen's approach does not specify content or grade-level. This nonspecific approach is the least structured in its adherence to the elements of CL. In this peer-mediated approach, students work in groups using one another as resources to complete the tasks. Group roles such as material manager, harmonizer, and resource person are assigned to students. The teacher's role is to facilitate the group work and emphasize that all skills and abilities are important and relevant for completing the task (positive interdependence). These approaches are described in more detail in Dyson (2001).

Substantial evidence exists to support the idea that students working in small cooperative groups can master material presented by the teacher better than students working on their own (Cohen, 1994b; Johnson & Johnson, 1989; Slavin, 1990, 1996).

A body of research in general education reports the benefits of CL (Cohen, 1994b; Johnson & Johnson, 1989; Kagan, 1990; Slavin, 1990, 1996). Substantial evidence exists to support the idea that students working in small cooperative groups can master material presented by the teacher better than students working on their own (Cohen, 1994b; Johnson & Johnson, 1989; Slavin, 1990, 1996). Other benefits of CL include higher achievement scores and social outcomes such as positive intergroup relations, the ability to work collaboratively with others, and the development of self-esteem (Cohen, 1994b; Johnson & Johnson, 1989; Slavin, 1990, 1996).

Research on Cooperative Learning in Physical Education

Although the evidence in general education to support teachers using CL is strong, research on CL in physical education is limited. Nonetheless, the studies that have been conducted indicate promising results. Grineski (1993) found that CL can enhance physical fitness and social interactions for elementary, kindergarten, and preschool children. Preschool children involved in cooperative games had higher rates of positive physical contact than children involved in free play, especially children with disabilities. In addition, cooperative games enabled players to demonstrate high rates of goal-related cooperative behaviors and lower rates of negative physical contact and negative verbal interactions. The CL structures facilitated successful student participation and positively affected player performance. Smith, Markley, and Goc Karp (1997) used CL with third-grade students in physical education classes. They found that students' social reasoning skills, interactions, and social participation improved after a six-week CL unit. With grade 5 and 6 students using CL, Dyson (2001) reported that both the teacher and the students emphasized improving motor skills, developing social skills, working together as a team, helping others improve their skills, and taking responsibility for their own learning. In the same school district at the high school level, Dyson and Strachan (2000) found that a physical education teacher believed that CL helped her students meet the following goals: developing motor skills, developing game strategies, actively participating, respecting one's peers, accepting responsibility, and improving communication skills. Grade 8 and 11 students stated that CL encouraged participation, was fun, and allowed them to develop motor skills and interpersonal skills.

Barrett (2000) investigated the use of two CL structures, Performer and Coach Earn Rewards (PACER) and Jigsaw II in Physical Education (Jigsaw II-PE), in which the two roles of performer and coach were used in two grade 6 physical education classes. These strategies used three elements of CL: cooperative interaction (positive interdependence), individual accountability, and group contingency. PACER and Jigsaw II-PE resulted in increased correct trials for participants and total trials for Jigsaw II-PE in sport skills units. Low-skilled male and female participants within PACER and Jigsaw II-PE classes also showed improved performances.

In another study, a teacher and her third- and fourth-grade students were followed over a two-year period to understand the process of implementing CL (Dyson, 2002). The teacher used Pairs-Check-Perform and Learning Teams as CL structures (Dyson & Grineski, 2001; Grineski, 1996). In this study the teacher and students held similar perceptions related to goals of the lessons, student roles, accountability, communication skills, working together, and practice time.

This was represented in the categories that emerged from the data: goals of the lessons, student roles, accountability, communication skills, working together, and practice time.

The findings from physical education research support the belief that CL can help students

- improve social reasoning skills,
- develop interpersonal skills,
- improve their active participation,
- develop motor skills and game strategies,
- improve working together as a team,
- assist others improve their skills,
- take responsibility for their own learning, and
- hold each other accountable for completing their tasks.

To introduce CL in physical education, a teacher can begin with students working in pairs and providing feedback to each other. Pairs-Check-Perform is based on Kagan's (1992) structure, Pairs Check. This structure requires individuals to stay on task and help others learn, and is useful when learning locomotor, manipulative, sport, gymnastic, or aquatic skills and strategies. The Pairs Check structure is similar to Mosston's (1981) reciprocal style of teaching, in which students are assigned to work in pairs, with each student given responsibility as either an observer or a performer. Later, students could work in groups of three in which the roles could include coach, encourager, and recorder. Initially, the coach watches for good form compared to appropriate learning cues; the encourager provides feedback to encourage and motivate group-mates (such as "Good follow-through" or "Nice parallel swing"); and the recorder writes the specific skill or tactical information (group-mates' progress) on the task sheet. For example, in a forehand tennis lesson, the coach's role is to watch that the performers are hitting the ball using good form (learning cues are side to net, racket, swing parallel, and follow through).

An example of a four-person activity could be a Jigsaw Perform (Aronson, 1978). In this CL structure each student is responsible for learning and performing a portion of the content, and then teaching that portion to group-mates. The Jigsaw Perform structure can be used in physical education for developing routines, creating stations, teaching dance, and teaching and reviewing motor skills and tactics. To be successful, the whole group needs to make sure that every student completes the tasks. That is, during Jigsaw Perform,

> *The Jigsaw Perform structure can be used in physical education for developing routines, creating stations, teaching dance, and teaching and reviewing motor skills and tactics.*

positive interdependence is strong because each student is dependent on others for information. For example, to create a dance routine, individual students are assigned a component or part of the dance to develop and are responsible for teaching that part to other group members. Students in small groups create a dance routine that matches a musical selection, uses steps outlined by the teacher, and uses specified body parts. Student groups take turns teaching their part of the dance routine to other group members, and then the group puts the dance together to perform it for the class.

Theoretical Connections Between CL and TG

Both CL and TG can be thought of as examples of situated learning. Situated learning theory is conceptualized as one component of a broader constructivist theory of learning in physical education (Kirk & Macdonald, 1998). Constructivist and situated learning perspectives have been promoted in the physical education literature (Chen & Rovegno, 2000; Dodds, Griffin, & Placek, 2001; Ennis, 2000; Kirk & Macdonald, 1998; Rovegno & Bandhauer, 1997; Rovegno & Kirk, 1995). The pedagogical emphasis is a focus on the student as an active, social, and creative learner (Perkins, 1999).

Situated learning theory investigates the relationships among the various physical, social, and cultural dimensions of the context of learning (Lave & Wenger, 1991). Situated learning is a type of social constructivism that provides a more holistic view of learning. The social and cultural situation of the teaching environment contributes significantly to what and how students learn (Kirk & Macdonald 1998). The deliberate organization and structures of CL and TG allow for participation to occur in a student-centered "learning curriculum" as opposed to a teacher-centered "teaching curriculum" (Lave & Wenger, 1991, p. 97). This moves students (learners) into situations in which they can also help their group-mates or teammates learn.

Kirk and MacPhail (2002) offered a connection between TG and situated learning. They suggested that TG can lead teachers to pay attention to the students' perspectives, skills, tactics, and game play. CL has many similarities to TG, with student-centered tasks that require student input and are meaningful, challenging, and authentic to students. The group dynamic in CL allows students to take on roles and responsibilities and provides students with the opportunity to achieve tasks while they are socially interacting.

Pedagogical Integration of the Models

Tactical problems, tactical awareness, and decision making are emphasized in the following example that integrates CL and TG (see figure 10.1). In soccer, maintaining possession of the ball is an important tactical problem for students to master. Using the triangle ball activity as a practice task for supporting the ball carrier can heighten the students' tactical awareness of maintaining possession of the ball. In the triangle ball activity, students are encouraged to make quick decisions as they pass the ball and run to support the ball carrier. Each student has a role: coach, organizer, encourager, and recorder. The students carry out their roles and provide feedback to each other to enhance learning. The recorder writes on the task sheet an assessment of each student based on the learning cues: call name and make eye contact, reach for ball (show a target), get into a supporting position, use a leading pass (to a partner on the move), give appropriate feedback, and receive feedback appropriately.

In addition, the triangle ball task sheet in figure 10.2 can be used to assess student learning. The triangle ball practice task sheet contains learning cues for the students. The teacher should review these learning cues with the students prior to sending them off to perform the task. Students should be encouraged to provide their teammates with specific feedback during the practice task. In the role of facilitator the teacher will actively monitor and interact with the students and encourage them to provide their peers with appropriate feedback to help them improve their skills.

1. Four players in a square, 3v1; three players work on the corners and sides of the square.
2. One of the four players works in the middle area and tries to intercept the ball as the other three pass it around.
3. Players with the ball can only pass and run along the perimeter lines of the square.
4. No diagonal passes.
5. Players in possession of the ball cannot move.

Teaching point:

Players should support the ball carrier on both sides.

X1 o ————> X2   —   Ball movement

                O   -----   Movement of support player

X3   ----------->

Figure 10.1 Triangle ball practice task.

Task

Play triangle ball and support the ball carrier on both sides.

Learning cues

1. Call name and make eye contact.
2. Reach for ball; show a target.
3. Move into a supporting position.
4. Use a leading pass (to a partner on the move).
5. Give appropriate feedback.
6. Receive feedback appropriately.

When you feel you are ready, complete the following form, rating each player's performance with each skill.

Awesome—uses the cues every time

Good—uses the cues most of the time

Needs work—rarely uses the cues

Name	Calls name	Reaches for ball	Uses a leading pass	Gives feedback	Receives feedback

Figure 10.2   Triangle ball task sheet.

Pedagogical Shift

Integrating TG and CL will require a pedagogical shift or change in teachers' mind-sets that will take time and effort. Mitchell, Oslin, and Griffin (2003) emphasized preparing students for TG: "A tactical approach requires that elementary students engage in game play independently in small groups; this requirement is a different way of learning for most elementary students" (p. 15). The TG or CL structure needs to be taught, reinforced, and reviewed for students. Physical educators need to understand the essential conditions needed for TG and CL to lead to positive outcomes. Putnam (1998) cautioned that "simply placing students in groups and asking them to cooperate will not ensure higher achievement or positive interpersonal outcomes" (p. 18). The process will require trial and error, but has many possible benefits for teachers.

Teachers can develop knowledge and experience in integrating these models from attending workshops, reading texts, and practicing TG and CL structures. Starting with familiar content and one or two learning activities can be helpful. Teachers will have to work with students to build interpersonal skills and small-group skills; these should be an integral part of every physical education lesson. Many students need to learn how to communicate more effectively with others. Therefore, lessons may go more smoothly if teachers spend the first several weeks of the school year engaging the students in activities that encourage them to have positive interactions (promotive face-to-face interaction). Students need to know how to give directions, listen to one another, work together, solve problems, and give and receive feedback. Activities that encourage these skills include Project Adventure activities (Rohnke, 1984), team building (Glover & Midura, 1992), and cooperative activities (Grineski, 1996). Because teachers may have many of these activities in their teaching arsenals already, they should start with what works for them.

> *Integrating TG and CL will require a pedagogical shift or change in teachers' mind-sets that will take time and effort.*

Teacher As Facilitator

Integrating TG and CL will require the teacher to guide the instruction and curriculum as a facilitator of learning who is not at the center of instruction. As the facilitator, the teacher sets problems or goals, and students are given an opportunity to seek solutions to these problems. For both CL and TG, being a facilitator is a complicated role. Quality facilitation is a learned skill that takes extended periods of time to develop, plan, and employ. Many teachers have difficulty releasing control to their students in a task or game. In TG, teachers need to learn how to guide their students through their questions and problems to help them determine their own solutions. The CL instructional model emphasizes working as a team and relying on each other to achieve the task. An integrated approach can assist the team to come up with the best possible solutions. For the teacher to act as a facilitator, the students need to be taught to organize equipment and be responsible for it, cooperate in their teams, coordinate teams or officiate games, give and

> *Quality facilitation is a learned skill that takes extended periods of time to develop, plan, and employ.*

receive feedback to their peers, coach, tutor, solve problems, and help their teammates learn.

Being Faithful to the Models

Metzler (2000) reminded us to be sure to preserve the fidelity of an instructional model when implementing it for the first time. Therefore, in an integrated CL and TG unit, teaching occurs in a deliberate manner to emphasize both social interaction and psychomotor (skill and tactical) outcomes. Teachers need to be aware of the salient features of each model to ensure the preservation of both. For example, in CL this can be accomplished by focusing on the five elements: positive interdependence, individual accountability, face-to-face interaction, interpersonal and small-group skills, and group processing. A common error that teachers make when trying to implement CL is failing to require positive interdependence in student tasks. If the students do not rely on each other to complete the task, then they are not positively interdependent. Similarly, using TG, teachers should focus on tactical problems, tactical awareness, and decision making. More specifically, questioning is a critical teaching skill in TG that enables the teacher to guide students to identify solutions to the tactical problems presented in games. Teachers need to know when to use questions and when to provide answers. They should preplan their questions and reflect on their efficacy after each lesson.

> *If the students do not rely on each other to complete the task, then they are not positively interdependent.*

Benefits of Integration

Because the integration of CL and TG is a complex and labor-intensive enterprise, a teacher may not be comfortable and effective teaching these instructional models for two or more years. There are, however, several benefits to the integration of CL and TG models: (1) The Game Performance Assessment Instrument (GPAI) (Mitchell & Oslin, 1999) complements the CL task sheet assessments by providing assessment of tactics during the game. The tactical emphasis of the GPAI draws attention to a focus on tactics in CL, not just skill development (see figure 10.3). (2) Both CL and TG have a focus on cognitive understanding, but the TG model emphasizes tactics in the game, in questions, and in assessments. This focus can help students develop tactical awareness and skillful decision making. (3) In CL, the tactical questioning can be expanded in the debrief to cover more affective or social issues: What happened? So what? Now what? In addition, questions can focus students on determining specific goals for the next lesson: What was one thing your team did well? and What is one thing your team needs to work on? (4) In both CL and TG, working in small-sided game situations allows for more touches of the ball and less complex situations in which students can problem solve and find solutions to tactical problems. In addition, staying in teams for an entire unit allows students in CL to develop teamwork, which can enhance positive interdependence and team affiliation. (5) Students taking roles can encourage positive interdependence in groups or teams and assist teachers with organization of their environment (e.g. role of equipment manager), (6) In both TG and CL, students assume responsibility in tasks and games. This empowers students to take control of their own learning. The appendix to this chapter provides a practical example of an integrated TG and CL lesson for setting up the attack in volleyball.

Task

In your groups, make sure that each teammate is observed. The recorder should check that everyone has a completed GPAI. The coach should discuss the observation with the teammates in a group-processing session after the game.

Components of game performance
(criteria for appropriate or inappropriate rating)

1. Decision-making criteria:	Player attempts to pass to well-positioned teammate
	Appropriate attack (spike, dink, long ball)
2. Skill execution criteria:	Ball reaches target
	- Forearm pass (bent knees, straight platform, move, square to target)
	- Set (soft hands, window, extended arms, square to target)
3. Support:	Attempts to make three hits
	Communicates with team members (e.g., calls for the ball)

(continued)

Figure 10.3   GPAI volleyball.

	Decision making		Pass execution		Support		Overall assessment (comments for individual or team)
	A	IA	E	IE	A	IA	
Name:							
Provide comments to justify your score:							
Name:							
Comments:							
Totals:							
Analysis of tactic:							Summary:
Suggested improvements:							

Key: A = Appropriate, IA = Inappropriate; or E = Efficient, IE = Inefficient

Figure 10.3 *(Continued)*

Conclusion

Remember my description of having the opportunity and instruction necessary to develop my kayaking skills? Similarly, in physical education I believe that we need to provide the opportunity and motivation for students to be physically engaged. I argue that a combination of Cooperative Learning and Tactical Games can provide the individual accountability and positive interdependence to facilitate successful completion of relevant tasks or specific goals to enhance student physical activity. The level of integration between the CL and TG models will depend on the needs and preferences of the physical educators. The goal should be to use the most effective combination to facilitate a student-centered learning environment in the gymnasium. Griffin, Oslin, and Mitchell (1997) provided some useful guidelines for implementation of the models: make explicit your core beliefs, think small, pick your favorite sport, make it yours, think "gamelike" and authentic, make the lessons reflect the lesson format of a game-practice-game cycle, plan the unit, and find company to reflect on your teaching and discuss how to enhance student learning. In addition, group processing can help teachers gain valuable information from their students. Both TG and CL can contribute to students' motor and social skills, but they also can enhance students' cognitive development through tactical awareness and skillful decision making. The road to implementation will be a labor-intensive process, but the potential benefits for students in physical education can be immeasurable.

Discussion Questions

1. What are the psychomotor, cognitive, and affective goals for your program? How can this integrated approach to teaching quality physical education achieve those goals?

2. How will you group your students? Take time to experiment so that you have truly heterogeneous groups that function effectively.

3. How will you assess your students? Two suggestions:

   a. Try to develop task sheets that can be used for teacher assessment or peer assessment.

   b. Make sure you have individual accountability for at least one task in every lesson.

4. How are the students positively interdependent on each other to achieve their tasks?

5. How can you incorporate group processing into each of your lessons? Remember that good questions can facilitate appropriate

cognitive responses during the lessons about skills and tactics and also enhance group processing.

References

Antil, L.R., Jenkins, J.R., Wayne, S.K., & Vadasy, P.F. (1998). Cooperative Learning: Prevalence, conceptualizations, and the relation between research and practice. *American Educational Research Journal, 35,* 419-454.

Aronson, E. (1978). *The jigsaw classroom.* Beverly Hills, CA: Sage.

Barrett, T. (2000). *Effects of two cooperative learning strategies on academic learning time, student performance, and social behavior of sixth grade physical education students.* Unpublished doctoral dissertation, University of Nebraska, Lincoln.

Bunker, D., & Thorpe, R. (1982). A model for the teaching of games in the secondary schools. *Bulletin of Physical Education, 10,* 9-16.

Chen, W., & Rovegno, I. (2000). Examination of expert teachers' constructivist-orientated teaching practices using a movement approach to physical education. *Research Quarterly for Exercise and Sport, 71,* 357-372.

Cohen, E.G. (1994a). *Designing group work: Strategies for the heterogeneous classroom groups.* (2nd ed.). New York: Teachers College Press.

Cohen, E.G. (1994b). Restructuring in the classroom: Conditions for productive small groups. *Review of Educational Research, 64,* 1-35.

Cohen, E.G., & Lotan, R.A. (1997). *Working for equity in heterogeneous classrooms: Sociological theory in practice.* New York : Teachers College Press.

Deutsch, M. (1949). A theory of cooperation and competition. *Human Relations, 2,* 129-152.

Dewey, J. (1924). *The school and society.* Chicago: University of Chicago Press.

Dodds, P., Griffin, L.L., & Placek, J.H. (2001). A selected review of the literature on the development of learners' domain-specific knowledge [Monograph]. *Journal of Teaching in Physical Education, 20,* 301-313.

Dyson, B. (2001). Cooperative learning in an elementary school physical education program. *Journal of Teaching in Physical Education, 20,* 264-281.

Dyson, B. (2002). The implementation of cooperative learning in an elementary school physical education program. *Journal of Teaching in Physical Education, 22,* 69-85.

Dyson, B., & Grineski, S. (2001). Using Cooperative Learning Structures to achieve quality physical education. *Journal of Physical Education, Recreation and Dance, 72,* 28-31.

Dyson, B., & Strachan, K. (2000). Cooperative learning in a high school physical education program. *Waikato Journal of Education, 6,* 19-37.

Ennis, C.D. (2000). Canaries in the coal mine: Responding to disengaged students using theme-based curricula. *Quest, 52,* 119-130.

Glover, D.R., & Midura, D.W. (1992). *Team building through physical challenges.* Champaign, IL: Human Kinetics.

Griffin, L.L., Mitchell, S.A., & Oslin, J.L. (1997). *Teaching sport concepts and skills: A tactical games approach.* Champaign, IL: Human Kinetics.

Grineski, S. (1993). Achieving instructional goals in physical education: A missing ingredient. *Journal of Physical Education, Recreation and Dance, 64,* 32-34.

Grineski, S. (1996). *Cooperative learning in physical education.* Champaign, IL: Human Kinetics.

Johnson, D., & Johnson, R. (1975). *Learning together and alone.* Englewood Cliffs, NJ: Prentice Hall.

Johnson, D.W., & Johnson, R.T. (1989). *Cooperation and competition: Theory and research.* Edina, MN: Interaction Book.

Johnson, D.W., Johnson, R.T., & Johnson-Holubec, E. (1998). *Cooperation in the classroom.* (7th ed.). Edina, MN: Interaction Book.

Kagan, S. (1990). The structural approach to cooperative learning. *Educational Leadership, 47,* 12-16.

Kagan, S. (1992). *Cooperative learning* (2nd ed.). San Clemente, CA: Kagan Cooperative Learning.

Kirk, D., & Macdonald, D. (1998). Situated learning in physical education. *Journal of Teaching in Physical Education, 17,* 376-387.

Kirk, D., & MacPhail, A. (2002). Teaching games for understanding and situated learning: Rethinking the Bunker-Thorpe model. *Journal of Teaching in Physical Education, 21,* 117-192.

Lave, J., & Wenger, E. (1991). *Situated learning: Legitimate peripheral participation.* New York: Cambridge University Press.

Metzler, M. (2000). *Instructional models for physical education.* Boston: Allyn & Bacon.

Mitchell, S.A., & Oslin, J.L. (1999). *Assessment in games teaching. NASPE assessment series.* Reston, VA: National Association of Sport and Physical Education.

Mitchell, S.A., Oslin, J.L., & Griffin, L.L. (2003). *Sport foundations for elementary physical education: A tactical games approach.* Champaign, IL: Human Kinetics.

Mosston, M. (1981). *Teaching physical education* (2nd ed.). Columbus, OH: Merrill.

Perkins, D. (1999). The many faces of constructivism. *Educational Researcher, 57,* 6-11.

Putnam, J.W. (1998). *Cooperative learning and strategies for inclusion: Celebrating diversity in the classroom* (2nd ed.). Baltimore: Brookes.

Rohnke, K. (1984). *Silver bullets.* Dubuque, IA: Kendall-Hunt.

Rovegno, I., & Bandhauer, D. (1997). Norms of the school culture that facilitated teacher adoption and learning of a constructivist approach to physical education. *Journal of Teaching in Physical Education, 16,* 401-425.

Rovegno, I., & Kirk, D. (1995). Articulations and silences in social critical work on physical education: Towards a broader agenda. *Quest, 47,* 447-474.

Siedentop, D., & Tannehill, D. (2000). *Developing teaching skills in physical education* (4th ed.). Mountain View, CA: Mayfield.

Slavin, R. (1990). *Cooperative learning: Theory, practice, research.* Englewood Cliffs, NJ: Prentice Hall.

Slavin, R.E. (1996). Research on cooperative learning and achievement: What we know, what we need to know. *Contemporary Educational Psychology, 21,* 43-69.

Smith, B., Markley, R., & Goc Karp, G. (1997). The effect of a cooperative learning intervention on the social skill enhancement of a third grade physical education class. *Research Quarterly for Exercise and Sport, 68* (Suppl.), A-68.

Integration of CL and TG: A Practical Example

Here is a practical example that has been used at the middle school level. The activities are designed to enhance students' psychomotor, cognitive, and affective capabilities by using TG integrated with a Learning Teams CL structure to teach volleyball (Dyson & Grineski, 2001). The structure of Learning Teams is based on Student Teams-Achievement Divisions (Slavin, 1990) and Learning Together (Johnson & Johnson, 1975). Learning Teams provide students with the opportunity to share leadership and responsibility roles and use collaborative skills to achieve group goals. The purpose of Learning Teams is to motivate students to be positively interdependent with their teammates, which is enhanced by students' taking on roles. In addition, the tasks are designed to help the students take responsibility in their group to complete their tasks. The task sheet (see figure 10.4) or a GPAI can also be used as a form of peer assessment. The intent of this lesson is to provide an example and framework for integrating TG and CL into physical education programs. Teachers should adapt this lesson to suit their contexts and their students' needs. Within the Learning Teams structure, students are taught roles such as coach, checker, recorder, organizer, and encourager. The teacher is in the role of facilitator.

The responsibilities of each role are as follows:

Coach—provides feedback to the group members to improve their performance

Checker—checks that every student completes the task

Recorder—records each student's performance on the task sheet

Organizer—organizes equipment

Encourager—encourages everyone to be involved and provides feedback to all group members

The coach explains the learning cues to the group, and the group practices the tasks. Remember that everyone participates in the tasks and everyone has a role. Students check off on the task sheet after their whole group has completed tasks 3, 5, and 6. Feedback cues can be on a clipboard or on a poster.

Task Sheet: Forearm pass for tasks 3, 5, and 6

> Task 3: Use the forearm pass to set up the attack in a practice task.
> Task 5: Play a modified 3v3 game:
>> a. Use a forearm pass as first contact on your side of court.
>> b. Use a forearm pass to set up the attack.
> Task 6: Create your own task and the learning cue focus for that task.

Student name	Belly to target G, D, or NW	Flat platform G, D, or NW	Move to the ball G, D, or NW
1			
2			
3			
4			
5			

Good = G; Developing = D; Needs work = NW

Group processing:

> 1. What are two things your team did well today?
> 2. What is one thing that your team needs to work on for the next lesson?
> 3. What happened? So what? Now what?

Figure 10.4 Task sheet: Forearm pass for tasks 3, 5, and 6.

Feedback Learning Cues

> Tasks 3, 5, and 6: Forearm pass: (1) ready position, (2) flat platform, (3) belly to target, (4) move to ball, (5) call ball "mine"

Tactical Problem: Setting Up the Attack

Task 1: Cognitive and Affective Task

The group or team decides on different roles. The teacher can assign roles for the students at first, eventually allowing the students to choose their own roles. Roles will vary depending on the lesson content. By trying each role, each student will have an appreciation for the others' roles. In a group of three (depending on the numbers in the class), the roles could include coach, encourager, and recorder. Initially the coach will watch for good form, the encourager will provide feedback about the skill, and the recorder will write the appropriate information on the task sheet. However, all students need to be as active as possible during the task; that is, the recorder should not get stuck recording throughout the task but should participate as a team member.

Task 2: Modified 3v3 Game

1. Set up to attack the ball.
2. Use a forearm pass as first contact on your side of court.

Task 3: Initial Psychomotor Task

- Offense tactic: Use the forearm pass to set up the attack in a practice task.
- Task: Tosser gives a *passable* toss to the passer, who forearm passes the ball to the setter. The setter catches the ball, then bounce passes it back to the tosser. Groups of three. Three to five trials to each position; then rotate. Practice on half of the court, two groups per court.
- Organization: Tosser (on the other side of the net), setter in setter position, passers in center, left back, and right back.
- Objective: Students use four of the five learning cues: (1) ready position, (2) flat platform, (3) belly to target, (4) move to ball, (5) call ball "mine."
- Variation: Free ball after *all* players have recorded their performance on the task sheet.

Task 4: Questions

The teacher poses questions and leads students to the appropriate responses.

Q: What do you need to do first to set up the attack?

A: A quality forearm pass

Q: Where must you pass the ball?

A: To the setter or target in the front line

Q: What are the learning cues for the forearm pass?

A: Ready position, flat platform, belly to target, move to ball, and call ball "mine"

Task 5: Modified 3v3 Game

1. Use a forearm pass as first contact on your side of court.
2. Earn 1 point for attempting a forearm pass at first contact.

Task 6: Cognitive and Affective Task

Students create their own task and the learning cue focus for that task.

1. Students sit down and discuss what task and goal(s) the group wants to practice. The recorder writes down the task and goal(s) on the recorder sheet.
2. Students attempt the task, trying not to forget their roles.
3. The recorder writes down the group members' performance. This could be different from the recorder sheet outline; this depends on what the group members decide are their group task and goal(s).

Task 7: Closure: Cognitive and Affective Task

Group processing (This is a debrief of the activities.)

1. What are two things that went well today?
2. What is one thing to work on next lesson?
3. What happened? So what? Now what?

11

Making Sense of Chaos: Australian Coaches Talk About Game Sense

Richard Light

T he Game Sense approach can appear chaotic. The game itself is chaotic. You go out and the game is chaotic and they're the conditions you have to train for. You have to replicate the game in training and develop players who can make sense of the chaos.

Les Bee, manager of coaching and officiating,
Victorian Coaching Centre, Australia

Perhaps two of the most basic questions coaches might ask themselves are, What makes good players in my sport and How can I develop those qualities in my players? Skill; fitness; physical attributes such as size, power, and speed; personal motivation; and technical proficiency all make important contributions to successful play. Something less tangible, however, is essential for a skillful player. Good players so often seem to be in the right place at the right time. They seem to have more time than other players, and they always seem to make the right decisions. They often exhibit an uncanny "sense of the game." Many coaches dismiss this elusive quality as something the player is born with that cannot be taught. Sociologist Pierre Bourdieu (1990) suggested that this "sense of the game" is indeed embedded in the body over a person's life. It is something learned through experience in particular contexts. It can, however, be fostered through activities that provide opportunities for learning guided by a coach's questioning. By adopting a Teaching Games for Understanding (TGfU) approach, or a variation of it such as Game Sense, coaches can develop players who know not only how to perform skills, but also where, when, and why to perform them. They can help develop players who, as Les Bee suggested in the opening quote, "make sense of the chaos."

From 1994 to 1998, Rod Thorpe regularly visited Australia, where he worked with the Australian Sports Commission (ASC, 1991) and Australian coaches to develop a systematic coaching approach known as Game Sense. Building on the existing practices of many Australian coaches, Game Sense offers a slightly more structured model than TGfU and is supported by a range of resources produced by the ASC. This chapter reports on interviews conducted with experienced Game Sense coaches working across a range of settings from grassroots sport to the most elite levels of high performance in Australian sport. Les Bee is the manager of coaching and officiating at the Victorian Coaching Centre (VCC), an organization that works at the grassroots level with community-based coaches. Ian Greener is the coaching and development manager at the Victorian Soccer Federation (VSF). Peter Spence is the operations manager at the Victorian Institute of Sport (VIS), where Jane Searle is the head netball coach. Nicole Goodman is the team leader of the accreditation standards, sport education section of the Australian Sports Commission.

This chapter identifies and discusses the main strengths of Game Sense as identified by the participant coaches, which are as follows:

- Development of the ability to "work off the ball"
- Transfer of training to the game
- Development of independent players
- Motivation of players in training
- Inclusive nature of Game Sense training

The chapter then addresses some challenges facing the Game Sense coach, which are also topics identified by the participant coaches. They are as follows:

- Repositioning the coach
- Chaotic appearance of Game Sense training
- Time restraints and the time required for long-term development

Working Off the Ball: Where, When, and How

Perhaps the strength of TGfU and Game Sense most emphasized in recent writing is the propensity to develop thinking players (for example, see Gréhaigne, Godbout, & Bouthier, 1999; Howarth, 2000; Kirk & MacPhail, 2002; Light, 2002). Technical approaches, on the other hand, develop skills out of context from the game and do not provide enough opportunity for learning how specific skills are used within the complex and changing environmental conditions encountered in games. The Game Sense approach gives meaning to skill development by placing it in authentic contexts. Skill is not neglected in Game Sense; it is developed through training activities that replicate, or at least resemble, the complex and fluid game environment in which players must engage physically, emotionally, and intellectually. Players of all levels are constantly perceiving and interpreting a changing physical environment and acting on this information (Abernathy, Kippers, Mackinnon, Neal, & Harahan, 1996; Kirk, Nauright, Hanrahan, MacDonald, & Jobling, 1996; Light & Fawns, 2001). This includes those players who are working off the ball.

Ian Greener from the VSF focuses his coaching on helping players develop knowledge of the where, the when, and the how of play in soccer. He does not, however, limit his focus to the player in contact with the ball. At any one time in territorial games such as rugby, soccer, or basketball, most players are not in contact with the ball. All the players in a team may focus on the ball during play and adjust their field position in relation to the ball's movement, but they typically come into contact with the ball only briefly and infrequently. Player movement off the ball is equally, if not more, important for the team's success than the manipulation of the ball.

During the 1993 World Youth Championships in soccer, Greener worked on the technical committee and recounted being amazed at how little time players spent "on the ball" during a game. In a 90-minute game, he estimated the ball to be in play for approximately 60 minutes. Within these 60 minutes, he found that each player averaged, at the most, two to three minutes in contact with the ball:

> So what are they doing for the other 57 minutes? They are running around making decisions. Three minutes of technique and 57 minutes of the where, when, and how: Where do I run, when do I run, and how do I run? *Where* meaning, I need to see where the ball is, where the players are. *When* meaning, Do I wait for the ball to be kicked, do I go too early or too late? And *how* meaning, Do I go quickly or slowly or do I go sideways? Do I pretend to run there and go there?

Game Sense offers coaches a means of working on the tactically informed movements of players working off the ball. This is an area of game play that involves relatively basic motor skills, yet demands well-developed tactical awareness, communication, and anticipation skills.

In light of Greener's observations, coaches may need to reconsider the amount of time typically devoted to ball manipulation skills. Game Sense offers coaches a means of working on the tactically informed movements of players working off the ball. This is an area of game play that involves relatively basic motor skills, yet demands well-developed tactical awareness, communication, and anticipation skills.

Transfer: Training for the Game

Much of the rationale for Bunker and Thorpe's (1982, 1986) development of the TGfU model arose from their concern about an apparent lack of transfer from training to performance in games. They argued that focusing on the refinement of technique produces technically skilled players who are not good games players. Les Bee (of VCC) suggested that players and coaches can become frustrated when they see little evidence of improved game performance through training. Bee sees this as the result of not training athletes in contexts that are close enough to game conditions. He suggested that the Game Sense approach addresses this problem by placing all learning in gamelike environments structured by the coach to develop particular skills and tactics: "It allows the coach to actually replicate the game, to put players in gamelike situations more often than in an actual game."

Peter Spence from the VIS was a physical education teacher before moving into professional coaching. He noted a similar problem in both school and club settings, where he began to develop coaching methods through which he could address this lack of transfer:

> I gradually became aware that there are athletes who train to train. They are good at training, but don't train to compete, irrespective of the level at which they are competing . . . [this situation] applies to entry-level and high-performance-level athletes. At the VIS we are very much into high-performance athletes. And we are very much attuned to the Game Sense approach.

Creating Independent Players

Game Sense coaching is a player-centered approach that places athletes in situations where they have to take control and make decisions. It empowers them and makes them responsible for their actions in training and in games. In sports such as soccer, hockey, rugby, and Australian football, in which the coach has little opportunity to make decisions during the game, players must be independent decision makers. Players must know the game and be able to make decisions for themselves. To develop such player autonomy, training must place them in situations that are similar to those they will encounter in the game and in which they are required to make decisions independent of the coach.

The Game Sense coach sets the environment and steps back to let the players figure problems out. The coaches in this study all identified creating coach-independent players as a primary aim of their coaching and as a strength of the Game Sense approach, as explained by Ian Greener:

> We want to produce players who are independent—where they don't worry if they look up and the coach is not there. It shouldn't make any difference. We want them to make the decision. . . . Our view is that if you set the right environment at training, then on the weekend, apart from the team talk before the game and at halftime, they look after themselves.

Lighting Up the Sport: Player Motivation

Physical education literature identifies the importance of enjoyment and fun for learning and for providing motivation for students (Hastie, 1998; Light, 2002; O'Reilly, Tompkins, & Gallant, 2001; Portman, 1995). Enjoyment is also important in attracting young people to community sports clubs and keeping them there. Affiliation, fun, and a sense of achievement are the primary motivations for young people's involvement in sport (Australian Sports Commission, 1991; Kidman, 2001). Les Bee suggested that Game Sense allows coaches to give the game back to children. He argued that Game Sense allows the players to take control and to set their own challenges instead of having them imposed by the coach. The Game Sense approach provides opportunities for enjoyment, creativity, expression, and innovation that lead to more positive experiences of sport for children and young people. This is supported by research on TGfU (Butler, 1996, 1997; Light, 2002). As Les Bee pointed out, games motivate players:

The Game Sense approach provides opportunities for enjoyment, creativity, expression, and innovation that lead to more positive experiences of sport for children and young people.

In Game Sense, coaching the game motivates [players]. The closer training is to the game, the more motivation there is. The further you get from the game, the less [players] are motivated. Actual games provide low repetition and high motivation, whereas drills offer high repetition and low motivation. Game Sense comes in here to offer increased repetition but staying close enough to the game to provide motivation.

Although elite-level sport, such as that practiced at the VIS, is primarily concerned with performance, Peter Spence argued that enjoyment is equally important in the quest for excellence at the highest levels of sport. Game Sense offers coaches a way to challenge and stimulate their athletes and encourage creativity:

> Game Sense can help athletes develop a real empathy for their sport, a real understanding, a real feel for it, a real love, a real passion. They get to feel the sport, they get to smell the sport and enjoy the sport. Without the enjoyment, you're not going to get excellence. I think a lot [of players] are disadvantaged by a skill-based approach. It doesn't light the sport up for them, and it doesn't develop skills that they can apply in action.

Inclusive Nature of Game Sense

One of the aims of VCC is to encourage lifelong participation in sport, especially for young people, through enjoyment and appeal. As such, the coaching approaches that are adopted need to provide for a wide range of abilities and interests. The propensity for Game Sense coaching to meet these requirements is one of VCC's primary reasons for promoting it. Les Bee views Game Sense as a "very inclusive coaching approach for players of all levels of ability," and one that is particularly effective for coaching young children and disabled athletes. The ways Game Sense relies on games that are modified to suit the abilities of learners make it invaluable in coaching athletes who have special needs. Peter Spence suggested that training needs to "light up the sport" through the provision of learning experiences that replicate game conditions and challenge players. This need not, however, exclude players of lesser ability in the mixed-ability groupings common to junior club sports or school sports. A good Game Sense coach can challenge and excite the better players and the less able or less confident players through the provision of appropriately structured challenges.

Bee suggested that approaches emphasizing the performance of technique are unkind to the less able: "If it's purely a technique approach, then only first-class passengers reach their destination. For the others, you're continually reinforcing what they can't do, and it eats away at their self-esteem."

Traditional approaches that teach predetermined "correct" techniques demand that players refine their technique, removing faults and striving to achieve a correct performance of the technique. This essentially involves highlighting what is technically wrong as the players practice and refine their performance. Although good teachers or coaches using a technical approach will provide as much positive feedback as possible, the feedback tends to be corrective and thus highlights what the player is doing incorrectly. In Game Sense coaching, on the other hand, there are few black and white answers. The questions asked tend to be open-ended; creativity is encouraged, and the less confident tend not to be so intimidated (Light, 2002).

Because Game Sense represents a significant break from traditional coaching approaches, it can be challenging for coaches to adopt. The following sections examine some of these challenges as identified by the coaches in this study.

Repositioning the Coach

The Game Sense coach sets the environment to maximize learning, but does not always determine exactly what players will learn. The coach encourages players to focus on particular aspects of play by asking questions, but needs to step back and let them learn. The emphasis on asking rather than telling places responsibility back on the players for their own learning and involves them intellectually in their training. This empowers players, develops player independence, and fosters good player relations and team spirit. The Game Sense coach is just as important as a traditional coach, but is less autocratic and far less visible, and the coaching is less explicit. The focus is on the players, not the coach. Players used to a directive, technical approach may expect the coach's role to be different from the role coaches typically assume in Game Sense environments. As Les Bee explained, "For players who always ask 'tell me what to do,' it's often a case of them hiding behind the coach and thinking that if [they're] unsuccessful, then it's [the coach's] fault."

Ian Greener said that he saw too many overly authoritarian coaches "standing there and rollicking the players, threatening them that if they don't achieve the end result, they'll be off the park [taken out of the game], but not helping them to understand." As he suggested, club committees and the parents of children playing in clubs often have a well-established perception of a committed coach that is at odds with the behavior of a Game Sense coach. The Game Sense coach may thus be accused of not being committed, as Ian Greener explained:

> For many coaches they think that if [they] don't stand there and rant and rave then [they're] not looked upon as a coach who is doing a good job. This culture means that there are times when I have been sitting there and people have said it looks as though [I'm] not interested in the game. . . . If you're in the coaches' box, you're almost obliged to jump up and down—that's the perception of what coaching is about.

Nicole Goodman from the ASC has been involved in the development and promotion of Game Sense and confirmed the difficulty that many coaches had in letting go of power. As she noted, coaches typically feel that they are supposed to "know it all." As she explained, "Game Sense encourages players to find answers for themselves rather than the coach being the 'font of all knowledge,' which can be a difficult concept for some people."

The Appearance of Chaos: Unleashing the Athlete

Les Bee commented on the often chaotic appearance of Game Sense training:

> Drills and a technique approach can appear very ordered and very well organized, and it looks good to parents. It looks like their kids are learning something, whereas the [Game Sense] approach can appear chaotic. But the game itself is often chaotic. It's organized chaos; the game is not ordered and organized. You go out and the game is chaotic, and they're the conditions you have to train for. You have to replicate the game in training and develop players who can make sense of the chaos.

Approaches to teaching and learning that are neat and well ordered attempt to reduce learning to a simple and linear process. As appealing as they are to those unfamiliar with the realities of learning, such approaches cannot account for the complexity of reality. Standing players in neat lines, running them along predetermined lines, and drilling a particular passing technique until it is "correct" may look good to the club administration or parents of junior players, but does it lead to better game performances? According to the coaches interviewed in this study, the answer is an emphatic no. As Peter Spence argued in the case of junior sport coaching, "Each kid is unique, yet the skill-based approach treats them like one size fits all. You've got to provide opportunities, stimulate them, and help them create. You don't have to help them, just provide opportunities."

> **S**tanding players in neat lines, running them along predetermined lines, and drilling a particular passing technique until it is "correct" may look good to the club administration or parents of junior players, but does it lead to better game performances? According to the coaches interviewed in this study, the answer is an emphatic no.

The performance of skills is deeply tied into the contexts within which they are performed (Brooker, 2000; Brooker, Kirk, & Braiuka, 2000; Light & Fawns, 2001). What works in neat lines at training typically breaks down under game conditions. Games are not neat, well ordered, and predictable. Players must perform within, and adapt to, a constantly changing, fluid environment. Spaces constantly appear and disappear, and players must keep track of the movements of opposition players and teammates within a context of changing conditions. Games are chaotic in so many ways. To replicate game conditions, Game Sense training often appears chaotic. Players standing in lines performing drills are learning something and that learning is often very explicit, but are they learning to play the game?

Learning in Game Sense training is game specific, deep, and lasting, but this learning takes time and is not readily apparent to the observer who is unfamiliar with the approach. As Ian Greener stated,

> If you want to impress the committee, then set up drills because it's all a pre-worked-out plan. Run here, knock it in there, run around the back, and join that group there. The committee will look at you and say, "He's pretty good, the players are moving along, it looks good." If you want to do Game Sense, it might look like a shambles. Stop, start, stop; everybody running about; a lot of questioning; and it can be untidy. The drills and activities probably look good, but for long-term benefit and understanding of the game, we have to go down the Game Sense way.

Game Sense training is less ordered than skill drills and is comparatively chaotic because it more closely resembles the game. As Peter Spence explained, this produces better players:

> There's always going to be an element of chaos, but out of the disorganization comes a high level of performance. If you keep closing things down and correcting things, you shut down the athlete and the teams don't develop. The control mentality breeds mediocrity. You've got to unleash the athlete.

Time Constraints: Quick Fix or Long-Term Development?

Coaches in Kidman's (2001) study on empowerment approaches to coaching in New Zealand identified the increased time needed for approaches such as the Game Sense approach as a problem. Junior sport coaches Hugh Galvan and Paul McKay noted how the extra time taken to develop players with these approaches presented problems for players and parents who wanted to see immediate results, and how the pressure for results can tempt coaches to find "quick fix" solutions. All coaches in the study conducted for this chapter suggested that such approaches take longer than technical approaches to get results, but achieve better long-term results. As Les Bee explained, this might be something that the coach should outline to those concerned with the team's progress:

> You are not giving specific instructions and don't get visible and immediate improvement. But it's a case of, I cannot teach you, I can only help you learn. I think it's important for the coach to outline these things if they are concerned.

The coaches in this study suggested that Game Sense involves a long-term learning process and can be seen as an investment in the players for the future. Jane Searle outlined how she has the benefit of working in what is explicitly seen as a development program in netball at VIS. This allows her time to develop her athletes free of the immediate pressure to win each week that is evident in most clubs and that can work to discourage coaches from adopting a Game Sense approach. As discussed earlier, parents and committee members may misinterpret the behavior of Game Sense coaches and see them as not working hard enough. Contrary to this perception, the Game Sense approach actually demands more work and time from the coach, but it is worth the time and effort, as Ian Greener explained:

To do a Game Sense approach initially takes a lot more work, but once you've got it going, then it starts to flow. Sometimes for 5 to 10 minutes it can be all disjointed and it's not quite working, but then suddenly it clicks. When I'm coaching this way, I've set the environment.

Game Sense involves a long-term learning process and can be seen as an investment in the players for the future.

I've got the players working well, and I stand back applauding, saying, "guys, brilliant, well done." It's a positive environment. That is one of the keys to successful Game Sense coaching.

Conclusion

TGfU and Game Sense both draw on many preexisting coaching practices in the United Kingdom, Australia, and elsewhere to provide a structured, systematic, and alternative approach to traditional coaching. Many coaches may thus recognize many Game Sense ideas and practices as something with which they are familiar. As Kidman (2001) suggested, coaches will interpret Game Sense, or TGfU, in different ways and will work it into their own coaching approaches and philosophies in particular ways. Indeed, the ways coaches in this study worked with Game Sense varied. Game Sense, however, is underpinned by a conceptualization of coaching that is distinctly different from what I have referred to as "traditional" approaches that focus on technical development and skill acquisition. Game Sense and variations such as Play Practice (Launder, 2001) can provide coaches with a way to develop more complete players with adaptable skills, tactical understanding, vision, and an ability to make informed decisions.

As Les Bee suggested in the opening quote, games are not neat and ordered but often chaotic, and good players must be able to makes sense of this chaos by training in ways that "replicate the game." Their skills and understanding must be developed in contexts that resemble those in which they must be performed. For too long, coaches have tried to force fit a template of order on an activity that is complex, dynamic, unpredictable, and often untidy. Game Sense provides a way through which coaches can strive to develop players who can "make sense of the chaos."

Discussion Questions

1. Identify some of the important decisions that offensive players typically need to make in territorial games when working "off the ball" and how a Game Sense (TGfU) approach to coaching can help them develop this often neglected aspect of their play.

2. Suggest how adopting a Game Sense (TGfU) approach might make young people's and children's experiences of sport more enjoyable and rewarding.

3. Drawing on your own experiences of coaching or games teaching in physical education, discuss the three challenges identified in this chapter that coaches typically face when adopting a Game Sense approach and suggest some ways you might address these challenges.

4. Game Sense (TGfU) coaching requires a repositioning of the coach that involves handing over much responsibility for decision making to the players and adopting a less directive coaching approach. This can cause problems for coaches used to being in a position of authority. How do you think this repositioning would change the ways coaches relate to, and interact with, their players?

References

Abernathy, B., Kippers, V., Mackinnon, L., Neal, R., & Harahan, S. (1996). *The biophysical foundations of human movement.* Melbourne, Australia: Macmillan.

Australian Sports Commission. (1991). *Sport for young Australians: Widening the gateways to participation.* Canberra: Australian Sports Commission.

Bourdieu, P. (1990). *The logic of practice.* Cambridge, England: Polity Press.

Brooker, R. (2000, September). *Contextual issues in teaching games in high school physical education.* Paper presented at pedagogy strand of 2000 Pre-Olympic Conference: International Congress on Sport Science, Sports Medicine and Physical Education, Brisbane, Queensland, Australia.

Brooker, R., Kirk, D., & Braiuka, S. (2000). Implementing a games sense approach to teaching junior high school basketball in a naturalistic setting. *European Physical Education Review, 6* (1), 7-26.

Bunker, D., & Thorpe, R. (1982). A model for the teaching of games in secondary schools. *Bulletin of Physical Education, 18* (1), 5-8.

Bunker, D., & Thorpe, R. (1986). The curriculum model. In R. Thorpe, D. Bunker, & L. Almond (Eds.), *Rethinking games teaching* (pp. 7-10). Loughborough, England: University of Technology, Department of Physical Education and Sports Science.

Butler, J. (1996). Teacher responses to Teaching Games for Understanding. *Journal of Physical Education, Recreation and Dance, 67* (1), 28-33.

Butler, J. (1997) How would Socrates teach games? A constructivist approach. *Journal of Physical Education, Recreation and Dance, 68* (9), 42-47.

Gréhaigne, J.-F., Godbout, P., & Bouthier, D. (1999). The foundations of tactics and strategy in team sports. *Journal of Teaching in Physical Education, 18,* 159-174.

Hastie, P. (1998). The participation and perception of girls within a unit of sport education. *Journal of Teaching in Physical Education, 17,* 157-171.

Howarth, K. (2000). Context as a factor in teachers' perceptions of the teaching of thinking skills in physical education. *Journal of Teaching in Physical Education, 19* (3), 270-286.

Kidman, L. (2001). *Developing decision makers: An empowerment approach to coaching.* Christchurch, New Zealand: Innovative Print Communications.

Kirk, D., & MacPhail, A. (2002). Teaching games for understanding and situated learning: Rethinking the Bunker-Thorpe model. *Journal of Teaching in Physical Education, 21,* 177-192.

Kirk, D., Nauright, J., Hanrahan, S., MacDonald, D., & Jobling, I. (1996). *The socio-cultural foundations of human movement.* Melbourne, Australia: Macmillan.

Launder, A. (2001). *Play practice.* Champaign, IL: Human Kinetics.

Light, R. (2002). The social nature of games: Australian pre-service primary teachers' experiences of TGfU. *European Physical Education Review, 8* (2), 291-310.

Light, R., & Fawns, R. (2001). The thinking body: Constructivist approaches to games teaching in physical education. *Melbourne Studies in Education, 42* (2), 69-88.

O'Reilly, E., Tompkins, J., & Gallant, M. (2001). They ought to enjoy physical activity, you know? Struggling with fun in physical education. *Sport, Education and Society, 6* (2), 211-222.

Portman, J. (1995) Who is having fun in physical education classes? Experiences of sixth grade students in elementary and middle schools. *Journal of Teaching in Physical Education, 14,* 445-453.

chapter

12

Implications of Models-Based Instruction for Research on Teaching: A Focus on Teaching Games for Understanding

Michael W. Metzler

You get what you teach for, so be sure you know how you are teaching.

I teach undergraduate and graduate courses on instructional models at Georgia State University. In both courses, I start out with this admonition: You get what you teach for, so be sure you (really) know how you are teaching. The kinds of things students learn are a direct result of how they interact with the content, and those interactions are almost entirely determined by the instructional model used by the teacher. A similar admonition applies to doing research on instructional models: You get what you ask and look for, so be sure you know what you are asking and how you are looking. The purpose of this chapter is to apply that same precaution to an emerging line of research on instructional models in physical education. Although some of this research can use questions and methods taken from earlier research on teaching in physical education, those questions and methods must be refined when applying them to research on instructional models. Using the same questions and the same methods will lead to largely misguided efforts to understand and use instructional models in our field.

Physical education has been taught in schools for well over one hundred years. The way it has been taught—that is, the instruction—has changed much in that time. For the most part, those changes have not been evolutionary; they have been marked by somewhat distinctive differences in instruction at identified periods: A "new way" to teach supplants the "old way," sometimes rather dramatically. To varying degrees, these changes have led to changes in the focus, methods, and application of research on instruction. The major premise of this chapter is that we are early in a new stage of instruction for physical education, a stage defined by the use of comprehensive and distinctive instructional models that promote well-articulated patterns of teacher and student behavior and lead to well-defined student outcomes. One of those models is Teaching Games for Understanding (TGfU). The purpose of this chapter is to present some guidelines for those who would do research on instructional models in physical education, using TGfU as the illustrative example.

Five Stages in the Development of Physical Education Instruction and Instructional Research

By my count, we have witnessed five major stages in the development of instruction for physical education. Shifts to new stages and events within stages influence how we teach physical education and how we do research on teaching. These shifts can and do change research purposes, paradigms, and the relationship between research and teaching. Because of space limitations, the following historical summary will be necessarily incomplete; I offer it to frame the main thesis of this chapter, that we are seeing the early signs of exciting new developments in instruction in physical education, which call for new ways to think about and conduct instructional research.

Stage 1: The PE Method

Oberteuffer and Ulrich (1951) considered the Physical Education (PE) Method as the predominant pedagogy for the first half of the 20th century. The PE Method was derived from the early gymnastics systems and was carried into sport-based school curricula. It was prescriptive, calling for the teacher to complete a well-defined set of operations in every class. It was also formal in that the teacher directed nearly every aspect of a lesson, with little opportunity for student choice or input. This combination offered little incentive for conducting research on teaching; the "one best way to teach" was known, so all we needed to help teachers learn to carry out the PE Method were good manuals to follow, such as *Successful Teaching in Physical Education* (Davis & Lawther, 1948).

Stage 2: Instructional Strategies

As the content and goals of physical education programs began to expand in the 1960s, new and varied ways to teach our subject matter developed. Even as Oberteuffer and Ulrich (1962) again discredited the PE Method, large parts of it carried over into the next stage but now included new and different kinds of task structures, called strategies, designed to accomplish short-term and often multiple objectives in a lesson or unit. Strategies had labels, such as station teaching, team teaching, and peer teaching. So, with new kinds of learning tasks, a new field of research on teaching emerged, with two major purposes: (1) to find links between theory and practice and (2) to test the effectiveness of each strategy in helping students learn content. An offshoot of the second objective was to test one strategy against another to determine which one was "the best" at helping students learn. That paradigm would dominate research on teaching for years and would later be labeled "Method A vs. Method B" (Graham, 1981), typified by titles such as "Effectiveness of Two Methods of Attaining a Full Draw by Beginning Archers" (Grebner, 1969).

Stage 3: The Spectrum of Teaching Styles

Teaching Physical Education (Mosston, 1966) is considered by many to be the best instructional book ever written in our field. It ushered in the third stage of development of instruction in physical education in its presentation of a series of teaching styles placed on a continuum (called the Spectrum) ranging from direct to indirect, based on a determination of who (teacher or students) controls the essential decisions made before, during, and after lessons. Terms such as *command style, practice style,* and *guided discovery* became part of our technical language and are still very much in our discourse on instruction today. The Spectrum generated an identifiable genre of research on teaching, much of it as "Style A vs. Style B." Some individuals became proponents of one style and set out to demonstrate the effectiveness of their preferred style over the others. Not surprisingly, a researcher's preferred style was often shown to be the "best way." Those damaging biases often led to serious methodological flaws, most of them originating in the *versus* paradigm itself (Byra, 2002; Goldberger, 1992), even though Mosston (1981) himself later advocated a *nonversus* approach. Studies from this stage included "A Comparison of the Effectiveness of the Command Method and the Task Method of Teaching the Forehand and Backhand Tennis Strokes" (Mariani, 1970).

Stage 4: Effective Teaching Skills

The concept of teaching effectiveness emerged in the 1970s and competed with the Spectrum for much of the following two decades, eventually winning out as the predominant view of instruction in physical education, although I suspect Spectrum loyalists would argue differently. The concept of teaching effectiveness is based on the hypothesized link between observable events in the classroom and student learning. Observable events could mean any combination of teacher or student behaviors carried out before, during, and after instruction. Student learning was typically defined in terms of achievement, which was assessed by measuring learning gains on skills, knowledge, or both. Once a correlation was made between observed teaching and learning processes and student achievement, or product, the next step was to devise ways to promote and maintain those processes across teachers, content, and contexts. Thus, several variations of process–product inquiry constituted the dominant paradigm in the heyday of teacher effectiveness research.

The main thrust of inquiry in this fourth stage of instruction was to demonstrate a correlation between what went on in the gymnasium or field and student learning. In one sense, it was an unbiased approach; if something a teacher did, or could get students to do, promoted more learning, that "something" was called effective teaching. This led to the investigation of a large number of discrete instructional skills and processes that were thought to increase student achievement. Some of these were based on the teacher's behavior, such as feedback, verbal and nonverbal interaction, planning, and the use of wait time after questions. Other processes were based on student behaviors, such as engaged time, management time, and Academic Learning Time (Metzler, 1979). In the end, the latter group of variables was shown to be better indicators of effectiveness; that is, what the teacher did mattered less than what the teacher could get students to do.

The stage of effective teaching skills saw the generation of a huge number of research studies in physical education (Rink, 1996), with titles such as "Relationship of Engagement and Practice Trials to Student Achievement" (Silverman, 1985) and "The Short Term Relationship of Teacher Feedback and Student Practice" (Rikard, 1991). It also spawned two excellent books, *Developing Teaching Skills for Physical Education* (Siedentop, 1976) and *Teaching Physical Education for Learning* (Rink, 1985).

One of the early and valid criticisms of the effective teaching movement was that it sometimes reduced empirically validated skills to simple, decontextualized rules (Fenstermacher, 1979). For example, if teacher feedback is *desirable,* then more must be better, regardless of the nature and quality of that feedback. If management time is *undesirable,* then little or none are the only acceptable levels regardless of contextual factors that a teacher could not control (e.g., class size). After over two decades of looking at narrowly defined conceptualizations of instruction, there was a shift to designing and implementing more comprehensive and expansive views of instruction and inquiry on it. We simply needed a bigger picture of both.

Stage 5: Instructional Models

The PE Method, instructional strategies, spectrum of teaching styles, and effective teaching skills are decidedly limited perspectives of instruction. Although each focuses to a different degree on one or more aspects of teaching, none of them address the full range of theoretical, design, planning, and assessment considerations in physical education instruction. Strategies, styles, and skills may be implemented within one or more of the models, but they are clearly not instructional models in and of themselves.

So, what then is an instructional model? Joyce and Weil (1972) provided the first definition:

> Models for teaching are models for creating environments: they provide rough specifications which can be used to design and actualize learning environments. Models are composed of interdependent parts. Content, skills, instructional roles, social relationships, types of activities, physical facilities, and their use all add up to an environmental system whose parts interact with each other to constrain the behavior of all participants, teachers as well as students. Different combinations of these elements create different environments eliciting different educational outcomes. (p. 25)

The Joyce and Weil text signaled the shift to models-based instruction in classrooms, but it would be a while before models were developed or adapted for physical education instruction.

The first such model was Teaching for Understanding described by Bunker and Thorpe in 1982 and expanded by Thorpe, Bunker, and Almond in 1986. It is significant that they used the term *model* (1986, p. 7) to separate their concept from other, less comprehensive views of instruction. Their model was revised and renamed Tactical Games by Griffin, Mitchell, and Oslin (1997). In this book, however, we are referring to it as Teaching Games for Understanding (TGfU).

The second model for physical education was presented by Hellison (1983) and eventually evolved into the Teaching Personal and Social Responsibility model (Hellison, 1995). A decade after Hellison introduced his model, Siedentop (1994) first publicly outlined his Sport Education model. Other models such as Cooperative Learning (Grineski, 1996) and Personalized Systems of Instruction (Metzler, 2001) were taken from classroom instruction and adapted for physical education. So, although we took a while to fully enter this stage, we developed an impressive array of models in a short time thereafter and an emerging line of inquiry on them.

Part of this development has included some nascent efforts to design models-based instruction for physical education, but this is still new enough that we have yet to establish our own "models way of thinking" (Joyce & Weil, 1972, p. 311) about physical education and sport instruction *and* its ancillary activity—models-based instructional research. But some signs indicate that things are changing. One clear sign was the first international conference that focused on teaching sport and physical education for understanding in 2001, which was devoted entirely to a single instructional model (i.e., TGfU) and attended by people from nearly two dozen countries. Other signs come from a number of physical education teacher education programs that have adopted a models-based approach to prepare new teachers and assist in-service teachers.

Doing Research on Instructional Models in Physical Education

The case I am making is that we are early in the fifth stage of development in how we conceptualize instruction in physical education, taking us *from method to models* over the past 50-plus years. Using the Joyce and Weil (1972) definition or the one presented in my own compendium (Metzler, 2005), we can identify at least eight such models designed expressly for physical education or adapted for use in our content: (1) Direct Instruction; (2) Inquiry Teaching; (3) Sport Education; (4) Peer Teaching; (5) Personalized Systems for Instruction (PSI); (6) Teaching for Responsibility; (7) Cooperative Learning; and, of course, (8) Teaching Games for Understanding.

> *The case I am making is that we are early in the fifth stage of development in how we conceptualize instruction in physical education, taking us from method to models over the past 50-plus years.*

Even though some research has been done on each of these models, we are still in the early stages of developing guidelines for inquiry, which are necessary to do the following:

1. Keep us from repeating some of the mistakes made in earlier stages
2. Bring the level of sophistication of models-based research up to that of models-based instruction (we cannot conduct inquiry on models with paradigms designed for strategies, styles, and skills)
3. Provide a better understanding of how an instructional model serves as the key mediating factor in the classroom actions of teachers and students
4. Allow better analyses of the relationship between instruction and student outcomes
5. Promote better transfer from research to practice

Based on these needs, I will present a series of guidelines that might apply to models-based inquiry in general, and I will use the TGfU model to illustrate each point.

As a caveat, it might appear that I address only process–product and other quantitative methods. I am defining *process* as anything done by teachers or students before, during, and after instruction, which is observed by, or reported to, a third party within a quantitative or qualitative tradition. *Product* is defined as any outcome from physical education instruction, whether it is measured with quantitative methods (such as a gain score) or captured with qualitative methods (such as student perceptions garnered from interviews). Only by expanding these boundaries can we determine parameters that encompass instructional models and inquiry on those models. Models are complex, comprehensive, and expansive ways to design instruction; research on them must be equally comprehensive and expansive.

Guideline 1: Be Sure It Is Models-Based Instruction and Models-Based Research

Separating teaching styles, instructional strategies, and effective teaching skills from instructional models can be difficult at times. For example, using the reciprocal style to put learners in pairs for short periods of time does not qualify one's instruction as the Peer Teaching model; similarly, putting a class in learning teams does not constitute Sport Education or Cooperative Learning.

By the same token, a model that studies tactical problems it is not necessarily TGfU, as Griffin and Placek (2001) so nicely pointed out in a recent *Journal of Teaching in Physical Education* monograph. Researchers in that monograph studied, among other things, how tactics were taught and learned (Rovegno, Nevett, & Babiarz, 2001) and how tactical knowledge and skills changed in a unit (Nevett, Rovegno, Babiarz & McCaughtry, 2001)—all outside of the context of the TGfU model. In the studies included in this monograph, the researchers were analyzing concepts, processes, and outcomes related to the teaching and learning of game tactics, but not within the TGfU model itself. That is an important distinction for researchers to make and for readers and teachers to understand.

Guideline 2: Be Sure to Ask the Right Research Questions

Method A vs. Method B and later Style A vs. Style B were popular paradigms in physical education research, and we still see some vestiges of them today as Model A vs. Model B inquiry (Ormond, Christie, Barbieri, & Schell, 2002). I am suggesting that the question, Which model is best? is inappropriate because of the problem of bias mentioned earlier and because that research design is simply invalid. Even if bias is sufficiently reduced, the intractable fact is that each model is designed to bring about a specified set of outcomes through well-defined and unique processes. Domain priorities, engagement patterns, and learning outcomes vary across models, so trying to test how well two models promote different kinds of outcomes with processes they do not hold in common is the empirical equivalent of comparing apples to oranges. Instead, we should be asking questions to explore how a model can achieve those outcomes for which it is designed and to determine the necessary contextual factors and processes for optimal implementation of each model. We should be asking questions such as, How effective is TGfU as a way to teach situated tactical decision making and skills to middle schoolers? and What are the essential prerequisites needed by learners to take full advantage of TGfU's features? We should not be asking, Do children learn tactics better with TGfU or Sport Education?

Guideline 3: Acknowledge That the Model Matters

How teachers instruct and how students are engaged with the content are as essential as the content itself. That is, it matters not only that students are trying to improve basketball skills or trying to decipher aspects of critical pedagogy in a soccer unit; it also matters how they go about learning those things. Each model is designed to promote differing types of engagement, some of which are quite divergent across several models. It is not sufficient just to state generally that some sort of physical education instruction took place; when models-based instruction is studied, the specific model must be identified and considered as one of many salient variables. The type of engagement promoted within an instructional model's design makes a quantitative and qualitative contribution to the teachers' and students' experiences and to the promotion of stated outcomes, so it behooves researchers to consider the model fully in their research plan.

How teachers instruct and how students are engaged with the content are as essential as the content itself.

Guideline 4: Make Sure the Model Was Implemented Faithfully

If *the model matters,* it also matters that the model is implemented with sufficient fidelity to its design. If TGfU is under study, then researchers must demonstrate that they used a reasonable version of that model, implemented within accepted standards for it. Like all other models, TGfU is rarely implemented exactly as it was designed; contextual factors, teacher innovations, and unforeseen events will result in less-than-exact versions in practice. At some point, changes can be substantial enough to cause the instruction to be something other than TGfU, even when that label is used and when, in practice, it appears to be TGfU at first glance. Acceptable fidelity can be achieved with several procedures:

1. The researcher must fully explain the model under study, noting all relevant features. It is not sufficient just to say that TGfU instruction was planned and implemented; key features of TGfU that determine salient processes and outcomes in the model must be made known.

2. The researcher must then document and confirm that the version of TGfU deployed in the study was acceptably faithful to its design. This can be accomplished by itemizing the key teacher or learner processes in the model and then verifying that those processes were adequately present. This benchmarking (Metzler, 2005) is a form of validation used to indicate the degree of fidelity in the delivery of a model (i.e., the planning and implementation of a TGfU unit) to better study the relationships between the model and other variables.

3. An instructional model is rarely implemented exactly within the designer's specifications. Therefore, the benchmarking process should make note of any changes in the model as it was implemented in a study. Griffin, Mitchell, and Oslin (1997) called for modified versions of games (game forms) for identifying tactical problems. This would suggest that teachers need to devise their own game forms and demonstrate that the

tactical problems are still present. Then, the researcher must describe how that relationship is maintained in the resulting new game form.

4. Another kind of validation should demonstrate that the necessary contextual and operational requirements for the model were met; that is, was it a true test of the model? In its design, every instructional model will specify essential contextual conditions needed for the model to have any chance of working. Questions about the length of the unit, teacher expertise and training for the model, appropriate content selection, class size, and student readiness for the model must be addressed as part of the research plan. For TGfU, some of those questions might be as follows:

   a. Do the students have the necessary cognitive and performance readiness for developing tactical awareness?

   b. Is there a reasonable time frame to learn all of the tactical skills and knowledge planned for the unit?

   c. Are time, equipment, and space resources adequate?

   d. Is the teacher knowledgeable enough about TGfU *and* the content?

> **O**nly over time, and with enough replication, can we really address the key compound question for TGfU: Under what conditions, for what content, and in which contexts will the model's design reach its full potential?

These factors might also be considered as variables to study in planned variations of the model by monitoring each one under differing amounts or conditions. Only over time, and with enough replication, can we really address the key compound question for TGfU: Under what conditions, for what content, and in which contexts will the model's design reach its full potential?

Guideline 5: Determine Appropriate Process Measures for Each Model

Each instructional model promotes certain and often unique patterns of teacher decision making and student engagement. Across models, these patterns can be quite divergent, requiring teachers to use a unique repertoire for planning, interaction, and assessment. Many of our notions of effective teaching are based on the repertoire needed for Direct Instruction (Rink, 1996): delineation of precise goals, clear and complete task presentations, maximum amounts of engagement, and the delivery of high rates of augmented feedback. Some of the repertoire needed for TGfU is quite different: using tactical problems as the organizing center, planning and analyzing the initial game form, determining tactical problems, letting students explore tactical problems (with cognitive and motor engagement), planning situated practice tasks, using key questions to promote tactical awareness, as well as using high rates of augmented feedback.

So, it stands to reason that researchers must be aware of the most appropriate teaching skills and types of student engagement called for by TGfU, that they must measure those processes accordingly, and that they must analyze those processes in the context of the model's design, not generically. Studying a well-known construct such as Academic Learning Time—Physical Education (ALT-PE; Metzler, 1979) will likely call for model-specific definitions of that variable in TGfU. Using the original definition of ALT-PE as the amount of relevant motor engaged time with a high rate of success (Metzler, 1979), one would likely find that TGfU students do not accrue much ALT-PE during the initial game form (it is likely too difficult for them to have success), nor will they accrue ALT-PE during discussions of tactical problems (they are cognitively engaged, not motor engaged). It would then appear that TGfU allows students little chance to accrue that essential type of engaged time, but we know better. That is, there are other criteria for effective engagement in TGfU, which can be uncovered only with new ways to define and measure ALT-PE.

> A second refinement of current ALT-PE practices will occur when we are able to relate ALT more carefully to the goals of a given learning environment. ALT-PE is, of course, a reasonably value-free notion. What counts as an instance of ALT-PE can be judged only in terms of the goals of the lesson. (Siedentop, 1983, p. 4)

Because each instructional model creates a well-defined learning environment, and many models have divergent processes and goals, it seems clear that we still need to develop model-specific definitions for some key process variables. This might open up a Pandora's box for researchers, reviewers, and readers, but if we really want to conduct good research on instructional models, we must recognize that generic definitions and instruments cannot always capture unique processes within a model such as TGfU.

The need to design model-specific protocols also applies to gathering qualitative data. Because models differ, we must develop protocols that are sensitive to those differences. For instance, student interview protocols would have to reflect aspects of content engagement, social phenomena, critical pedagogy, and learning outcomes that are unique to the design of TGfU instruction. A researcher should not just ask learners "about physical education," as though all physical education units and learning environments were the same.

Guideline 6: Relate Processes to Specifically Planned Outcomes in the Model

Similar to the need to devise appropriate process measures is the need to capture outcomes that are appropriate and unique to each model and to then relate processes to outcomes. The critical test for any instructional model is to establish that it actually works to promote the types of outcomes predicted from its theory and design. Although some earlier guidelines serve to establish how faithfully a model is implemented, it is still necessary to demonstrate that the model works and to explain why it works.

Demonstrating a model's effectiveness requires measurement techniques sensitive to changes in learning over the course of a unit of instruction and which reflect the specific, major outcomes intended by the model's design. For the TGfU model, effective teaching is indicated by gains in tactical skill and knowledge demonstrated in authentic game forms. The version of TGfU designed by Griffin, Mitchell, and Oslin (1997) includes the Game Performance Assessment Instrument (GPAI), which can be modified for any game form taught with the model to produce scores that can measure students' tactical learning over time. The GPAI also takes the guesswork out of what should be assessed in the model, which helps teachers and researchers alike.

But quantitative outcome data are not the only kind that should be generated. Models-based inquiry should also include analyses of outcomes that can be revealed only with qualitative methods such as student journals, various types of interviews, and reports from third parties. Those kinds of evidence will allow researchers to go beyond the obvious (i.e., "students changed"), toward a more complete understanding of the relationships among theory, design, implementation, and outcomes. This level of understanding can come only from a rich and varied base of evidence to analyze a model from many perspectives. Given the zeal of TGfU advocates and the epistemological views of many of them, I have no doubt they will soon provide this type of evidence on TGfU instruction.

Conclusion

I started this chapter by making a case that we are witnessing a new shift in how physical education teachers view and conduct instruction in schools. But what does this current shift in our views of teaching mean for models-based instruction and inquiry on it? The biggest realization for me is that it will fundamentally change how we teach physical education and how we conduct inquiry on instruction. Models such as TGfU are here to stay, and I think it is only a question of how pervasive models-based thinking becomes for physical education teachers and researchers. My hope is that it thrives. If instructional models are here to stay, they will have direct implications for models-based inquiry, regardless of which model is being studied.

Models such as TGfU are here to stay, and I think it is only a question of how pervasive models-based thinking becomes for physical education teachers and researchers.

First, we cannot conduct models-based inquiry at the same relatively low level of complexity used with strategies, styles, and skills. Models use unique, sophisticated, and comprehensive plans designed to lead students to multiple, subtle, and complex outcomes, so it stands to reason that models-based inquiry must be conducted commensurately. We need to ask *compound* questions about models, which will call for multitalented researchers, or teams of researchers who come together to study a model from a variety of perspectives. Second, we will need to completely abandon *versus* paradigms in research on instruction. Instead, we should make planned variations of instructional models, and we should study those to fine-tune each design and to better know when and how to use it.

Third, there should be more direct interaction between teachers who use instructional models and those who research the models. This would mean less reliance on static, typically *post-hoc* methodologies, and more use of real-time analyses in which the researcher observes what is going on and is able to interact on the spot with teachers and students. Fourth, and related to the previous point, we need to study the interactions among a model's design, content, context, and outcomes *simultaneously.* Models create dynamic environments that can be fully understood only when their component parts are studied at once.

The fifth implication comes to me from using a models-based approach in our teacher education programs at Georgia State University. We admonish our preservice and in-service teachers: You get what you teach for, so be sure you know how you are teaching. Many instructional models have been shown to be effective in various content areas and now have a growing base of support for their use in physical education. They can and do work! So, there needs to be congruence among a teacher's intended outcomes, the selected model, and how the model is implemented. The same goes for models-based research: Be sure you know what you are asking and how you are looking. Research plans must be developed that match the model, teacher expertise, instructional processes, and data analyses to verify that the model is being studied in a way it should be studied.

Now more than ever, we need coherent, comprehensive, and effective ways to teach our subject matter in school and sport settings. If models-based instruction and models-based inquiry are to meet that challenge, we must enter this new stage by looking ahead, not behind, so that this stage can provide some new ways to teach physical education and sport that are effective, sustainable, and beneficial to both teachers and students.

Discussion Questions

1. Ask your instructor to describe the kind of instruction he or she experienced in physical education as a student (specify a grade level). Think of how you were instructed in your own physical education program at that same grade level. What are the similarities? What are the differences?

2. What do you know *from research* about instruction in physical education?

3. Why do we know less about instruction from research than we do from other sources (journals, workshops, other teachers)?

4. Why is a *versus* approach to research on instruction in physical education inappropriate?

References

Bunker, D., & Thorpe, R. (1982). A model for teaching games in secondary schools. *Bulletin of Physical Education, 18,* 5-8.

Byra, M. (2002). A review of spectrum research. In M. Mosston & S. Ashworth (Eds.), *Teaching physical education* (5th ed., pp. 318-335). San Francisco: Benjamin Cummings.

Davis, E.C., & Lawther, J.D. (1948). *Successful teaching in physical education* (2nd ed.). Englewood Cliffs, NJ: Prentice Hall.

Fenstermacher, G.D. (1979). A philosophical consideration of recent research on teaching effectiveness. *Review of Research in Education, 6,* 157-185.

Goldberger, M. (1992). The spectrum of teaching styles: A perspective for research on teaching in physical education. *Journal of Physical Education, Recreation and Dance, 63* (1), 42-46.

Graham, G. (1981). Research on teaching in physical education: A discussion with Larry Locke and Daryl Siedentop. *Journal of Teaching in Physical Education, 1* (1), 3-15.

Grebner, T. (1969). Effectiveness of two methods of attaining a full draw for beginning archers. *Research Quarterly, 40,* 50-54.

Griffin, L., Mitchell, S., & Oslin, J. (1997). *Teaching sports concepts and skills: A tactical games approach.* Champaign, IL: Human Kinetics.

Griffin, L., & Placek, J. (Eds.). (2001). The understanding and development of learners' domain-specific knowledge [Monograph]. *Journal of Teaching in Physical Education, 20,* 299-416.

Grineski, S. (1996). *Cooperative learning in physical education.* Champaign, IL: Human Kinetics.

Hellison, D. (1983). Teaching self responsibility (and more). *Journal of Physical Education, Recreation and Dance, 54,* 23, 28.

Hellison, D. (1995). *Teaching responsibility through physical activity.* Champaign, IL: Human Kinetics.

Joyce, B., & Weil, M. (1972). *Models of teaching.* Englewood Cliffs, NJ: Prentice Hall.

Mariani, T. (1970). A comparison of the effectiveness of the command method and the task method of teaching the forehand and backhand tennis strokes. *Research Quarterly, 41,* 171-174.

Metzler, M. (1979). The measurement of Academic Learning Time in physical education. (Doctoral dissertation, The Ohio State University, 1979). *Dissertation Abstracts International, 40,* 5365 A.

Metzler, M. (2005). *Instructional models for physical education* (2nd ed.). Tempe, AZ: Holcomb-Hathaway.

Metzler, M. (2001). *Mastering the basics with the Personalized Sports Instruction System.* Boston: Allyn & Bacon. (Series includes six PSI-based student workbooks)

Mosston, M. (1966). *Teaching physical education.* Columbus, OH: Merrill.

Mosston, M. (1981). *Teaching physical education* (2nd ed.). Columbus, OH: Merrill.

Nevett, M., Rovegno, I., Babiarz, M., & McCaughtry, N. (2001). Changes in basic tactics and motors skills in an invasion-type game after a 12-lesson unit of instruction. In L. Griffin & J. Placek (Eds.), The understanding and development of learners' domain-specific knowledge [Monograph]. *Journal of Teaching in Physical Education, 20,* 352-369.

Oberteuffer, D., & Ulrich, C. (1951). *Physical education: A textbook of principles for professional students* (3rd ed.). New York: Harper & Row.

Oberteuffer, D., & Ulrich, C. (1962). *Physical education: A textbook of principles for professional students* (4th ed.). New York: Harper & Row.

Ormond, T., Christie, B., Barbieri, D., & Schell, B. (2002). A comparison of sport education and the traditional unit approach: Game play, activity levels, and knowledge. *Research Quarterly for Exercise and Sport, 7 3*(1 Suppl.), A-77-78.

Rikard, L. (1991). The short term relationship of teacher feedback and student practice. *Journal of Teaching in Physical Education, 10,* 275-285.

Rink, J.E. (1985). *Teaching physical education for learning.* St. Louis, MO: Mosby.

Rink, J.E. (1996). Effective instruction in physical education. In S. Silverman & C. Ennis (Eds.), *Student learning in physical education: Applying research to enhance instruction* (pp. 171-198). Champaign, IL: Human Kinetics

Rovegno, I., Nevett, M., & Babiarz, M. (2001). Learning and teaching invasion-game tactics in 4th grade: Introduction and theoretical perspective. In L. Griffin & J. Placek (Eds.), The understanding and development of learners' domain-specific knowledge [Monograph]. *Journal of Teaching in Physical Education, 20,* 341-351.

Siedentop, D. (1976). *Developing teaching skills for physical education.* Boston: Houghton Mifflin.

Siedentop, D. (1983). Academic learning time: Reflections and prospects. In F. Rife & P. Dodds (Eds.), Time to learn in physical education: History, completed research and potential future for Academic Learning Time in Physical Education [Monograph]. *Journal of Teaching in Physical Education, 1,* 3-7.

Siedentop, D. (1994). *Sport education: Quality PE through positive sport experiences.* Champaign, IL: Human Kinetics.

Silverman, S. (1985). Relationship of engagement and practice trials to student achievement. *Journal of Teaching in Physical Education, 5,* 13-21.

Thorpe, R., Bunker, D., & Almond, L. (Eds.). (1986). *Rethinking games teaching.* Loughborough, England: University of Technology, Department of Physical Education and Sports Science.

13

Teaching Games for Understanding and the Delights of Human Activity

R. Scott Kretchmar

T he experience of swing is what hooks people on rowing. The appetite for swing is limitless.

Craig Lambert (1998)

Teaching for delight is an unusually ambitious goal. It would be safer to teach for more modest ends, perhaps for satisfaction or simply for fun. Why then should Teaching Games for Understanding (TGfU) practitioners aim for something different—something as lofty, difficult to achieve, and potentially hard to pin down as delight?

Answers to this question are not hard to find. It is possible that TGfU techniques are uniquely suited for delight. Understanding itself might be a singularly potent catalyst for special movement experiences. And, it is also possible that aiming for delight would help instructors achieve more in physical education classes than they would with lesser affective goals. Many of us, in all probability, embrace an active lifestyle because we find movement genuinely delightful, not just fun.

The purpose of this chapter is to examine teaching for meaningful experiences. Specifically, the theory and practice of TGfU pedagogy will be analyzed and conclusions will be drawn about its potential as a "pedagogy for delight." This journey will require visits to several philosophical locations.

In this chapter you will do the following:

- Examine the significance of the subjective domain
- Distinguish delight from fun
- Review examples of activity-based delight
- Survey the potential of TGfU methodologies to promote delight
- Review doubts about the utility of TGfU as a resource for delight
- Draw conclusions about TGfU and delight

Importance of the Subjective Domain

To my knowledge, delight was not an explicit objective for the founders of TGfU. But Bunker and Thorpe (1982) *were* concerned about affect, specifically about the mechanistic, mind-numbing, repetitive drills that provided some skill, but left learners confused about how anything fit together and why they were doing what they were being directed to do. Much like Jewett and Bain (1985), Siedentop (1994), and others who focused on the subjective, early TGfU theorists realized that the magic of physical activity could not be found in isolated technique. This holistic philosophy put TGfU in a good position to pursue an ambitious affective end such as delight.

Arguably, however, TGfU has not pursued this purpose in any systematic way (Holt, Strean, & Bengoechea, 2002), nor, to be perfectly fair, has any other methodology in our field. Physical educators, for the most part, continue to be more comfortable with the objective, the concrete, the measurable, and the public. We tend to underplay the subjective, the personal, the idiosyncratic, and the private. Accordingly, our textbooks and public messages continue to focus on heartbeats over heartaches, gut measurements over gut feelings, muscular excitation over personal joy, and long life over a meaningful existence.

As a result, we have developed a battery of tools to measure the objective, everything from calorimeters to impedance machines, scales to skill tests, heart rate monitors to blood pressure cuffs. We can now light up virtually any part of the body—from regions of the brain to individual cells—to better see what is "really" going on when people move.

In contrast to these sophisticated methods for measuring objective change, we are still very limited when it comes to assessing the subjective domain. We rarely ask our students about it. We don't know very well how to measure it. We don't even know exactly what to call it. So we tend to label it *fun* or *enjoyment* and then pile this whole boatload of diverse experiences into a single, undifferentiated basket. This mixture of subjec-

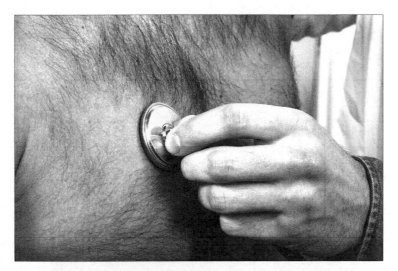

Our textbooks and public messages continue to focus on heartbeats over heartaches, gut measurements over gut feelings, muscular excitation over personal joy, and long life over a meaningful existence.

tive apples, oranges, and pineapples makes any meaningful accountability for specific affective accomplishments virtually impossible. Consequently, we are forced to aim at a subjective conglomerate called *fun* and to count teaching as affectively successful when it is achieved.

The result is an ironically lopsided profession. The irony resides in the fact that we never live objective heartbeats or blood pressures or brain

Prudence, duty, and careful planning have too often trumped spontaneity and play.

waves, but we spend most of our time trying to change and measure them. We have become lopsided because we have so focused on the healthful consequences of activity that we have tended to overlook the human significance of movement. Jump Rope for Heart has too fully supplanted jumping for joy. Prudence, duty, and careful planning have too often trumped spontaneity and play.

The point here is not to choose between health and meaning, but rather to find an appropriate balance between them and to appreciate their close interrelationships. Movement can and should be healthful and joyous, often at the same time, and possibly with one facilitating the other. But balance is the key, and currently the subjective needs more attention. This attention starts with a closer look at human experience and a description of the differences that can be found there.

Qualities of Delight in Movement (Comparisons With Fun)

Delight, first and foremost, is a memorable experience. Its subjective qualities are such that it stands out from the ordinary. We do not encounter delight all that often, but when we do, it tends to stick in our memory. When we say we delight in the company of a great opponent, we remember who we played and what happened. When we report a delightful experience with jogging, playing golf, or swimming, we refer to an engagement that stood out from our typical performances, perhaps some quality of movement—good timing, effortlessness, or harmony with the sporting environment—that usually does not show up.

Fun, by way of contrast, is more common and ordinary. Events that are merely fun usually recede into the background over time. Days or even hours after the pleasurable occasion, we cannot remember the details. Thus, although episodes that include fun are pursued and enjoyed, they are also often quickly forgotten.

This difference between fun and delight is exemplified in an account of rowing recorded by Craig Lambert. He was surprised by delight one afternoon on the Charles River near Boston and could not forget the encounter.

> The boat is perfectly level. Set up beautifully, we skim the surface on an invisible laser beam running from horizon to horizon. There is no friction; we ride the natural cadence of our strokes, a continuous cycle. The crew breathes as one.

Inhale on the recovery, exhale as we drive our blades through the water; inspiration and expression. In. Out. Row with one body and so with one mind. Nothing exists but: Here. Now. This. Rushing water bubbles under our hull, as if a mountain brook buried within the Charles flows directly beneath us. I have never heard this sound before, but I know it means we are doing something right. Rowers have a word for this frictionless state: swing. The experience of swing is what hooks people on rowing. The appetite for swing is limitless. (Lambert, 1998, pp. 124-125)

It would not do for Lambert to say that this experience was merely "agreeable" or "fun." Such language would cheapen and otherwise incorrectly describe the event. The experience of "swing" was special, indeed memorable, a temporary possession that Lambert hoped to get hold of repeatedly during his lifetime.

This account provides clues for further characteristics of delight. It seems to be rare, elusive, and difficult to produce on command. Delight hides and sometimes defies our efforts to find it. It often requires extra preparations on our part to make it feel welcome. In this sense, delight tends to be a high-demand subjective state.

We do not, strictly speaking, plan for delight. When we look hardest for it, it may even conceal itself more completely. In a way, delight surprises us. It shows up, often unexpected and unannounced, just as it did for Lambert. Nevertheless, although we cannot summon delight directly, we

The appetite for swing is limitless.

can lay the groundwork and otherwise prepare ourselves for it. To make the arrival of delight more likely, we may need to practice at length, train faithfully, better focus our attention, or simply work longer and harder.

Fun, on the other hand, usually resides out in the open and requires relatively little on our part to locate and secure it. When we seek fun, we typically find it. We gravitate toward favorite foods, movies, CDs, novels, amusement parks, friends, lovers, sports, and coffee shops and almost always have a good time when we are in their company. In the process, fun makes relatively few demands on us.

Delight is not as enduring. Like a fickle guest, it is liable to leave without giving a moment's notice.

We may only need to be in a decent mood, relatively alert, and modestly persistent. Thus, when we plan for parties, or trips to amusement parks, or games of golf, we almost invariably thereby plan for and achieve at least some modicum of fun. And when we locate fun in these places, it tends to stick around—at least for the duration of the event.

Delight is not as enduring. Like a fickle guest, it is liable to leave without giving a moment's notice. It is like a fragile spell that gets cast over us. Even turning our attention to it will often kill it on the spot or at least send it packing. Lambert was in the presence of "swing" for only moments, during only one outing on the river. Although this delightful experience might return, and although Lambert continued to work hard to make sure that it did, he was still not privy to its schedule.

Lambert learned that, in addition to being unpredictable, fragile, unusual, and memorable, delight is also personal. Delightful experiences speak to us individually, in terms of our unique aspirations and our own idiosyncratic stories. Because of this, delight stirs us, moves us, or carries us away.

When Lambert found himself under the spell of delight, he was figuratively transported to a very personal and special place—in this case, to a world inhabited only by members of what Lambert called the rowing tribe, a place where the common friction of a boat against the river, uncertain teamwork, and the everyday sweaty effort of pulling oars through water magically took on very different characteristics. Lambert was carried away on the wings of delight, as it were, to his own rowing place (Kretchmar, 2000).

Fun in physical activity, as we all know, is not usually personal in this sense, and it hardly carries us anywhere. Fun typically does not add any important chapters to our stories and does not come equipped with wings. I have never heard it said, for example, that someone was moved, stirred, shaken, or carried away by fun. If delight speaks more to our heart, fun usually lives on our skin. Thus, although fun is pleasant and desirable, it is still not particularly personal.

These reflections on delight lead to a final characteristic, a most important one. Delight is a condition of rest, of fulfillment (Drost, 1995). Delight is dependent on a union with some object or goal that is regarded as good. To experience delight, one must achieve a close tie with something that is desirable but often lies at a distance or is typically out of reach.

Delight, in our physical education language by this account, more often attaches to genuine achievements than either strivings (the arduous process of seeking achievements) or gratuitous accomplishments (the possession of things that are not worth seeking or having). Delight in movement is a change from seeking to finding, from trying to learn to having learned, from hoping-to-possess to having-in-hand. But, more than that, what is found, learned, or possessed is typically difficult to secure. Otherwise, the union would not be noteworthy.

These significant unions in education typically come in stages. Every learning acquisition is a step in a progression to further unions and higher levels of learning. Thus, in teaching toward delight, we are actually teaching toward progressive delights—that is, temporary and special affective states that are memorable in their own right but are also motivators for additional delights at even higher levels of skill, knowledge, or understanding. Seeking delight, therefore, turns out to be a journey that can be taken by beginners, intermediates, and advanced performers alike.

Delight, as we have seen though this brief description, cannot be sought everywhere. It is harder to find in the domains of general health, prudent behavior, entertainment, stimulation, variety, novelty, or anything else that is grounded in an impersonal duty, superficial diversion, or easily forgettable activity. Some degree of fun might be found in those places, but usually not delight. Delight, we discovered, resides closer to the heart, in domains that are far more personal. Furthermore, although a degree of fun can be found in seeking, trying, attempting, hoping, planning, learning, or any other form of striving, delight requires having, possessing, and forming a union with some special object or objective.

Delight resides close to the heart, in domains that are very personal.

In short, physical educators who teach toward fun, on the one hand, or toward delight, on the other, move in two very different directions. The direction toward fun is well marked in today's literature by a variety of tips and techniques, and most of us have our favorite strategies for making activity enjoyable. Without question, all of us must spend at least some of our time and effort promoting this base-level affective goal.

However, the road to delight deserves our attention too. This pedagogical pathway has barely been cleared and has far fewer signposts. Nevertheless, with a description of delight now in hand, we have some clues about a pedagogy for delight. One of them tells us that delight often accompanies very personal and special unions or possessions, so this might be a good place to start.

Special Activity Possessions That Have the Potential to Delight

As TGfU has evolved, a number of sources for affective success have been identified, including affiliation, friendship, and social approval; knowledge and understanding; skill achievement; excitement/sensation; teamwork; victory; and self-direction (Werner, Thorpe, & Bunker, 1996). The focus here, however, will be on performance as a source of delight, on the actual playing of games. This focus is consistent with the holistic underpinnings of TGfU, which suggest that knowing is not independent of performing, or more specifically, that tactical thinking is not independent of skillful doing (Kirk & MacPhail, 2002). In short, an important goal of TGfU has always been to teach students to play well and to enjoy activity.

The path to playing well is, of course, an educational journey marked by new feelings, sensations, emotions, insights, and skills. The journey, therefore, is not uniform, even, or linear. Various breakthrough experiences or leaps forward occur occasionally and count as special learning events. These learning advances are difficult to put into words, but they stand as potential sources for delight. Here are some examples:

Ten Aspects of Movement Journeys That Lead to Valuable Possessions

From mechanically correct to expressive movement

From acting to being

From repetitive, effective movement to inventive (clever, unique) movement

From inventive movement to creative (artistic) movement

From seeing one's opponent as a threat or enemy to viewing one's opponent as a facilitator, partner, or friend

From movement as a mere obligation to movement as part of one's own story

From the lived constraints of being unfit to the freedom of good conditioning

From movement as aesthetically distasteful (e.g., hurried, awkward, difficult) to movement as beautiful (e.g., smooth, graceful, effortless, balanced)

From fearing and avoiding a difficult motor task to meeting and overcoming a genuine challenge

From thinking through a technique or strategy to spontaneously intuiting a right move

In a sense, these are different ways to talk about one process—the journey from moving poorly to moving well. Nevertheless, each separate journey from the aesthetic to the expressive, from experiences of inventive movement to those of interpersonal cooperation is subjectively a distinct possession and thus a potential source of delight. The question remains, however, whether these activity resources are effectively and uniquely tapped by TGfU methodologies.

Promoting Activity Delight Through TGfU

Verbal, propositional, explicit, or what is sometimes called declarative knowledge is a signature feature of TGfU methods. Coming to understand tactics at this explicit level can in itself be delightful. But in the current context, tactical and other explicit knowledge become primarily tools, means to an end, not a source of delight in themselves. If TGfU is a powerful pedagogy for activity-based delight, it is because understanding is a powerful catalyst. In other words, physical education students who understand their movement (in some verbal, explicit way) will learn faster and better than students who lack such understanding.

This utility role for understanding might be captured in five statements that can be found as assumptions or claims in the TGfU literature. (See, for example, Thorpe et al., 1984; Werner et al., 1996.) These are assertions about how and why understanding enhances motor learning and overall play.

1. Explicit understanding provides context. Students who see the context for skill and tactical development will improve more quickly.

2. Explicit understanding enhances motivation. Students who know why they are practicing a given skill will work harder at it and learn it faster.

3. Explicit understanding enhances the transfer of skills. Students who know temporal and spatial tactical strategies for a type of game will be able to perform more quickly and effectively in a variety of games of that type.

4. Explicit understanding enhances psychomotor skill development. Students who understand technique and strategy first, or during the learning process, will more quickly develop the skills and sense-perceptual capacities needed on the court or field.

5. Explicit understanding enhances creativity during performance. Students who know how a game works will be less tied to rote actions and better able to develop novel movement patterns.

If these five claims are true, a strong case can be made for TGfU as a pedagogy for activity-based delight. With the aid of understanding, students would encounter the 10 performance acquisitions sooner and at higher levels in TGfU curricula than they would under other instructional methodologies. More creativity, more authorship, more aesthetic intrigue, increased effortless movement—all of this because explicit understanding expedites the motor learning journey. But some would ask whether this catalyst is, in fact, as effective as TGfU theorists believe it may be.

> *If these five claims are true, a strong case can be made for TGfU as a pedagogy for activity-based delight.*

Doubts About TGFU As a Pedagogy for Delight

TGfU shares a fate with many other physical education pedagogies—namely, an absence of well-controlled research that conclusively documents its relative success. Although TGfU might be expected to outperform curricula that are grounded in skill and drill methods and that treat the learner less holistically, such superiority is difficult to show definitively (e.g., Chandler, 1996; French, Werner, Rink, Taylor, & Hussey, 1996; McMorris, 1998; Rink, 1996). It is even more difficult to judge the efficacy of TGfU compared with other pedagogies that are like it, that is, ones that are more or less subjectively inspired, such as Siedentop's (1994) pedagogy for play, Jewett and Bain's (1985) pedagogy for purpose, or even Metheny's (1968) pedagogy for symbolic meaning.

However, such comparisons are crucial if we are to match educational goals with their most potent methodologies. A step toward this end can be taken by raising key issues about the efficacy of TGfU as a pedagogy for delight. Here are some of the central points on which the promise of TGfU as a promoter of affective excellence hinges:

■ *The need for more empirical research.* To my knowledge, as implied earlier, research to date has not verified, let alone strongly supported, any of the five empirical claims about the utility of understanding. If explicit understanding is in fact a potent catalyst for faster and better learning, TGfU may well be a premier pedagogy for activity-based delight. If not, it may still offer superior techniques for promoting fun. But in this case, other pedagogies should be selected if one is pursuing delight.

■ *The need for a clearer notion of understanding.* Because understanding is the lynchpin for TGfU techniques, practitioners must be absolutely clear about what understanding is, what forms it takes, when it is best employed, and so on. In fact, it is doubtful that good empirical research can move forward until and unless understanding—at its various levels and in its various forms—is fully defined, operationalized, and also placed in broader learning contexts (Kirk & MacPhail, 2002; Rink, 2001).

■ *The need for an examination of time use and setting.* TGfU devotes considerable time to the acquisition of understanding and to participation in simulated activities. Both techniques are thought to promote fun or enjoyment. Their efficacy in providing access to delight is less clear, particularly if delight, as speculated, is a high-demand affective state. If this is true, the manner in which TGfU balances brief introductory experiences with sustained challenges may well affect its potential as a methodology for delight.

■ *The need for an examination of purpose.* TGfU's focus on explicit understanding may both underestimate the scope of knowing and constrain its capacity to generate activity-based delight. Some have argued that performers, like musicians, poets, writers, dancers, and athletes, come to understand tacitly (e.g., Polanyi & Prosch, 1975) and that this tacit form of understanding is what produces the 10 opportunities for activity delight described previously. Ironically then, it is understanding that produces delight, but not the kind of understanding about which we typically think. Moreover, explicit knowing may be only one very uncertain and occasionally useful route toward tacit understanding. These speculations may constitute the more radical truth of holism, namely, that uniquely human understanding works in verbal and nonverbal ways, at explicit-abstract levels and at tacit-concrete levels. In the extent to which TGfU relies on verbal, abstract, explicit forms of understanding, it may impede other levels of understanding that carry their own delights.

Conclusion

In this day and age when we are worried about reducing obesity and promoting active lifestyles, wouldn't it be wonderful if we could somehow wave a magic wand and give our students the marvelous experiences of delight that are available in the movement domain? And wouldn't it be great if everyone could have experiences of swing similar to Lambert's rowing in a frictionless state? Of course it would, but these are probably unrealistic objectives. Nevertheless, steps in that direction can be taken by focusing on a few take-home points and conclusions.

- In physical education too many practitioners ignore the subjective. They dismiss it by dumping a rich variety of affective states into one large basket called enjoyment or fun. They also dismiss it by aiming too low, by settling for mere satisfaction when they could be targeting something more memorable, more meaningful.

- Distinguishing among subjective states is not only possible, it is also a professional responsibility. Fun is not the same thing as delight, and we can describe in concrete terms how and why they are different. Once differences are clear, it becomes our responsibility to target affective goals as carefully as our more objective, empirically measurable health and skill outcomes.

- When we know what delight is, we can develop pedagogical strategies that are designed to produce it, or at least to lay the groundwork for its more regular appearance. It is one thing to move an arm or a leg into a correct position. It is another to enable a person to move into the right position gracefully, expressively, on the so-called "wings of delight."

- Not all pedagogies are equal when it comes to teaching toward delight or toward any other advanced and highly valued affective state. Some will be better; some will be worse.

- TGfU holds considerable promise as a pedagogy aimed at affective excellence. As a holistic approach that relies on understanding and meaning, not just on rote movement, it is well positioned to pursue ambitious subjective goals. On the other hand, if holism requires a rethinking and revaluation of tacit understanding, TGfU may embody theoretical flaws.

- At a practical level, TGfU also carries potential advantages. If explicit understanding is, in fact, a powerful catalyst for better play, many of the 10 learning acquisitions associated with delight will be expedited in TGfU curricula. On the other hand, important questions remain about the efficacy of explicit understanding in certain contexts, at various levels, at different times, and in relationship to other learning considerations.

In this chapter I have raised questions that may seem bewildering. But ultimately the issue here is very simple. Many of us have chosen physical education for a career because we have had our own love affair with movement. We have personally experienced some of the 10 wellsprings of delight—from moving gracefully to playing expressively, from solving a movement problem creatively to hitting a ball effortlessly. It was probably delight, therefore, that got our attention initially. It was also probably delight that brought us back. And it may well have been delight that has kept us exercising, moving, and competing across the years.

If so, it might be good for us to work harder at sharing some of this outstanding subjective stuff with our students. We know that they are always interested in having some fun in our classes, but we know too that the attraction of movement does not need to stop there.

Discussion Questions

1. Why do kinesiologists avoid the subjective? Is it a matter of convenience? Laziness? A lack of confidence? An unrealistically strong reliance on empirical measurements? Do other subjects face similar difficulties? What about English? What about music?

2. Can you come up with other subjective end points besides fun and delight? What would they be, and how do they differ from these two conditions?

3. Could you map out a subjective progression as part of a unit plan? Where do learners start subjectively? By what steps do they progress? Even though there will certainly be important individual differences here, is there not also a partly common human pathway that nearly all of us take?

4. If you were to have a class debate on the following issue: It is better to base physical education on sound, measurable health benefits than on meaning and other subjective goals, where would you stand? What arguments would you use to defend your position?

References

Bunker, D., & Thorpe, R. (1982). A model for the teaching of games in secondary schools. *The Bulletin of Physical Education, 18,* 5-8.

Chandler, T. (1996). Teaching games for understanding: Reflections and further questions. *Journal of Physical Education, Recreation and Dance, 67* (4), 49-51.

Drost, M.P. (1995). In the realm of the senses: Saint Thomas Aquinas on sensory love, desire, and delight. *The Thomist, 59* (1), 47-58.

French, K, Werner, P., Rink, J, Taylor, K, & Hussey, K. (1996). The effects of a 3-week unit of tactical, skill, or combined tactical and skill instruction on badminton performance of ninth-grade students. *Journal of Teaching in Physical Education, 15,* 418-438.

Holt, N., Strean, W., & Bengoechea, E. (2002). Expanding the Teaching Games for Understanding model: New avenues for future research and practice. *Journal of Teaching in Physical Education, 21,* 162-176.

Jewett, A., & Bain, L. (1985). *The curriculum process in physical education.* Dubuque, IA: William C. Brown.

Kirk, D., & MacPhail, A. (2002). Teaching games for understanding and situated learning: Rethinking the Bunker-Thorpe model. *Journal of Teaching in Physical Education, 21,* 177-192.

Kretchmar, S. (2000). Moving and being moved: Implications for practice. *Quest, 52,* 260-272.

Lambert, C. (1998). *Mind over water: Lessons on life from the art of rowing.* Boston: Houghton Mifflin.

McMorris, T. (1998). Teaching games for understanding: Its contribution to the knowledge of skill acquisition from a motor learning perspective. *European Journal of Physical Education, 3,* 65-74.

Metheny, E. (1968). *Movement and meaning.* New York: McGraw-Hill.

Polanyi, M., & Prosch, H. (1975). *Meaning.* Chicago: University of Chicago Press.

Rink, J. (Ed.). (1996). Tactical and skill approaches to teaching sport and games [Monograph]. *Journal of Teaching in Physical Education, 15,* 4.

Rink, J. (2001). Investigating the assumptions of pedagogy. *Journal of Teaching in Physical Education, 20,* 112-128.

Siedentop, D. (Ed.). (1994). *Sport education: Quality PE through positive sport experiences.* Champaign, IL: Human Kinetics.

Thorpe, R., Bunker, D., & Almond, L. (1984). A change in focus for the teaching of games. In M. Pieron and G. Graham (Eds.), *Sport pedagogy: Olympic Scientific Congress readings,* Vol. 6 (pp.163-169). Champaign, IL: Human Kinetics.

Werner, P., Thorpe, R., & Bunker, D. (1996). Teaching games for understanding: Evolution of a model. *Journal of Physical Education, Recreation and Dance, 67* (1), 28-33.

14

Future Prospects for Teaching Games for Understanding

David Kirk

I magine that I want to teach a class of 8-year-old students basic safety principles in a gymnastics lesson. In this situation, with this aim, direct instruction is the right instructional strategy to use. Now imagine that I want the same children to learn some of the basic principles of playing a game as a team member, including how to work with others and the relationship between being in space and having time to make decisions and execute movements. Would direct instruction work in these circumstances? Michael Metzler claimed it would not. He argued that I would need to use other instructional strategies that would allow me to design appropriate learning experiences that would be likely to produce the desired learning outcomes.

In his recent book *Instructional Models for Physical Education,* Metzler (2005) argued that we need more models-based instruction in physical education (see chapter 12 for more about models-based instruction). This is because models-based instruction brings into close alignment instructional strategies and subject matter with intended learning outcomes, all considered within specific sets of circumstances. Understood in terms of the scenario that opens this chapter, Metzler's key insight might not seem particularly revolutionary or novel. In fact, it sounds like common sense. Unfortunately, although it makes perfect sense, it is not at all common.

Plenty of evidence indicates that physical educators do not use much models-based instruction, except for using the direct instruction model, sometimes inappropriately (e.g., Curtner-Smith, 1999; Green, 1998). One of the instructional models in Metzler's book is the Tactical Games model, also called Teaching Games for Understanding (TGfU). Those of us who have been using TGfU have been practicing a models-based approach to instruction all along, possibly without realizing it. Models-based instruction is currently scarce in physical education, and this is partly why TGfU has yet to become commonplace in our schools.

As a form of models-based instruction, TGfU proposes that good games players are good thinkers as well as good technicians. In other words, TGfU suggests that the development of cognitive processes such as thinking strategically and decision making are as important to becoming a good games player as is physical dexterity. Also consistent with models-based instruction, TGfU asserts that all students must learn domain-specific knowledge to become good games players, and that the subject matter of games play offers different challenges to learners than the subject matter of other forms of physical activity in physical education. Perhaps more radically, and in acknowledgment of these previous two issues, TGfU requires teachers to step outside the comfort zone of direct instruction and to design learning experiences that give learners some responsibility for their learning.

TGfU asserts that students must learn domain-specific knowledge to become good games players, and that the subject matter of games play offers different challenges to learners than the subject matter of other forms of physical activity in physical education.

TGfU does indeed align learning outcomes with subject matter and instructional strategies, but this is not the reason it has yet to become common practice. More telling and consistent with many of the other instructional models Metzler includes in his book, TGfU proposes learning outcomes that challenge conventional ways of thinking about learning in physical education and requires teachers to use strategies other than direct instruction to achieve these outcomes. Laker (2000) suggested in his book *Beyond the Boundaries of Physical Education* that physical educators have for too long clung to an outmoded traditional role as expert teachers of sport skills. Meanwhile, according to Laker (2000), the emerging need in troubled times is for physical education to contribute to "the complete development of the individual" (p. 3).

Advocacies such as Laker's for a broader set of learning outcomes for physical education are not new. What is new in an age of increasing accountability is the existence of statutes requiring publicly funded schools to deliver learning outcomes, as they now must in parts of the United Kingdom. Along with this accountability to the law has come a realization that if we say we can deliver a wide range of learning outcomes in physical education, we need to be sure the outcomes are achievable and that we can show they have been achieved. The exclusive use of direct instructional strategies that keep kids "busy, happy, and good" (Placek, 1983); under control; and relatively safe are no longer sufficient in the current educational climate.

I believe that TGfU is, at this moment in the history of physical education, very well placed to become common practice for very sound educational reasons. What are games of the kind we commonly find in physical education programs if they are not, as the philosopher Bernard Suits (1967) once noted, rule-bound activities and elaborate exercises in problem solving, with the added spice of associated physical challenges? To be a good games player is to be a good solver of complex problems, a good strategist, a good team worker in achieving shared goals, and an effective mover. TGfU can, in the hands of skillful and knowledgeable teachers, assist all young people to become competent games players and to gain the satisfaction of contributing to a game well played.

TGfU is very well placed to become common practice for very sound educational reasons.

The idea of TGfU has been around for at least 20 years. It has become popular with many teachers and coaches, and since the late 1980s has been studied by a growing number of researchers. It has influenced new developments, such as Alan Launder's (2001) "play practice" approach, and Horst Wein's (2001) soccer development model. It is based on a sound educational rationale. It is well suited to meet the current challenges for accountability in educational systems. Are its future prospects assured? I think not.

To be a good games player is to be a good solver of complex problems, a good strategist, a good team worker in achieving shared goals, and an effective mover.

To assure the future of TGfU, we must resolve a number of ongoing issues, each of which I will discuss in this chapter. First, I will consider the way we do research and how we design research studies. Second, I will discuss the need to continue to develop the TGfU model. Third, I will explore some new concepts for thinking about, and tools for measuring, learning in games. Finally, I will consider the challenge of incorporating TGfU into teacher and coach education programs. I will conclude this chapter by looking at each of these issues in relation to the future prospects of TGfU.

Design of Research Studies and Practice-Referenced Research

Researchers began scrutinizing TGfU empirically in the late 1980s. Much of this research has taken the form of experimental studies that have compared TGfU with the forms of games teaching it is assumed to replace, traditional technique-led approaches (e.g., Griffin, Oslin, & Mitchell, 1995; Lawton, 1989; Oslin, Mitchell, & Griffin, 1998; Turner & Martinek, 1992). Rink, French, and Tjeerdsma (1996) noted that research on TGfU has reported positive learning outcomes for students. The most powerful finding across the studies reviewed by Rink and her colleagues (1996) was that students taught from a TGfU perspective tend to perform better on tests of tactical knowledge than those taught from a technique-led perspective. Some studies (e.g., Griffin, Oslin, & Mitchell, 1995; Lawton, 1989) have suggested that a TGfU approach may be perceived by students to be more enjoyable than the technique-led approach, and so students may be more highly motivated to participate.

Rink and colleagues (1996) also noted that, despite some positive findings, the studies reviewed could not provide conclusive support for TGfU over technique-led approaches. They argued that this was the result of different research designs that made comparisons difficult because studies varied according to the game chosen, the age of participants, the length and nature of the intervention, the variable chosen for investigation, and the ways these variables were measured.

Although the fact that early research on TGfU adopted this comparative experimental design is understandable, the assumption that TGfU is mainly about teaching tactics and traditional approaches are mainly about teaching techniques is false. If we remind ourselves of the key premises of model-based instruction, we can see immediately that this way of characterizing the key features of each approach is too simplistic. The issue is not about tactics versus techniques. Thorpe and Bunker have always argued that both tactics and techniques are important in developing good games players. The issue, instead, is about learning outcomes and how these might be achieved using particular instructional strategies and subject matter presented as learning experiences.

In the traditional approach, the almost universal use of direct instruction encouraged a concern for the technique of individuals and small groups of players. In large, mixed-ability physical education classes, the hidden curriculum of control added a further incentive to teachers to teach games in a particular way. In a sense, the focus on technique was merely a means to an end (class control and safety) rather than an end in itself. Although ostensibly the ultimate goal may have been playing a game, I suggest that the learning outcomes of control and safety were and continue to be the main concerns of many teachers because control and safety are key institutional imperatives of the school (Kirk, 1999). The strenuous defense of the importance of technique provides a convenient justification for this direct instructional approach and its hidden curriculum of control.

TGfU, in contrast, has quite different learning outcomes in mind. Of course, safety and control are important here also, but good teachers have learned how to build these dimensions into the small-group, task-based learning that characterizes TGfU lessons. Strategic thinking, decision making, and effective movement execution are key aspects of good game play. TGfU disrupts the conventional institutional imperatives for social control because this approach works toward learning outcomes that are organic to game play. TGfU has never been about the mere development of tactical awareness. It has always been about developing good games players.

Part of the confusion surrounding learning outcomes in games teaching has centered on the place of techniques and skills in game performance. Bunker and Thorpe consistently made an important but often overlooked distinction between a technique and a skill. A technique is a means of executing movement efficiently and within the rules of a game for a specific purpose, but is practiced and performed outside of an actual game context. An example of a technique is the lateral pass in rugby, often practiced unopposed or in drills. A skill is the appropriate practice and performance of a technique in a game situation (Thorpe, 1990). In the "textbook" technique becomes a skill when speed, direction, and spin are modified to produce a catchable pass in a given situation. Thorpe, Bunker, and their colleagues were concerned primarily with the development of these two key features of game play, tactics, and skills.

Disregard for Bunker and Thorpe's distinction between a technique and a skill and subsequent confusion surrounding the relationships among techniques, skills, and tactics has been at the heart of confusion about the relationship

> *T*GfU disrupts the conventional institutional imperatives for social control because this approach works toward learning outcomes that are organic to game play. TGfU has never been about the mere development of tactical awareness. It has always been about developing good games players.

between TGfU and traditional approaches. This confusion has managed to become a formalized part of our research designs. Given what I have said so far, I hope it is clear that it makes little sense to compare TGfU with traditional approaches and to hope to come up with conclusive findings about which is best. If you want to teach for control and safety, use the traditional method. If you want to help young people become good games players, use TGfU.

So what are the alternatives? I think our research on TGfU needs to be practice referenced. What I mean by this is that the research is designed to fit the routine circumstances in schools in which teachers and students work and so seeks to deal with the real-time issues teachers and learners face on a day-to-day basis. Within this kind of design, TGfU units of work are implemented as faithfully as local circumstances allow, outcomes are set according to these circumstances, and data is collected appropriate to these outcomes. At least two examples of this approach are already in the literature: our own studies in Australia (Kirk, Brooker, & Braiuka, 2000) and Inez Rovegno and her colleagues' work (Rovegno, Nevett, & Babiarz, 2001).

> **R**esearch is designed to fit the routine circumstances in schools in which teachers and students work and so seeks to deal with the real-time issues teachers and learners face on a day-to-day basis.

Rovegno and colleagues (2001) called their studies descriptive, but I think this is too modest a label. Practice-referenced studies of TGfU seek to describe a "teaching experiment" (Cobb & Bowers, 1999) as it happens, for sure. But they also seek to make judgments about the impact of these experiments on student learning, based on the goals and learning outcomes established by the teacher for that particular lesson with those particular students. This practice-referenced approach, in short, is concerned with making judgments about the usefulness of TGfU for achieving learning appropriate to the model itself and to the circumstances in which it is being applied. I believe we need to give up the comparative experimental designs and focus our research program around practice-referenced studies of TGfU. In my view, this is the way for research to support the development of TGfU and to provide evidence of the learning it can facilitate.

Developing the TGfU Model

Bunker and Thorpe first published their TGfU model back in 1982. Review figure 1.1 (on page 3) which shows the original Bunker-Thorpe model.

Until recently, there had been no published attempts to revise the model during the past 20 years, either in light of how teachers and coaches actually use the model or in light of new theories of learning and teaching. This is somewhat surprising given the interest the approach has generated, and it suggests that a revision of the model and an associated program of research into its use are long overdue.

At the heart of this approach is the use of modified games to suit the developmental level of learners. All TGfU teaching and coaching takes place within the framework of game play and the modified game form. The logic is simple and compelling. Games, particularly team games, are tactically complex. One needs to simplify the game demands to suit the level of ability of the learner and gradually increase complexity as learning progresses. So, modifications are made to rules, playing areas, and equipment. Techniques are developed using drills and other training practices common to the traditional approach. A technique is only introduced, however, when the players reach a level of game play that requires the use of that technique. As the players' expertise develops, the game form is changed to continue to challenge them in terms of game appreciation, tactical awareness, decision making, and execution of technique.

Len Almond (2001) outlined some of the theoretical foundations to this original model. Although I believe the rationale for the model itself to be robust, researchers have generated new insights that may help make the model even more robust and useful. Ann MacPhail and I (Kirk & MacPhail, 2002) provided some pointers as to how the model might be revised by drawing on new knowledge from a situated learning perspective in particular. Our revised model is shown in figure 14.1.

We have changed some of the terminology: game concept, thinking strategically, movement execution, and situated performance. We have also added a number of mediating processes between the revised Bunker-Thorpe categories as a means of adding points of focus for teachers. These processes include emerging understanding, cue perception, technique selection, skill development, and a construct from Lave and Wenger's (1991) theory of situated learning, legitimate peripheral participation in communities of practice. This latter notion raises a key issue with respect to young people's motivation to participate wholeheartedly in the physical education learning process. The situated learning perspective demonstrates that motivation is enhanced when young people find their learning experiences to be meaningful and authentic (Kirk et al., 2000; Rovegno, 1999). Holt, Strean, and Bengoechea (2002), in another recent revision of the TGfU model, also raised this issue regarding the affective dimension of young people's experiences with TGfU.

Holt and colleagues (2002) proposed some modifications to the TGfU model regarding what they contend is an underdeveloped dimension of game play—young people's motivation and affective behavior. They

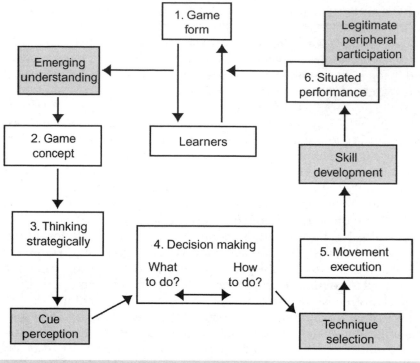

Figure 14.1 Kirk MacPhail revision of the TGfU model.

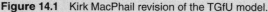

Adapted, by permission, from D. Kirk and A. MacPhail, 2002, "Teaching games for understanding and situated learning: Rethinking the Bunker-Thorpe model," *Journal of Teaching Physical Education* 21(2):179.

*T*he situated learning perspective demonstrates that motivation is enhanced when young people find their learning experiences to be meaningful and authentic.

also argued for the integration into the model of the four pedagogical principles of game play developed by Thorpe and his colleagues. Holt and colleagues (2002) consider these principles (sampling, modification-representation, modification-exaggeration, and tactical complexity) to be essential to the implementation of the TGfU model.

An explanation in any detail of the reasoning behind these revisions is beyond the scope of this chapter. I mention them merely to emphasize the need for ongoing revision of the model as it is tested periodically against the literature and, most important, as we study whether and how teachers use the model to teach games for understanding. We need a program of research focused on these latter two questions, of whether and how the model, in whatever form, is operationalized in practice. If the model serves, as I suspect it does, as a means of *thinking* about how to teach for understanding, rather than as a blueprint for planning lessons, then we must refresh and update that thinking on a regular, periodic basis if TGfU is to remain robust and useful in the future.

Conceptualizing and Measuring Learning in Games

Earlier, I suggested that it was incorrect to assume that TGfU was about developing tactical understanding and traditional approaches were about developing technique execution. Lying beneath this assumption is an issue that has dogged physical education throughout its modern history in public school systems: mind–body dualism. However hard we try, we seem to have difficulty escaping dualistic ways of thinking about physical education. This is especially so when it comes to making judgments about learning. Even at the level of matriculation of physical education in the United Kingdom, where the subject is studied in high school and counts toward university entrance, so-called theoretical and practical lessons continue to be taught and assessed separately.

The recent emergence of new lines of research on learning in physical education, some of which have focused particularly on learning in games, is beginning to provide us with opportunities to bury dualistic thinking for good. These new approaches are beginning to provide us, first of all, with a new vocabulary for thinking and talking about learning in the physical domain. And second, they are providing us with a clearer sense of how we might make valid assessments of learning, particularly in game contexts.

Alternative approaches to the once dominant process–product paradigm have drawn on information processing and constructivist theories of learning, such as Solmon and Lee's (1996) use of the mediating process paradigm and Luke and Hardy's (1999) metacognitive approach. Both approaches have studied learning in physical education generically, however, without reference to specific content. As Rink (1999) noted, a potential shortcoming these approaches share with the process–product paradigm is that generic definitions of content miss key qualitative dimensions of students' experiences of learning. This means that learning gymnastic activities, for example, may involve different thought processes, metacognitive strategies, and in-class behaviors than learning to play games.

One important line of research to emerge from these criticisms is the study of learners' domain-specific knowledge (Alexander & Judy, 1988; Dodds, Griffin, & Placek, 2001). Much of the research on domain-specific knowledge has been carried out within a games context, and most of this research has used the comparative experimental design I criticized earlier. Despite this body of research, Dodds and colleagues (2001) suggested that there has, to date, been scant examination of the ways domain-specific and strategic knowledge interact in the learning process.

A second emerging line of research on learning is studies of alternative conceptions of the domain-specific knowledge learners bring with them to new learning experiences. The University of Massachusetts team of Griffin and Placek (2001) and their colleagues have shown us that studies of learners' prior knowledge in science suggest that groups of learners possess diverse conceptions of domain-specific knowledge (Wandersee, Mintzes, & Novak, 1994). Rovegno (1999) argued that more attention needs to be paid to the social and cultural origins of children's conceptions of domain-specific knowledge because many games feature large in the popular media domain.

A third line of research in physical education has developed and applied a situated perspective on student learning to identify physical-perceptual, social-interactive, and institutional-cultural dimensions of the situatedness of children's learning in physical education (Kirk, Brooker, & Braiuka, 2000; Rovegno, Nevett, & Babiarz, 2001). This work goes some way toward providing concepts that permit us to make judgments about players' domain-specific and strategic knowledge in interaction. For example, in a recently published study of modified basketball, Rovegno and her colleagues (2001) argued that rather than teaching children to pass and catch in a traditional static format, children should be taught, from a situated perspective, to throw catchable passes. The "catchable pass" involves players making interpretations and decisions about the positions of other players, the speed of the pass, and the ability of the thrower and catcher. The term *throwing the catchable pass* is worth committing to memory. It captures precisely the kind of insight the situated learning perspective can generate. It is just one example of a relational construct that offers a strikingly new perspective on learning to play games and that holds significant implications for teachers.

Each of these emerging lines of research has raised questions about conventional practice around TGfU. For example, it seems to be common practice in TGfU for teachers and researchers alike to assess players' domain-specific knowledge of rules, field positions, and tactics using paper-and-pencil tests. In light of the issues raised by Dodds and her colleagues (2001) about the interaction of domain-specific and strategic knowledge; by Rovegno and her colleagues (2001) about the mutuality of game play; and by Kirk, Brooker, and Braiuka (2000) about the social-interactive and relational nature of game play, such tests now appear to have doubtful value. The task of recalling the principles of play for a class test is not of the same order as using these principles appropriately in a game. These emerging lines of research and the new constructs they provide suggest that we might now be in a position to dispense with such crude assessments and use in their place forms of description and analysis of game play that are organic to the game form, the players' levels of ability, and the intended learning outcomes of a lesson.

The development of tools for measuring game performance such as the Game Performance Assessment Instrument (GPAI; Oslin, Mitchell, & Griffin, 1998) already move us forward to more valid means of making judgments about learning in game contexts. The challenge that remains for such instruments may be to address the question of the unit of analysis. Typically, our judgments about learning in games tend to be focused on individuals, in part because of the institutional requirements of schools. Although doing this is not inappropriate, we should also recognize that individual performance is affected by the actions of teammates and opponents because of the social-interactive character of game play. At some point in the process of measuring learning in games, we need to be able to account for this characteristic, exemplified in Rovegno and colleagues' (2001) notion of "throwing the catchable pass." In short, we need to be able to treat the group as well as the individual as a unit of analysis. This is a topic for future intensive work by researchers.

Incorporating TGfU in Teacher and Coach Education

The final issue I want to raise in relation to the future prospects of TGfU is that of the preparation of teachers and coaches in effectively using the TGfU model. The more I have worked with TGfU both as a teacher educator and as a researcher, the more I have become convinced that TGfU is more demanding of teachers' pedagogical content knowledge and subject matter knowledge than is the traditional approach. Unfortunately, as Siedentop (2002), among others, argued, the rise of kinesiology-based preprofessional programs has led to a situation in which teachers increasingly lack precisely these forms of knowledge, and subject matter knowledge in particular.

To teach games from a TGfU perspective, teachers and coaches need to have a sound understanding of the game concept; of the relationship of time and space; and of issues such as cue perception and its relationship to decision making, technique selection, and so on. Without some firsthand experiential knowledge of these aspects of game play, I believe it is very difficult to teach for understanding. I am not suggesting that good teachers and coaches need to have been champion games players. I am saying, though, that this is not the kind of knowledge one can gain from viewing a videotape or reading a textbook.

A TGfU approach, or any other approach based on a similar rationale, must be embedded in all teacher and coach education courses. For those who might suggest, in the spirit of inclusivity, that there should also be space for traditional technique-based approaches in teacher and coach education courses, they need to determine if their primary intended learning outcomes are for social control and safety or for mastery of isolated techniques. If we want students to learn to be good games players, we must use TGfU or a comparable approach. If we are determined to use a traditional approach, we must not try to fool ourselves into believing that we are teaching students to become good games players.

> *A TGfU approach, or any other approach based on a similar rationale, must be embedded in all teacher and coach education courses.*

Even if you agree with my argument, you might be thinking that this could be harder to do than it sounds. There is indeed massive resistance to using a TGfU approach, particularly among primary and elementary school generalist teachers, because this approach potentially risks exposing teachers' lack of experience and competence as games players. But even middle and secondary school teachers may be resistant because most are themselves successful products of the traditional approach. Some of these student teachers may know less about games than they think, and TGfU again threatens to move them from the comfort zone.

Behind all of this is my conviction that we must convince teacher educators that the future of physical education lies in models-based instruction. Perhaps TGfU, Siedentop's Sport Education model (Siedentop, 1994), and Hellison's Personal and Social Responsibility model (Hellison, 1995) can be the vanguard in convincing teacher and coach educators of the value of models-based instruction. Unless this happens, however, there may be no future for TGfU as a common practice in school physical education.

> *If we want students to learn to be good games players, we must use TGfU or a comparable approach.*

Conclusion

I began this chapter with a scenario that posed the question of what the best instructional strategy would be to teach a class of 8-year-old students basic safety principles in gymnastics. I suggested that direct instruction might be the best approach in this circumstance. But I argued, following Metzler, that this strategy probably would not be appropriate if I wanted to teach the same children how to play games. The point of the scenario is that instructional strategies must be aligned with intended learning outcomes, content, and context. When these four factors are aligned, Metzler suggests we are using a models-based approach to instruction. I then went on to examine one instructional model in detail, the Teaching Games for Understanding (TGfU) model.

TGfU is an instructional model well placed to become common practice in physical education. But its future is not assured. Much of this chapter highlighted the issues that we must address and resolve: research design and the wider use of practice-referenced research; ongoing revision of the TGfU model; better constructs for theorizing and tools for measuring learning in games; and the incorporation of TGfU into teacher and coach education. Behind this work lies the challenge of moving toward models-based instruction, where we can work with closely aligned instructional strategies, subject matter, and learning outcomes. If we can resolve these issues satisfactorily, I believe TGfU has a real chance to be at the heart of future good practice in physical education.

One additional issue may be worth mentioning. The issue involves a tendency within the academic community to seek to contain and normalize new or radically innovative educational developments. There are many complex reasons for this, but not least of these are the rules and procedures for securing tenure and promotion in the university system. In the case of TGfU, I have observed this tendency in operation as conventional canons of procedure are applied through peer scrutiny of research. I suspect that this normalizing tendency lies behind the extensive use of comparative experimental studies of TGfU. We must, of course, observe and uphold what we believe to be tried and tested procedures for doing and judging the worth of research. But we must not allow these procedures to stifle the radical intent inherent in ideas like TGfU. In terms of the future prospects for TGfU, the academic community could kill the momentum of this movement by applying the normalizing hand of conventional procedure. I urge physical educators to be watchful and to resist this normalizing tendency wherever it may arise.

Discussion Questions

1. Explain why TGfU might be considered a form of models-based instruction.
2. Consider the differences between a skill and a technique in the context of learning to play a game, and the implications of these differences for research on TGfU.

3. How have new theoretical perspectives on learning and instruction affected the conceptualization of the Bunker-Thorpe TGfU model?

4. When considering the assessment of learning to play games, why is it important to consider the unit of analysis?

5. Why might teachers resist using the TGfU model?

References

Alexander, P.A., & Judy, J.E. (1988). The interaction of domain-specific and strategic knowledge in academic performance. *Review of Educational Research, 58,* 375-404.

Almond, L. (2001, July). *Reflecting on the development of TGfU.* Keynote speech presented at the Teaching Games for Understanding Conference, Plymouth College, NH.

Bunker, D., & Thorpe, R. (1982). A model for the teaching of games in the secondary school. *Bulletin of Physical Education, 10,* 9-16.

Cobb, P., & Bowers, J. (1999). Cognitive and situated perspectives in theory and practice. *Educational Researcher, 28* (2), 4-15.

Curtner-Smith, M.D. (1999). The more things change, the more they stay the same: Factors influencing teachers' interpretations and delivery of the National Curriculum Physical Education. *Sport, Education and Society, 4* (1), 75-98.

Dodds, P., Griffin, L.L., & Placek, J.L. (2001). Chapter 2. A selected review of the literature on development of learners' domain-specific knowledge [Monograph]. *Journal of Teaching in Physical Education, 20,* 301-313.

Green, K. (1998). Philosophies, ideologies and the practice of physical education. *Sport, Education and Society, 3,* 125-143.

Griffin, L.L., Oslin, J.L., & Mitchell, S.A. (1995). An analysis of two instructional approaches to teaching net games. *Research Quarterly for Exercise and Sport, 66* (Suppl.), 65-66.

Griffin, L.L., & Placek, J.H. (2001). The understanding and development of learners domain-specific knowledge: Introduction [Monograph]. *Journal of Teaching in Physical Education, 20,* 299-300.

Hellison, D. (1995). *Teaching responsibility through physical activity.* Champaign, IL: Human Kinetics.

Holt, N.L., Strean, W.B., Bengoechea, E.G. (2002). Expanding the Teaching Games for Understanding model: New avenues for future research and practice. *Journal of Teaching in Physical Education, 21,* 162-176.

Kirk, D. (1999). Embodying the school/schooling bodies: Physical education as disciplinary technology. In C. Symes & D. Meadmore (Eds.), *The Extra-ordinary school: Parergonality and pedagogy* (pp. 181-196). New York: Peter Lang.

Kirk, D., Brooker, R., & Braiuka, S. (2000, April). *Teaching Games for Understanding: A situated perspective on student learning.* Paper presented at the annual meeting of the American Educational Research Association, New Orleans, LA.

Kirk, D., & MacPhail, A. (2002). Teaching games for understanding and situated learning: Rethinking the Bunker-Thorpe model. *Journal of Teaching in Physical Education 21* (2), 177-192.

Laker, A. (2000). *Beyond the boundaries of physical education: Educating young people for citizenship and social responsibility.* London. Routledge/ Falmer.

Launder, A.G. (2001). *Play practice: The games approach to teaching and coaching sports.* Champaign, IL: Human Kinetics.

Lave, J., & Wenger, E. (1991). *Situated learning: Legitimate peripheral participation.* New York: Cambridge University Press.

Lawton, J. (1989). Comparison of two teaching methods in games. *Bulletin of Physical Education, 25,* 35-38.

Luke, I., & Hardy, C.A. (1999). Pupils metacognition and learning. In C.A. Hardy & M. Mawer (Eds.), *Learning and teaching in physical education* (pp. 38-58). London: Falmer.

Metzler, M.W. (2005). *Instructional models for physical education* (2nd ed.) Tempe, AZ: Holcomb-Hathaway.

Oslin, J.L., Mitchell, S.A., & Griffin, L.L. (1998). The Game Performance Assessment Instrument (GPAI): Development and preliminary validation. *Journal of Teaching in Physical Education, 17,* 231-243.

Placek, J. (1983). Conceptions of success in teaching: Busy, happy and good? In T.J. Templin & J.K. Olson (Ed.), *Teaching in physical education* (pp. 46-56). Champaign, IL: Human Kinetics.

Rink, J.E. (1999, April). *What do students learn in physical activity and how do they learn?* Keynote presentation at the Association Internationale des Ecoles Superieures d'Education Physique World Convention Proceedings, Conference, Besancon, France.

Rink, J.E., French, K.E., & Tjeerdsma, B.L. (1996). Foundations for the learning and instruction of sport and games. *Journal of Teaching in Physical Education, 15,* 399-417.

Rovegno, I. (1999, April). *What is taught and learned in physical activity programs: The role of content.* Keynote presentation to the Association Internationale des Ecoles Superieures d'Education Physique World Convention Proceedings Conference, Besancon, France.

Rovegno, I., Nevett, M., & Babiarz, M. (2001). A field-based project on learning and teaching of invasion game tactics in fourth grade: Introduction and theoretical perspective. *Journal of Teaching in Physical Education, 20,* 341-351.

Siedentop, D. (1994). Introduction to sport education. In D. Siedentop (Ed.), *Sport education: Quality physical education through positive sport experiences* (pp. 38-58). Champaign, IL: Human Kinetics.

Siedentop, D. (2002). Content knowledge for physical education. *Journal of Teaching in Physical Education, 21,* 368-377.

Solmon, M., & Lee, A. (1996). Entry characteristics, practice variables, and cognition: Student mediation of instruction. *Journal of Teaching in Physical Education, 15,* 136-150.

Suits, B. (1967). What is a game? *Journal of Philosophy of Science, 22,* 148-156.

Thorpe, R. (1990). New directions in games teaching. In N. Armstrong (Ed.), *New directions in physical education,* vol. 1 (pp. 79-100). Champaign, IL: Human Kinetics.

Turner, A.P., & Martinek, T.J. (1992). A comparative analysis of two models for teaching games: Technique approach and game-centered (tactical focus) approach. *International Journal of Physical Education, 29* (4), 15-31.

Wandersee, J., Mintzes, J., & Novak, J. (1994). Research on alternative conceptions in science. In D. Gabel (Ed.), *Handbook of research on science teaching* (pp. 177-210). New York: Macmillan.

Wein, H. (2001). *Developing youth soccer players.* Champaign, IL: Human Kinetics.

Index

Note: The italicized *f* and *t* following page numbers refer to figures and tables, respectively.

About the Contributors

Joy I. Butler, EdD, is an assistant professor in the Curriculum Studies Department at University of British Columbia, Canada. She has taught the TGfU approach as a high school physical educator in England from 1984 to 1989, where as department chair she developed a physical education curriculum based on the constructivist principles. In 1993, she received her EdD in curriculum and teaching from Boston University, where she previously received her MEd in human movement. In 2003, Butler co-authored a chapter to *Teaching Games for Understanding in Physical Education and Sport: An International Perspective.* This included an historical context, defined the positive aspects of TGfU, and questioned the merits and demerits of the tactical and technical debate. Butler is also a member of AIESEP and AAHPERD.

Connie S. Collier, PhD, is an associate professor of sport pedagogy at Kent State University. She studied at The Ohio State University from 1990 to 1994, during the time Daryl Siedentop was piloting the Sport Education Model within the Columbus area schools. She has taught physical education using the SEM principles for over ten years and has co-authored two presentations with Judith L. Oslin on Teaching Games for Understanding. She has been invited to speak in multiple professional development workshops, which focused on promoting innovative curricular approaches to urban physical education specialists. Collier currently serves as chair of the Curriculum Instruction Academy for NASPE and is also a member of AERA, AAHPERD, and Ohio AHPERD.

Ben Dyson, PhD, is the academic coordinator and associate professor of physical education teacher education at the University of Memphis. He has taught at elementary, middle school, and high school levels. For the past 11 years, Dyson has taught physical education teacher education at three different universities in Canada and the United States. Dyson received his PhD from The Ohio State University. He has presented at state, national, and international conferences on cooperative learning and has published several articles in practical and academic research journals. He also worked on the NASPE/NCATE Task Force to rewrite the national standards for physical education teacher education.

Linda L. Griffin, PhD, is a professor and chair of the Department of Teacher Education and Curriculum Studies in the School of Education at the University of Massachusetts at Amherst. She received her PhD from

The Ohio State University in 1991. She has 14 years of teaching and coaching experience and has spent 13 years as a teacher educator/researcher and has authored or coauthored 20 publications on TGfU. Griffin has coauthored two books with Steve Mitchell and Judith L. Oslin, which focus on elementary and secondary physical education and promote the use and implementation of the tactical games approach. In 2003, Griffin was a keynote speaker at the second TGfU conference in Melbourne, Australia. She has served as president of the Research Consortium for AAHPERD and is a member of AIESEP, AERA, and Massachusetts AHPERD.

Kath Howarth, PhD, is an associate professor of physical education at the State University of New York at Cortland. She was awarded a PhD in physical education from Temple University in 1986 and has taught in physical education programs in England and the United States for 25 years. Howarth played and coached lacrosse in England, and she coauthored a book on women's lacrosse as part of a series of sport skills games books in England. She is a member of AERA and AAHPERD.

David Kirk, PhD, has been a physical education teacher, an educator of physical education teachers, and a researcher in physical education since 1979. He was a professor of human movement studies at the University of Queensland, Australia, from 1995 to 1998. He is now a professor of physical education and youth sport at Loughborough University, England. Kirk is recognized internationally for his research in physical education, having published many articles in academic and professional journals. He has authored or coauthored seven texts, including the critically acclaimed *Schooling Bodies: School Practice and Public Discourse, 1990-1950* (1998). Kirk earned his PhD from Loughborough University, England, in 1986. He was awarded the President's Prize of the International Olympic Committee in 2001 for research and development in physical and sport education, and the Outstanding Scholar Award of the American Educational Research Association's Special Interest Group in Research on Learning and Instruction in Physical Education in 2003.

R. Scott Kretchmar, PhD, is a professor of exercise and sport science at Penn State University in University Park, Pennsylvania. He has written extensively on the value of games, play, and competition. Kretchmar, a Fellow in the American Academy of Kinesiology and Physical Education, is former president of the International Association for the Philosophy of Sport, and served as editor of the *Journal of the Philosophy of Sport.* He has been named an Alliance Scholar by the American Alliance for Health, Physical Education, Recreation and Dance (AAHPERD) and a Distinguished Scholar by National Association for Kinesiology and Physical Education in Higher Education (NAKPEHE).

Richard Light, PhD, is a senior lecturer in social theory in human movement education at the School of Policy and Practice at the University of Sydney, Australia. He has had a long career in coaching at all levels from primary school sport to elite level rugby and martial arts. He was head rugby coach at Kinky University in Osaka, Japan, from 1990 to 1993, and he convened the Second International Conference on Teaching Sport and Physical Education for Understanding in Melbourne. Light is a member of AIESEP and the International TGfU Task Force. He received the Australian Association for Research in Education (AARE) Doctoral Thesis Award for comparative study on the social dimensions of young men's rugby in Australian and Japanese high schools.

Barbara J. McCahan, PhD, an associate professor and chair of the Department of Health, Physical Education, and Recreation at Plymouth State University. She has been teaching in physical education for the past 12 years and has been professionally active in promoting constructivist pedagogy in physical education for the past seven years. She was coadvisor of a major's Teaching for Understanding club and has written several works promoting TGfU in community recreational settings. She is a member of AAHPERD and ACSM.

Michael W. Metzler, PhD, is the associate dean of Georgia State University's College of Education. He received his MS and PhD in physical education teacher education from East Stroudsburg University in 1976 and The Ohio State University in 1979, respectively. Metzler is the author of *Instructional Models for Physical Education,* and he received the 2003 NASPE Curriculum & Instruction Academy Honor Award. He has also been an international consultant on physical education teacher education in Singapore, United Arab Emirates, and Australia.

Steve Mitchell, PhD, is a professor of physical education teacher education at Kent State University. He has 20 years of teaching and coaching experience and has authored or coauthored 15 publications on TGfU. Mitchell has coauthored two books with Linda Griffin and Judith L. Oslin, which focus on elementary and secondary physical education and promote the use and implementation of the tactical games approach. Mitchell was awarded a PhD in teaching and curriculum from Syracuse University in 1992. He also belongs to AAHPERD and Ohio AHPERD.

Judith L. Oslin, PhD, is a professor at Kent State University. She has coauthored two books with Linda Griffin and Steve Mitchell, which focus on elementary and secondary physical education and promote the use and implementation of the tactical games approach. In 2001, Oslin gave the keynote address at the first TGfU conference in New Hampshire. She has conducted studies on the tactical games approach, written multiple chapters and articles on the subject, and has conducted numerous workshops and presentations at the international, national, and local levels. She also belongs to AERA, AAHPERD, and Ohio AHPERD.

Kevin Patton, EdD, is an assistant professor at the University of Northern Colorado. He recently completed his work at the University of Massachusetts at Amherst. He received his MA in physical education pedagogy from California State University at Chico, and he is a member of AERA and AAHPERD.

Jean-François Richard, PhD, is an associate professor and department chair at the Department of Elementary Education and Educational Psychology, Faculty of Education, Université de Moncton, Moncton, New Brunswick, Canada. Having received a doctoral degree in physical education from l'Université Laval (Québec City, Canada), Richard presently teaches and does research in the fields of curriculum planning and classroom assessment. To his credit, he has been a regular contributor to the growing body of knowledge in relation to games education. Since 1996, most of his work pertaining to games education has been centered on different aspects of assessment in a TGFU setting. Professionally, Richard has also taught K-8 physical education for six years and has coached ice hockey and track and field from novice to elite levels. In 1999, the Canadian Association for Health, Physical Education, Recreation and Dance acknowledged his contributions to physical education by naming him Young Professional of the Year for the province of New Brunswick.

Steven Tan, PhD, is the associate dean of professional development at Nanyang Technological University. Since 1999, he has been involved in the review and development of teacher education programs at NIE and has conducted numerous TGfU workshops. As part of his teaching and research, he conceptualized and helped develop a team research project whose aim is to extend the knowledge base beyond effective curricular implementation and into successful student learning outcomes. Tan was awarded his PhD in physical education from the University of Georgia in 1995. He is also a member of the Teaching Games for Understanding Task Force under the auspices of AIESEP.

Adrian P. Turner, PhD, is an associate professor of sport pedagogy at Bowling Green State University. He has been a physical education teacher educator for 10 years and has conducted 17 in-service workshops on the TGfU approach for physical educators and coaches. He received his MS and PhD in physical education from the University of North Carolina at Greensboro and has taught courses to preservice physical education teachers in advanced performance and content development in both invasion and striking/fielding games. Turner is a member of AAHPERD and Ohio AHPERD. He received the Authors and Artists Award from Bowling Green State University in 2001.

Nathalie Wallian, associate professor at the University of Franche Comte, France, has been successively a primary school teacher, then a physical education teacher at the International College of Strasbourg, and finally in charge of physical education teacher education at Besan n Department of Physical Education. Her thesis topic laid on an historical approach of the school game didactics. She now teaches educational sciences, swimming, and research methodology in physical education. Her current research interest is on language interactions within the teaching/learning system, where she develops a semioconstructivist approach focusing on student-centered teaching. In charge of the new master degree of Sport, language, and intervention, she is also member of the AIESEP Board and reviewer at the *Physical Education and Sport Pedagogy Journal.*